B.V. Raman

HINDU ASTROLOGY
AND
THE WEST

Books on Astrology by Dr. B. V. Raman

Astrology for Beginners
A Manual of Hindu Astrology
A Catechism of Astrology
Hindu Predictive Astrology
How to Judge a Horoscope Vol. I
How to Judge a Horoscope Vol. II
Three Hundred Important Combinations
Prasna Marga Vol. I
Prasna Marga Vol. II
Prasna Tantra
Notable Horoscopes
My Experiments with Astrology
Nirayana Tables of Houses
Bhavartha Ratnakara
Ashtakavarga System of Prediction
Graha and Bhava Balas
Hindu Astrology and the West
Planetary Influences on Human Affairs
Muhurta or Electional Astrology
Studies in Jaimini Astrology
Klachakra Dasa
Raman's One Hundred Ten Years Ephemeris (1891-2000)

|| श्री: ||

HINDU ASTROLOGY
AND
THE WEST

(Revised and enlarged edition of the book previously
published as 'A Hindu in America')

BANGALORE VENKATA RAMAN
Editor : THE ASTROLOGICAL MAGAZINE

UBSPD
UBS Publishers' Distributors Ltd.
New Delhi Bombay Bangalore Madras
Calcutta Patna Kanpur London

UBS Publishers' Distributors Ltd.
5 Ansari Road, New Delhi-110 002
Mumbai Bangalore Madras
Calcutta Patna Kanpur London

Fifth Edition	1992
First Reprint	1993
Second Reprint	1994
Third Reprint	1996

Printed at Ram Printograph (India),

CONTENTS

PREFACE TO FIRST EDITION

In recent times quite a number of Indians have been going to Europe, America and other parts of the world and readers will no doubt have heard from some of them their own impressions about the countries they happened to visit. However my trip to Europe and America could of more than casual interest because it not only fell to my lot, as a humble exponent of astrology, to represent India at important conferences but also to tell the American people something about the greatness and scientific character of Indian astrology, our ancient cultural heritage and ways and values of life thus creating in the minds of a number of Americans interest in our ancient culture.

After the Conferences, I visited important places in America, giving lectures, addressing group-meetings and holding discussions with persons eager to understand India and her culture in their true perspective.

One's impressions about a country, its people and their ways of life are generally coloured by one's own way of looking at them. Thus one used to Western ways of life and habits may not perhaps find anything uncommon in many of the customs and habits of Americans whereas one used to Indian ways of life and thinking and with convictions rooted in Indian traditions may find several things uncommon and somewhat strange. Therefore my assessment of America and her way of life are bound to differ from the impressions gathered by other visitors.

Many Europeans and Americans have written about their experiences in India. But there are very few books written by Indians about their experiences in the West. To Indians, especially conservative Hindus who contemplate visiting the West, this book is bound to make a fascinating appeal. But to the Westerner, especially to the American, the description of the experiences of an Indian (the first Indian ever to speak in public on astrology in the West), as his deeply ingrained conceptions meet unaccustomed ways of life to which, however, astrology offers access as a common heritage, should prove of equally great interest.

I must express my grateful thanks to Dr. Hans A. Havemann a distinguished scientist, thinker and admirer of Indian culture and now Head of Institute of Technology, Aachen, W. Germany and Mr. Cyril Fagan, a great researcher and savant, now settled in U.S.A., for their excellent 'Foreword' and 'Introduction' respectively contributed to this book. They forcefully sum up the scope and object of this publication.

It is hoped that this book will help all those Indians, who wish to know something about the great American people and their country.

Bangalore
16th March, 1969
B. V. RAMAN

PREFACE TO FIFTH EDITION

AFTER the first edition was published in 1969, I visited U.S.A., Europe, Japan, etc., in October 1970 with Mrs. Rajeswari Raman, alone in April 1971, and in October 1972 and with Mrs. Raman in May 1981 delivering lectures, addressing group-meetings and holding discussions with scientists and leading astrological savants. In fact the highlights of these visits were the opportunity given to me to deliver a lecture at the United Nations, New York; and successful demonstration--lectures by Mrs. Rajeswari Raman in Europe and America on Yoga, and the interest she was able to create in the minds of ladies in these countries for a correct appreciation of Yoga in the daily life of a woman.

The special features of this edition are :

(1) A new chapter on our 1981 visit giving details of our meeting with Swami Muktananda in his Asram at South Falsburg, New York;

(2) Publishing in full two of my important lectures delivered at London on "Nadi Astrology" and "The Techniques of Prediction". These lectures will go a long way in enabling the reader to understand the significance of *Nadi Astrology* and the *Shodasavargas*.

How the average Western citizen reacts to Hindu Astrology and how Western astrologers have begun to appreciate the importance of Hindu Astrology, as compared to their own systems, have been clearly explained in these pages. It is a matter of gratification that it was possible for me to make the Western astrological savants conscious of the pracitical utility of the Hindu system.

It is my hope that my impressions recorded in these pages and the responses of the Western audience to my appeal for an objective consideration of Hindu Astrology will be viewed with indulgence by my esteemed readers, especially because of my frank assessment of the relative merits of the Hindu and the Western systems of Astrology and the values and ways of life.

I am thankful to UBS Publishers' Distributors Ltd., New Delhi for bringing out this exhaustive edition attractively.

Dr. B. V. Raman

"Sri Rajeswari"
Bangalore-560 020
1st January, 1992

FOREWORD

• *Dr. Hans A. Havemann*

. The quest for knowledge and for co-ordination of knowledge gained—a process which establishes understanding—is certainly one of the noblest qualities of humanity. and through the ages has been and still is the main spring for its development. It has led man to believe in a grand unity and oneness of the cosmos pervading all occurrences and establishing a harmonious relatedness not only on the purely terrestrial plane but throughout the universe and its heavens.

Astrology can be interpreted as the ceaselessly undertaken attempt based on the belief to correlate the heavenly bodies with events on this earth and thereby, to derive insight into their otherwise unexplainable courses Thus, these bodies were individually bestowed with qualities. character and meaning, capable of entering into mutual relationships as they moved in their orbits. *e.g.*, as planets around—as one thought—the earth. Eventually, the conception of relatedness was modified to an assumption of influences, if not of forces which were believed to determine destinies of all dimensions; the fate of the individual and the fate of nations as they write their history.

Once this relationship was held acceptable, it should then also become possible to predict from the stars future happenings more or less precisely and thus to approach

---

* Director, Institute of Technological Studies. Aachen, West Germany.

one of the most intriguing problems of mankind : the shape of things to come.

It is not surprising that the most eminent minds have been attracted by this idea and have devoted their efforts to meet this challenge. Their findings were preserved and in many cases handed down across dividing expanses of time and distance—from the Mayans in America, the Egyptians, the Chaldeans, the Hindus—from the dawn of history right to this century.

One country where these traditions are eminently alive permeating virtually all social layers and activities is India—as I have witnessed during many years of life there. The more profound aspects have in no small measure been influenced by the author Prof. B. V. Raman, who, through his THE ASTROLOGICAL MAGAZINE and a proud number of books, has initiated a veritable renaissance of classical Hindu astrology. He is therefore uniquely qualified to convey Eastern astrological history and thought to the West, and to seek a meaningful confrontation. The transcript of his observations should arrest the attention of the reader from East and West alike especially where human reactions are revealed as deeply ingrained conceptions meet, during this mission, unaccustomed ways of life.

However, in East and West, life poses identical fundamental problems for the individual as also for social entities and thus the appeal of astrology is universal. It can therefore serve as common ground for mutual understanding and thus as a bridge and a connecting link between East and West. It is this cause which the author serves and which should assure him of our compliments and good wishes.

Technical University   DR. HANS A. HAVEMANN
Aachen, West Germany
13th March, 1969

INTRODUCTION

By Cyril Fagan

The opening chapters of recorded history find the people of the world scattered in groups all over the face of the globe. To protect themselves and their acquisitions from the in-roads of alien groups they formed themselves into nations and chose the strong men among them to be their chieftains. In course of time some nations prospered better than others, which made their neigbhours envious and avaricious. This inevitably led to war and pillage; and the chieftain of the victorious nation was proclaimed ruler or king of the conquered land, whose people were enslaved.

But in those far-off days groups of people and even nations were isolated and out of touch with the rest of humanity. So, in the ensuing years, they developed a language, customs and Government of their own: and the units of humanity that composed the nation, being small and petty in themselves, identified themselves with their people as a whole or their ruler, taking strength and finding protection in such identification, thus isolating themselves still further from the rest of humanity. Then with the advance of knowledge the powerful nations sent their well-equipped armies over the world subduing those not so endowed and colonised their land.

But now the pendulum is swinging in the opposite direction, and the people of the oppressed lands are clamouring for total independence and the eviction of the settlers; and so the world is being broken up into a multitude of smaller nations, each at other's throat; and this fractionalization of the people of the world into self-contained groups goes on in space causing greater conflict with mounting sorrow and despair. But this is a retrogressive step and a fatal one. The advance of science has become so great in all directions that isolation is impossible and independence impractical; for we are rapidly becoming almost totally dependent on one another. Modern means of travel is speedily destroying the practical worth of frontiers, while the camera and other scientific apparatus are laying bear the most guarded of national secrets. In every respect the people of the world are becoming vulnerable to one another. Isolation and separatism are things of the past. All attempts to restore or preserve national languages, customs, culture and the glories of ancient times, is doomed to complete failure, for we are now on the threshold of the Aquarian Age, when the whole relationship of the human race will undergo a profound revolutionary change. In a little over 400 years hence, the vernal equinoctial point will slip backward into the tail-end of the constellation Aquarius, when the much-heralded Aquarian Age will technically commence: but its shadow is already upon us.

In the coming age, nations, separate communities, tribes, sovereign governments, monarchies, republics, national frontiers and customs, barriers and, in fact, everything and every institution that divides man from man will be things of the past; for all the people of the world, irrespective of race or colour, will be just one big happy family; speaking one language and intermarrying one another. National, political and religious labels, which now sever the world into contending camps, such as American, Indian, Russian, British, German, French,

Communist, Capitalist, Christian, Hindu, Moslem and so forth will vanish. The hierarchical class and caste systems will be no more: and colour barrier will cease to exist. In such a society there will obviously be no need for armies or armaments of any description. This delightful state of affairs will not be brought about by conquest; but by a complete psychological revolution taking place in the consciousness of all individuals. and which, most appropriately, will originate in India the home of spiritual fluorescence.

Today the intellect has developed out of all proportion to the heart, so that we have become intellectually top-heavy: but our hearts are withered. But in the Aquarian Age the heart will again begin to function and more arid intellectualization will give place to compassion, love, ecstasy, beauty and humility. As astrologers, we know that the Sun is the symbol of the Atman. the self, the 'I', the 'Me' and the 'Mine' and the world today is fundamentally motivated by a concern for *self*—the only devil that exists —with its self-isolating process and search for security and self-glory at the expense of the rest of mankind and which is the prime cause of antagonism and war. But in Aquarius the Sun is debilitated, and so the emphasis on *self* will vanish to give place to an abiding concern for *others*; for love and self cannot co-exist. Where one is, the other is not. Thrice holy is he who is in a state of love, for he walks with Reality, which knows no centre nor boundary.

Most fitting is it that Sri Bangalore Venkata Raman, the distinguished scholar, author and editor of THE ASTRO-LOGICAL MAGAZINE and, himself, a most worthy scion of Aquarius, should leave his beloved Bangalore and fly to America. when Uranus was exactly in conjunction with his natal Sun in his Varshaphal for that year, to expound to the rapt audiences, who attended the many lectures arranged for him in the principal cities of the United States of America, the astrological lore and culture of ancient Aryavarta. Such a venture has no parallel in the annals of Hindu civilisation. It would have been unthinkable a century ago. By this unique act—consciously or unconsciously—Prof. Raman quickened the advent of the Aquarian Age; and for this he deserves well of those who desire, above all things, peace on earth and good-will to all human beings.

In the following pages, Prof. B. V. Raman reveals himself, as an unusually keen observer, with an eye for the historical. His detailed descriptions of his travels, of the cities and places he has visited and the customs and social mores of the people, present a vivid picture of the American scene, which will long tarry in one's memory.

For one steeped in Eastern Jyotisha (astrology), his grasp of the details and problems of Western astrology is astonishing; but it is feared he is a little too tolerant of its frailties and inconsistencies. Yet, as a true child of Aquarius, he freely admits that the East has as much to learn from the West; as the West has from the East.

Tuckson,
U.S.A.
15th March 1969

CYRIL FAGAN.

Dinner meeting at Washington (page 31)

The Author with the office bearers of N.E.A. (page 41)

Speaking at New England Astrological Association, Boston (page 41)

The Author with the office bearers of N.E.A. (page 43)

Sitting : L to R Dr. Percy Ryberg, the Author and Dr. Guttman
(page 23)

At the United Nations with Mr. K. Balaraman and Mr. Dayal, the then Indian Ambassador to Nepal (page 90)

L to R : Dr. Ryberg, Mrs. Jayne, Mr. Jayne, Mr. Emerson, Dr. Wagner, Mr. Ralph and Mr. Hans Niggeman (page 93)

At the office of "Life and Time" : Sitting : The Author and Miss
Diana Fetter. Standing : Charles Jayne and Al Fa (page 92)

The Author with Dr. Bruce Gordon Kingsley (page 78)

At the first Temple and College of Astrology, Los Angeles (page 78)

Signing Autographs at the Temple of Astrology, Los Angeles (page 79)

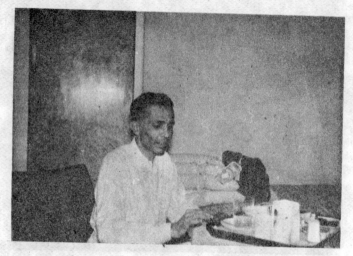

On Board 'Queen Mary'—The Author taking his lunch (page 96)

On Board 'Queen Mary'—Mr. Massey serving lunch (page 96)

With reporters at Los Angeles (page 78)

Dr. Curtis and Miss Elizabeth Grover and the Author
at Cambridge (page 108)

The Author at Charles Dicken's House, London (page 125)

The Author at the Tower of London (page 115)

At London with British Astrologers Dr. W. J. Tucker and Messrs Edward Whitman, J J. N. Rowell and M. K. Gandhi (page 109)

With eldest son late B. Surya Prakash on arrival at Bombay from London (page 130)

Mrs. Rajeswari Raman welcoming Dr. Raman on his return from U.S.A (1959) (page 130)

Charles Jayne and Barbara Somerfield at New York (page 203)

Send off to the Ramans at Bangalore Air Port (page 184)

The Ramans at Vienna, with Countess Wassilko (page 185)

Dr. & Mrs. Raman with the Indian Ambassador Mr. Dhamija
at Amsterdam (page 191)

Reporter of a leading Rome newspaper interviewing
the Ramans (page 187)

Dr. & Mrs. Raman at the British Museum, London (page 192)

The Ramans with Michel Gaquelin at Cambridge (page 192)

The Ramans with Mr. Al Morrison, President, Astrologers' Guild of America (page 194)

Visiting Liberty Statue, New York (page 194)

Lecturing at the United Nations, New York (page 199)

At Athens, Greece, the Author with the Ambassador of Japan
and his wife (page 207)

Mrs. Rajeswary Raman preparing to give a demonstration of meditation techniques at New York.(page 195)

At New York with Scientist Dr. John Nelson (page 195)

I The Preparation

I had been receiving invitations from Europe and America for the past many years to attend conferences. Several hurdles were in the way of my accepting these invitations. Thanks to the persistent persuation of my wife Srimathi Rajeswari, in April 1959 I decided to respond to the invitation to address the International Congress of Astrology at New York, besides accepting invitations from a number of astrological and cultural groups throu- out America and Europe to deliver lectures. Leading American and European astrologers assured me of "most warm and cordial receptions."

So when I decided to go to America, I was somewhat perplexed at the persistent opinion, still current with conservative Hindus, that anybody who went to Europe or America should be prepared to compromise in matters of food and drink, opinions which are thoroughly wrong and which perhaps deter many conservative Hindus from undertaking these trips. But I have always held the belief and this was amply justified later on, that one can go to any part of the world and keep up one's convictions in regard to food and drink. However, I wanted to discuss the matter with some of my friends who had been over- seas. But there was no unanimity between any two opinions. A good friend and well-wisher of mine, eminent in the social life of the country, suggested that I should be a "Roman while in Rome" and that I should not hesitate to adapt myself to the food habits of the countries I would be visiting. And he also told me that after my return to India he would be the first to see that I went back to my old food habits. Needless to say that the advice of this friend was not quite helpful to me. Then I discussed the matter with another friend—an international figure, who often visits the Continent and America on lecture tours. He said that *Satwic* (by which he meant vegitarian) food could be had everywhere in America and that he had no objection to take such food, no matter who prepared it or how it was prepared. He was also emphatic that it was perfectly possible to live in America as a non-smoker and a teetotaller. But mine was not merely the problem of getting vegitarian food. It was a question of my not taking any cooked food at all, the fear being that while cooking there might be a mixing-up of non-vegitarian stuff by the use of common vessels, etc. Mrs. Rajeswari Raman was emphatic that I could live quite comfortably on milk, fruits, raw-vegitables and corn flakes and that there was no point in thinking about what food to take. Mrs. Rajeswari's suggestion was seconded by another family friend—a High Court Judge—that fruits and milk would be quite adequate as they would keep my health in good condition. Circular letters had been issued in advance to all those who had extended to me invitations for dinners, etc., informing them about my food and drink taboos; and it must be said to the credit of American friends and also hotels in America that great consideration was shown to my wishes and feelings in these matters. Throughout my stay in Europe and America I lived on fruits, raw-vegitables, milk, corn flakes and eatables taken from home. I not only enjoyed good health but was in the best spirits despite the strenuous programme that had been scheduled for me.

A number of friends and well-wishers favoured my undertaking the trip by steamer as in their opinion travel by air would not be quite safe. But I was personally not inclined to go by steamer as it would mean waste of time. Mrs. Rajeswari favoured my going by air. After these decisions were over and the passport was obtained, I went to Madras to get my visa from the United States Consul. The Consul showed interest in my lecture tour, issued the visa without much delay and wished me every success in my efforts to expound astrology in America. There were the usual Health Certificate, Income-tax clearance Certificate, etc., and these were all obtained without much difficulty. Having secured these documents, I applied to the Reserve Bank for dollar and sterling exchange. After prolonged correspondence, the authorities were good enough to grant some dollar and sterling, hardly adequate to meet my expenses in America. In the meanwhile however several friends assured me that they would take care of my expenses during my stay in the United States. Passage money to and fro—is usually allowed to be paid in rupees in India. But just at the last moment, a few days before my departure, my Travel Agent informed me that the authorities had agreed to passage money being accepted in rupees only upto New York and back. I had engagements to fulfil in different parts of U.S.A, and travel expenses within U.S.A. would come to not less than 5 to 6 hundred dollars. The dollar exchange sanctioned was not adequate even for a ten-day stay in U.S.A. Thanks to the magnanimity of American friends, particularly to Mr. Paul Sherbert and Dr. Hans Havemann, I was enabled to tide over the exchange difficulty.

After these preliminaries were settled, and as the day of my leaving India came nearer, I was visited by scores

of friends, relatives and admirers to wish me a safe and
successful trip. Several dinners were given and the last
few days before my departure were so crowded that it
began to cause considerable physical strain. On the 3rd
evening, I was entertained by the staff members of my
office and Press and my Auditor Sri S. Srikantaiya, and
I was presented with an address, in which, among other
things Mrs. Rajeswari assured of loyal co-operation and
efficient discharge of office work during my absence. And
these assurances were fully kept up.

2 The Journey

The inevitable moment came and after traditional send-off at my residence by Mrs. Rajeswari and family members, I left for the Air Port on 4th October 1959 at precisely 12–20 noon. There was a large gathering of friends, admirers, relatives and members of the staff of *Raman Publications* and Press to bid me *Bon flight*. At the Air Port, I met Mr. Karmarkar Central Government Minister and had a brief talk with him. He wished me success in my mission. It was difficult for Mrs. Rajeswari and children to reconcile themselves to a long separation but Mrs Rajeswari bravely controlled her feelings. She told me after my return how at the moment of my boarding the plane she felt a sense of desolation, which she had to suppress lest it would grieve me.

I boarded the plane at 2–40 p.m. and a few minutes later, Bangalore landscape had disappeared and I was in the midst of the sky. Bangalore from air looked like Walt Disney's wonderland which I later visited at Los Angeles. The sight you see until leaving Mysore State is soothing to the mind, the eye travelling over thousands of resplendent pools which dot the land like pimples on a charming face. The flight from Bangalore to Bombay was quite pleasant. At the Bombay Air Port, I was met by my eldest son Mr. B. Surya Prakash, and my good old friend Mr. Mick d'Souza, Editor-in-chief, *Indian and Eastern Engineer,* and quite a few others. A dinner had been arranged by

Mr. Salivateesvaran at his residence near Churchgate, in the evening. The same night I took off for London by Air India International at 12 midnight.

Just before getting into the Air Port at Bombay, I could see the planet Saturn who bears the horrid reputation of being the inexhaustible source of misfortune and evil fates, going down the western horizon and he had completely set by the time I boarded the plane. The God of sorrow had disappeared. Poor Saturn has won no favour with the astrologers. In fact he is wholly innocent troubling himself not at all with our world or its inhabitants. But instead of blaming ourselves, we blame this God of fate.

The night flight was quite pleasant and enjoyable. Just before the plane took off, the air hostess explained the use of lifebelt in the "event of emergency landing on sea which was most unlikely". The plane I travelled in was a Constellation with wide-vision windows and good and well-placed lighting. The plane was completely air-conditioned and pressurised. The air-conditioning system also provides for auxiliary ventilation. Most of the passengers in the first class in which I travelled were Indians and first class passengers are provided with slumberettes—fully reclining arm chairs with cushioned foot-rests which, at a button's press, turn into bedlets. One can conveniently stretch oneself and relax. The Constellation flies at an altitude of over 20,000 feet cruising at a speed of about 300 miles an hour and the night flight was thoroughly enjoyable. As the plane gathered speed, the landscape of India became hazy and we were speeding over the blue waters of the Arabian Sea.

As a student of stars, I went on contemplating, through the windows of the plane, on the grand and silent spectacle of the stars. What greater delight can be conceived on a fine night than to be away from the earth and its inhabitants, be nearer the stars and get a clearer and a more sublime view of the heavens? In the first class we were about seven passengers and we could look through the windows on both sides of the plane. I could see Sagittarius sinking in the south-western sky and Pisces already on the meridian. I somehow missed Perséus, which, three hours earlier, was fully above the horizon but Revati racing to reach the meridian was quite resplendent. The air hostess issued us tooth paste for next morning's use and my attention was distracted. Suddenly my thoughts were transformed to the constellation of Orion— Mrigasira—my own birth star. The plane was going west and Mrigasira was above the eastern horizon. Somehow I tried to get a glimpse of my own star. But how could I get it when as a dazzling sextuple system it is in the very heart of the nebula! I was about to become despondent but lo! I could snatch a few glimpses of the ever-smiling Satabhisha—my wife's birth star—in the constellation of Aquarius. The despondency ceased and my thoughts soared into higher and sublimer regions. What enormous distances must separate the stars to admit of their free revolution in the outer space! At what depths and at what distances from our tiny earth must these celestial gems pursue the paths traced for them by destiny! Then why not man, a puny creature, bound to the earth by bonds of passion and attachment, humbly acknowledge and pursue the path chalked out for him, by the same destiny, trying to understand what this destiny is and how it is patterned by the ever-merciful Almighty. These thoughts plunged me into sleep. It was already daybreak when I was awakened by the air hostess, to see the Suez Canal over which the plane was flying at a low altitude to enable the passengers to have a clear view of the Canal, which was the seat of an armed conflict a few years ago. As the blazing Sun was slowly emerging up the horizon, and as I was just sipping my favourite cup of coffee, I could get a general view of the Suez Canal. It is an artificial waterway about 100 miles long connecting Port Said on the Mediterranean Sea and Suez on the Red Sea. By 7–45 a.m. (Cairo time) the plane made a perfect landing at Cairo Air Port. Passengers were served with soft drinks (coffee and fresh lime-juice) at the Air Port restaurant. I preferred fresh lime-juice served by Arabs in their traditional robes.

While on the plane I became acquainted with the pilot, Captain D'Souza who showed a keen interest in and understanding of astrology vis-a-vis Indian culture. I was also introduced to Captain Nadkarni, who was proceeding to London. Mr. Nadkarni is a keen student of astrology and I had some interesting discussion with him. Leaving Cairo at 8–30 a.m. on the 5th, the plane arrived at Zurich at 3–5 p.m. (C.E.T.). The flight was excellent with occasional bumping of the plane due to heavy air-packets. On the plane, special arrangements for my diet had been made and I was served with milk, raw-cucumbers, apples, grapes, bananas and plenty of dry fruits. At Dusseldorf which I reached at 5–15 p.m. a funny incident occurred. There was a passenger—Mr. X—from Bangalore who was taking his father to London for medical treatment. At the Air Port alcohol was sold without any tax to passengers who held direct tickets to New York. Mr. X suggested that since I was going direct to New York, I could buy a bottle and give it to him. This annoyed me a bit, as being a teetotaller, the very thought of alcohol being purchased in my name was repugnant to my sense of decency. Capt. Nadkarni, who was with us and who saw my annoyance, took Mr. X away for a while and within a few minutes, Mr. X was apologising for the liberty he had taken with me. I arrived at Northolt Air Port at London at 6–30 p.m. (G.M.T.) the flight from Dusseldorf taking just 50 minutes. As the aircraft approached London, perhaps the second largest city in the world, I could see the Thames, some of the narrow streets and the constant stream and flow of activity. Throughout the flight landings and take-offs were perfect and the service of attendants courteous. At London the Air Port formalities took about an hour and Captain Nadkarni was very helpful in not only enabling me to pass through the customs and other formalities but also in suggesting that I stay with him during the night. The British Customs were courteous and the least annoyance is caused to the passengers. From the Air Port, I drove straight to Shaftesbuty Hotel and I had my first view of the great City of London. Though expensive, and considered to be a first class hotel, the accommodation was not quite convenient. Continuous flight of 30 hours had tired me a bit and since I had to resume my flight to New York the next day, I spent the night quietly at the hotel.

On 6th October, I left London at 12–30 p.m. (G.M.T.) by Pan American 707 Boing Jet Plane. Nothing has so revolutionised air travel since the Wright Brothers proved to the world that man could fly, and their pioneer hop was just 24 feet shorter than the Jet plane's 144 foot fuselage. The flight was most thrilling. I had enough experience of having travelled in aeroplanes in India since 1947, but this way my first flight in a Jet Plane. Flight by Boeing 707 is an entirely new experience. The plane ascends to 30,000 feet in 15 minutes. It flies at an altitude of about 40,000 feet, cruising at about 600 miles an hour. At this height clouds are rare and turbulence is practically non-existent. Smooth and almost vibrationless in flight the Being 707 produces a sensation of being suspended motionless in space while the Atlantic ocean skims by in a spectacular panorama far below. A specific object on the horizon at Jet altitude would be about 200 miles distant. 20 minutes later we can find the same object sliding by directly beneath the plane and this can give one a real measure of the speed of the Boeing. One of the Captains, with whom I became friendly, explained to me that the flight looks incredibly quiet and smooth because of the placement of the engines. They are suspended from the wings in revolutionary new pods, far from the cabin itself. Another basic reason, the Captain said, for the Boeing's vibration-free flight is the engine itself. With no propeller, pistons, magnato, electrical ignition and fuel mixture mechanism, there is nothing that can vibrate. The driving force of a Jet is the release of gas at high velocity. In operation, air scooped in through a large opening in front is compressed mechanically. This compressed air superheated by the engine's burner raising its temperature even further. As this air forces its way towards the only avenue of its escape—the exhaust jet—it passes through turbines and finally emerges under tremendous speed at the rear of the engine. It is this release of gas that propels the plane, entirely free of vibration and at fantastic speeds.

I travelled in the *Deluxe* class, which provides the ultimate in luxury service. I was the only Indian amongst more than 100 passengers on their way to New York. As soon as the jet plane took off from London, meals were served to the passengers. Meals, supplied on the Boeing jet, are said to be prepared by Maxim of Paris. The names on the menu-card made no sense to me, and especially so to a vegetarian. Just before meals, vintage vines were liberally served. I found that not one passenger was a teetotaller. All the passengers in the *Deluxe* class feasted themselves on continental delicacies with "Charles Heidsieck Champagne" followed by finest cocktails and light beverages. I was the only exception. The meals, I learnt, were entirely non-vegetarian. The steward could not understand why I neither took the meals nor the drinks. I told the steward that I was strict vegetarian. He said : "I shall give you rice, beer, boiled potatoes, fish and egg". And I retorted, "I do not eat fish, I do not eat eggs, I do not eat any boiled food." "Then what will you eat" ? asked the steward. I said : "I would take fruits, corn flakes, milk, coffee, curds and buttermilk." "Alright, I can give you all this in plenty except corn flakes. I cannot understand how milk could be vegetarian. You are a strange gentleman. It is the first time I have ever come across such a 'strict vegetarian' in the Pan American" laughed the steward. Then I had a plentiful supply of fine Californian fresh grapes, apples, bananas and milk and I enjoyed a fine fruit meal. But for a halt of 30 minutes for refuelling at Gander Airport (Newfoundland), it was a non-stop flight from London to New York. The airliner landed at New York La Gaurdia Airport exactly at 4-30 p.m. (New York Time). It is amazing that the Jet Plane has made it possible to span the Atlantic in as little as 8 hours. The Panorama that stretches from the European to the American Continent is most thrilling.

3 New York

The Customs examination at New York Air Port was not irksome. "What is your occupation" asked the Customs Official, a Negro gentleman. "I am a writer" I said. "Is it possible to live in India by writing" asked the official. "Quite possible" i replied. "I doubt it very much. India is a strange country but I like it", said the official.

As I drove to the city from the air port, darkness was just setting in and I had my first glimpse of "the most exciting city in the world"— New York—with its wonderful skyscrapers, and limousines rushing at terrific speeds in four lanes. For the initial half hour as our car was speeding at 60 miles an hour, I was on my nerves fearing that an accident was inevitable any moment. My fears were allayed by my friends that what I was seeing was the normal New York traffic, that the drivers had such perfect control over the steering wheel that accidents were most unlikely. In my home town Bangalore, 25 miles per hour is the maximum speed while in the heart of the city you cannot go more than 10 to 15 miles. I have been driving cars for over 12 years and perhaps I should get a training for a year or two, if I am to sit at steering wheel at New York. My friend Dr. Havemann who was then in New York and who fully agreed with me, said that it took a month for him to get used to driving his car in New York.

Immediately I reached Hotel Taft, the place of residence during my stay at New York, at about 8 p.m. I had a number of visitors including Mr. & Mrs. Charles Jayne, Mrs. Marcia Roof, Dr. Havemann, and some newspaper men. Continuous flight from Bangalore to New York made me feel a bit tired physically and I was suffering from a nasty attack of headache ever since I landed at New York. When I went to the drug store nearby to get some aspirin tablets I found that the shelves were full of bottles, containing tranquillisers. When I was looking at these bottles, the salesman remarked : "They are not for you, sir. Tranquillisers are for Americans only. *Indians do not generally suffer from complaints requiring use of tranquillisers."

On the morning of the 7th, I had a number of visitors, most of them being readers of The Astrological Magazine and my other writings. My first public appearance at New York was on the same day at 3 p.m. when I addressed the International Congress of Astrology at Hotel New Yorker. Dr. Ziegler, Organiser of the Congress, introducing me to the audience said: "It is my great privilege to introduce to astrologers gathered at this Congress, Bangalore Venkata Raman, India's foremost exponent of Astrology, writer and lecturer—and the first Indian to ever speak on Astrology on the soil of America. He has come here as the representative of India. As the foremost authority on Hindu Astrology, and as Editor of The Astrological Magazine which is perhaps the only journal of its type in the world, Professor Raman is eminently qualified to represent his great country. It is

*Things have changed now. Quite a number of people mostly in urban areas have become addicts to tranquillisers to get sleep and "relief from tension" a concomitant of increasing industrialisation.

a unique opportunity for us—the American astrologers—
to honour him and to hear him speak on India's great
heritage. He comes from far off India and he is our
honoured guest."

I spoke on "India's Contribution to Astrology." In
the course of my address, I explained the distinctive
features of Hindu astrology and said that long before the
dawn of what is popularly called the period of authentic
history great strides had been made in almost all branches
of knowledge in India and that it was not quite safe to
assume as correct the opinions of scholars who had tried
to trace the origin of Hindu astrology, to Grecian or
Chaldean sources. I pointed out salient features of
Hindu astrology and to what extent it can be adapted by
Western astrologers. After the address, several questions
were put by members of the audience pertaining to Hindu
astrology, Karma Theory, Indian social life etc., and it
was nearly 7 p.m. by the time I was released. Among the
speakers at the Congress were Dr. Davidson, Dr.
Macdonald, Jessie Smith Miller, Mrs. Lee Mefadden,
Rolle Nardie, and Mrs. Clara M. Darr. Tape recordings
from Dr. W. J. Tucker, Dr. Mandal, Dr. Falconer, Mrs.
George Haas, and Miss Constance Sharpe of London were
much appreciated as also papers from Messrs. Willy
Bischaft, W. E. Witte of Berlin, A. M. Grimm, Dr. Walter
A. Koch and Hans Genuit of Germany, Mr. Won M. Von
Ploennies of Australia, Won Koeing of Canada and Dr.
Matsubara of Japan. Dr. Davidson's talk on Medical
astrology was stimulating. I was so pressed for time with
discussions, group meetings, visitors calling at the hotel,
etc., that I had to miss several items. It was a pleasure
to make the acquaintance of a number of intelligent
astrologers, including Mr. & Mrs. Wagner, editors of the
widely circulated *Horoscope*.

The same evening at 6–30 p.m. a dinner was given to me at the Cosmopolitan Club by Mr. Ronald Freelander of the Asia Society. At 7–45 p.m. we drove to the French Institute, where I delivered a lecture, under the auspices of the Asia Society, on "Astrology in Indian Social Life". The Asia Society was formed for the purpose of helping the United States and Asia "to know and to appreciate each other better". It has as primary areas of interest "education in the United States concerning Asia and encouragement of exchange of ideas, people and fine arts". The then President of the Society was Mr. John D. Rockefeller, Chairman Dr. Graysen L. Kirk, Executive Director Mr. Paul C. Sherbert, and Associate Director Mr. Ronald Freelander. The Society has its headquarters in its own building in east sixty-fourth street in New York.

My lecture was presided over by Mrs. Horace R. Lamb. She is considered an authority on Asian studies. She is in fact an interpreter of Asia, especially India to American audiences. Introducing me to the large gathering present at the French Institute, Mrs. Lamb observed : "Today we have a wonderful person to lecture to us on one of the most fascinating aspects of Indian Culture, *viz.*, Astrology. He is Bangalore Venkata Raman, Editor of The Astrological Magazine and an authority in this subject. His activities cover a wide range—writing books, interpreting astrology on scientific lines and public lectures. He has to his credit outstanding predictions made in respect of individuals and nations. Prof. Raman wrote, in his magazine, about Hitler's fall, the death of Mussolini, the end of Second World War, Indian Independence, etc., long before the events happened. In India, unlike in the West, astrology has been part of the

general scheme of Indian Culture, and astrology is widely
used by the educated public, the science having attained
considerable perfection centuries ago."

After explaining the social and cultural background
of India, and how "astrology permeates Indian life and
culture in all their ramifications", I observed : "One
should have the critical spirit of the scientist if one were
to grasp the correct significance of astrology in the life of
an Indian." Dismissing the baseless theory still current
with some European and Indian scholars that Aryans
originally inhabited Central Asia and that they later on
migrated into India, and upholding the authenticity of
the indigenous sources of history and astronomy which
have been lending strong confirmation to the view that
India is the original home of the Hindus and of their
ancient civilisation and culture, I said that "it is the
Indian or Hindu culture that imparted to the whole of
India a strong and stable cultural unity that has successfully withstood powerful onslaughts of socio-political
revolutions". I pointed out the originality and antiquity
of ancient Indian achievements and explained how the
totality of the spiritual, intellectual and cultural life of
India contains astrology in perfect integration with itself
constituting a coherent whole, whose coherence was not
merely coherence in a general sense but also expressed
itself as coherence which rests on vigorous philosophical
thinking. "It can be clearly stated", I said, "that never
during the last 5 or 6 thousand years of so-called historical times has there been one age in India in which signs
and symptoms of astrological principles and ideas were
missing. At the moment, astrology still holds a remarkable position in India even though an organic relation

with our *modern Universities may be wanting and
present day academical science which is largely western,
may be ignoring it. It exists as fresh as ever and occupies
an important place." Then I dealt elaborately with the
philosophical aspect af astrology, the characteristic
features of Indian social set-up—Varnashrama Dharma
or the so-called caste system, as it existed in the ancient
times and as it contiues to exist even today, the significance of the ashramas or four well-defined stages of life
and how the social and moral philosophy of India considers the caste system and the ashramas to be conditioned
by four ends or aims of life called purusharthas. Then I
gave an exposition of the theory of Karma and pointed
out that Karma is the common factor between astrology
and Vedanta. After dealing with the uses to which astrology was put in India and explaining the profoundity of
Indian astrological attainments, I concluded my lecture
with the following remarks : "Why does astrology have
such an importance in India despite the fact that the
objective traits of technological culture of the West are
exerting a strong influence on India's social life ? It is
not easy to answer this question satisfactorily. There
appears to be something inherently vital in India's way of
life and India's cultural pattern that the attacks from
industrial culture have not been able to penetrate deep

------

* Events have been moving fast in India. Some of the Indian
Universities have shown willingness to introduce astrology as an
optional subject. On 29th April 1976, I addressed a meeting of the
Vice-Chancellors of all Universities in Madhya pradesh and my
plea for the introduction of astrology well received. The Kumaon
University (U.P.) conferred on me the honorary degree of D. Litt,
for my "contribution to the cause of Astrology" and this forebodes
well for the future of astrology. The Karnataka University,
Dharwad has now a post-graduate diploma course in Astrology.

into the soul of India. The integration of ancient ideals and values into the life and thought of the average Indian is so powerful that it is acting as a shock-absorber. The long history of India shows the process of assimilation. Many an attempt was made in the past to foist on India new ways of living, believing and thinking. Each attempt failed in the sense that the best in it was assimilated. This assimilation makes the culture of India one of integrated humanism. The philosophy of astrology is in tune with the philosophy of the people—the common factor being Karma. The Universe is the Brahman and the individual is the Atman. The physical aspect of the Universe—Brahmanda—has as its counterpart the physical aspect of man Pindanda. Therefore changes occurring in the Universe must have their repercussions on the individual also."

The lecture was followed by questions and answers—questions ranging from Mr. Nehru's attitude towards astrology to the third World War and covering such topics as the role of astrology in the stability of marriages, etc. Several members of the audience rushed to the dais to congratulate me on what they termed my 'wonderful lecture'. Mr. Ronald Freelander, who proposed a vote of thanks, found the talk "very interesting". He said : "This is perhaps the first time, that a lecture of this type dealing with one of the most fascinating aspects of Indian culture has been delivered at the Asia Society by a scholar of the eminence of Prof. Raman. From what he has told us about the useful part played by astrology in the lives of Indians, it seems clear that astrology in that ancient land has been fulfilling a useful function. We keep an open mind on the subject and, after hearing this talk we would wish to know more about the subject."

At the Asia Society lecture I could spot only three Indians—a lady from Bangalore and a Parsi couple from Bombay. After the lecture, they also complimented me for having presented before the Americans a clear "perspective of astrology", and they said that such would go a long way in creating in the minds of the American people great respect for and understanding of Indian Culture.

The next evening, a lecture was delivered at Hotel New Yorker on the "Outlook for 1960". In the course of the lecture, the salient features of mundane astrology as recorded in ancient classical works were dealt with in detail. The audience – mostly astrologically minded—sought clarification of several aspects of Hindu astrology.

On the 10th October, I addressed the Special Conference of Astrologers held at Hotel Astor under the joint auspices of Astrologers' Guild of America and Astrological Research Associates. The Special Conference was attended by a large number of delegates from different parts of America. It was opened by Mrs. Mabel Leslie Fleisher, Second Vice-President of the American Federation of Astrologers. I was introduced to the audience by Mr. Alfred C. Emerson, Vice-President of the Astrologers' Guild of America, in the following terms : "The Special Conference is being held to honour the eminent Prof. B. V. Raman of India and Mr. W. O. Suchar of England. Prof. Raman comes from a country, which has a vital ancient culture and which had developed astrology to considerable perfection. As the leading astrologer of India and Editor of the widely read and influential periodical THE ASTROLOGICAL MAGAZINE, Prof. Raman is most qualified to expound Hindu astrology. Apart from being a pioneer author and editor, he has considerable

prestige as a Mundane astrologer who has many successful predictions of world events to his credit."

In my address on "Astrology in India" I dealt with
the greatness of ancient Hindu achievements and the
originality of ancient Hindu astrology and how many a
gap in the western system could be filled up by a liberal
indent on the Indian systems. On behalf of the Organisers, Mr. Emerson expressed gratefulness for my "interesting and stimulating talk" and remarked thus : "The
response to your efforts was highly gratifying and the
subject has held your audience spell-bound. It has also
done much to increase the interest in the ancient science
of Hindu Astrology which is well worth an extensive
study. We are proud to have such a distinguished astrologer from the East in our midst and I want to thank you
again on behalf of the members of *Thē Astrologers' Guild*,
for your splendid contribution to the success of our
Conference."

There were several notable speakers at this Conference. Dr. Richard Wagner's "Report on Dr. R.
Tomaschek's Study of the Correlations of Earthquakes
and Planets" was very instructive. Dr. Tomaschek, a
former Director of the Institute of Physics at Munich,
has arrived at significant conclusions on the correlations
between earthquakes and planetary movements and Dr.
Wagner's talk brought to focus, the main stream of
researches conducted by this German scientist. The
lecture of Mr. Charles A. Jayne Jr. on U.S.A. *vs* Soviet
Union and Major Planetary Cycles" was highly stimulating. He explained how certain major planetary cycles
clearly denoted the evolution of political thinking and
based on this theory, he anticipated the waning of
communism in Russia in due course. He demonstrated

the effects of long-term cycles of Jupiter and Saturn and Saturn and Uranus on the rise and fall of civilisations.

Mr. Paul Grell, Executive Secretary of the American Federation of Astrologers, gave a talk on "The Planets". His approach was more akin to the Hindu approach. According to Mr. Grell "what the horoscope indicates is the resultant of our Karma and man must try to overcome the Karmic indications". I felt that Mr. Grell had a very sound knowledge of the theory of Karma. Mr. Vernon Clark spoke on "A recent Experiment with Twenty of America's and Britain's Leading Astrologers". In the experiment he conducted, the astrologers were required to match charts with brief case-histories of 5 men and 5 women. It was under the strict supervision of two practising psychologists with no bias in favour of astrology. His investigation revealed that the findings of the majority of astrologers, regarding the mental charcteristics of the natives of the horoscopes entrusted to them were correct. Such experiments, familiar to psychologists, go a long way in making the scientific minded to realise what astrologers can do under such test conditions.

Other speakers were Dr. William Gutman, M.D., on "The Scientific basis for Cosmic Influence" and Mathilda Shepiro on "The Approach to the Chart As a Whole" Mr. W. O. Suchar, who also spoke has a new theory of prediction to offer, based on the heliocentric system. He is director of the Landvidi Research Centre in England, a movement, directly connected with the work of the late Rudolph Steiner. He appears to have done good work on what he calls the "horoscope of death".

4 New York—2

In New York, apart from the lectures I delivered at the Special Conference, at the Asia Society and other places I also addressed some group meetings not only at my hotel but also at the residences of some friends. In these meetings, I was generally called upon to speak on ancient Indian Culture, values and ways of life and the place of astrology in the daily life of an average Indian. Generally my expositions used to be listened to with great interest. Thanks to the inadequate publicity given by our official representatives, the average educated American seems hardly to know anything about India. In all such group meetings, I endeavoured to impress that the soul of India, in spite of the cultural and industrial impacts the country has been subject to for the past 200 years, is intact and that the ancient way of life—simple living and high thinking, belief in the existence of a Higher Power shaping human destiny, and patterning of life on the principles of the theory of Karma or Moral Causation—is still conspicious by its presence. I also took the opportunity to bring home to the American people that ancient Indians had made considerable advances even in physical sciences, having anticipated thousands of years ago, theories regarding the origin and evolution of the solar system, which are the wonders of even present-day scientists.

A group meeting worth mentioning is the one held at the residence of Dr. Percy E. Ryberg, M.D., thanks to the initiative of Mr. Charles A. Jayne, Editor, *In Search*. Those who attended the meeting were Dr. Richard M. Barry, a cancer specialist ; Mr. Vernon Clark, psychologist ; Dr. James Stephenson, physician ; Dr. William Guttman, physician ; Mr. E. Douglas Dean, E.S.P. specialist ; Dr. E. R. Wagner, chemist; Mr. Willi Suchar, Director, Landvidi Institute ; Mr. Paul R. Grell, Secretary, American Federation of Astrologers , Mr. Hans Niggerman, exponent of Hamburg School of Astrology ; Mr. W. L. Heller, Miss Irene Carotneff, Mrs. Ellen Resch Mrs. Maria J. Wehrheim, Mrs. Vivia Lang and Mrs. Margaret Morrel, all astrologers ; and Mr. Charles Emerson, Vice-President of Astrologers' Guild of America Mrs. Ruth Ferguson ; Mrs. Marcia Roof, and the host Dr. Percy Ryberg.

The meeting commenced at about 8–30 p.m. and lasted for over three hours. I explained the basis and antiquity of Hindu astrology, how astrology in India is an integral part of the general scheme of Indian Culture, the part played by astrology in Indian social life and how it could be made use of for the amelioration of several social and psychological ills facing modern man. Mr. Vernon Clark was called upon to explain the experiments he had recently carried out—getting information about the mental dispositions of his patients on the basis of astrology. I felt that the medical men and the psychologists who attended the meeting were impressed. It was gratifying to find that not only great interest was being seriously taken in astrology but also the importance of astrology being increasingly realised. At this meeting Mrs. Marcia Roof gave a short talk on a thesis she was writing on astrology for a Radcliffe College Degree. The thesis incorporated the finding of a survey among people seriously interested in astrology conducted by the Astrological Research Associates. Amongst the sponsors of the project were my humble self, Mr. C. E. O. Carter, Dr. Mark Edmund Jones, Brigadier Firebrace, Mr. Dane Rudhyar, Miss Margaret Morrel and Miss Margaret Hone. Mrs. Roof then mainly dealt with socio-psychological aspects of astrology and not the techniques *per se*. She told me that for the questionnaires sent by her, she received exceedingly helpful replies from astrologers in India. I felt that Mrs. Roof's thesis on astrology—perhaps the first of its type to be submitted for a University degree in the West—was bound to evoke much interest.

On Sunday the 11th October, my good friend Dr. Havemann took me round New York and I visited a number of museums including the Hayden Planetarium. I spent a quiet evening with Dr. Havemann and his family in the doctor's fine cottage at Scarsdale, a beautiful suburb of New York, resembling the *malnad* area of Mysore. Mrs. Havemann had a surprise in store for me. She had prepared a South Indian meal—rice, vegetables, etc. The couple assured me that the meal was absolutely vegetarian, similar to what we would take in our hometown, but Mrs. Havemann had to be disappointed because of my food habits. Of course the couple appreciated my feelings and I was immediately served with a fine fruit meal which I greatly enjoyed.

Dr. Hans Havemann is a German scientist and was for some time a Professor at the Indian Institute of Science at Bangalore. He is now the head of a technical university in West Germany. While in Bangalore, I got the doctor interested in astrology. It was a great surprise to find that Dr. Havemann had become a good astrologer. He had acquired a sound knowledge of the Western system of astrology and was able to work solar charts, progressions, etc., and interpret them. Unassuming by nature and sincere in friendship, Dr. Havemann is a gentleman to the core and my stay in New York would not have been as enjoyable and pleasant as it was, had it not been for Dr. Havemann's help and assistance.

Despite the heavy programme I had to keep up, I missed no opportunity of sight-seeing. New York, the largest city in the United States, and perhaps the third largest in the world, is at the mouth of the Hudson river, in the south-eastern New York State. The width of the city, east-west, is 24 miles and the length, north-south, is about 35 miles. In one of the museums I visited, the following details about this great city were gathered. In 1626, there were about 200 inhabitants ; 1000 in 1656 and 1400 in 1670. By 1871 the population was nearly a million. Today the population is almost about 8 millions. There has been a rapid growth of population in the course of 200 years, and it would be interesting from an astrological point of view to study how such a rapid growth of population became possible. Almost every national and racial group is represented among the people in the city. Until 1664, the city was named Amsterdam. After the long strife between the English and Dutch, in 1664 when the city was taken possession of by the English the city was re-named as New-York.

The diversity of New York has become a legend. There is an endless variety of things to see, provided you have the time, the resources and the patience. I visited the harbour, the Statue of Liberty, Wall Street, the Lower East side, Greenwich village, the Times Square, Rockefeller Centre, Central Park, the Metropolitan Museum of Art, Natural History Museum, the Hayden Planetarium, United Nations, the Upper East side, Harlem, Brooklyn,

Coney Island, the Bronx, several churches and one or two theatres in Broadway.

Starting from Times Square where I was staying, my hosts drove me round the city. In a single day we covered the Wall Street in lower Manhattan, Fifth Avenue with its fine shops, residences and clubs ; Riverside Drive overlooking the Hudson's, Park Avenue which continues Fourth Avenue above 8th street to the Grand Central Terminal, and thence from 46th street to the Harlem river, lined with fine apartment houses in the middle section above 45th street ; the Bowery where most people live unconcerned even about themselves, and Broadway which extends more than 18 miles from the southern tip of Manhattan to the northern limits of the city, and then from 34th street to Columbus Circle at 59th street, the centre of the automobile, theatre, movie pictures, restaurant and night life district.

It was lunch time when we had been up the one hundred and two story Empire State Building—supposed to be the world's* tallest. Over a thousand feet below, the enormous mass of people moving in the streets look like insects. From its tower, a 50 mile panorama is visible. New York is the city of sky-scrapers. For a time the commercial sky-scraper became the symbol of the United States. But for one going from a city like Bangalore, where you are always bathed in sunshine, it will not be difficult to realise that the sky-scrapers have reduced the narrow-streets between them to sunless caverns besides adding to the congestion of the surrounding streets.

I very much enjoyed my visit to the Rockefeller Centre, the largest privately owned business and amuse-

---

* Pan American Airways Building is now said to be the tallest in the World.

ment centre in America. It is a towering sky-scraper city with its flowered plaza, theatres, radio and television studios, restaurants, science museums and shops, and covers about 23 acres between fifth and sixth Avenues from 48th to 51st streets. There are 15 separate buildings and the five edifices of the western section of the Centre comprise Radio City. This is the home of the several large corporations including the National and American Broadcasting systems.

Wall Street, with its crowding towers, is the nerve centre of America's pre-eminence in trade and finances. I was told by the friend who took me round the Wall Street, that here the securities are bought and sold in a matter of moments. The street itself is narrow and short extending only some seven blocks from Broadway. Most of the major banking houses maintain headquarters here. It is an international money market and annual transactions soar into billions of dollars. Trading can be watched from a gallery.

The Statue of Liberty in New York harbour is a well-known landmark. A gift of France for the 100th anniversary of American Independence it rises from Bedloe's Island 300 feet above the harbour. The statue is 2 miles from New York City and it can be reached by a steam launch. From the top of the statue, the city of the sky-scrapers, New York, presents a magnificent appearance. It is interesting to see the huge piers which line both sides of river Hudson, with tugs warping ships into their berths and manoeuvring them from pier to pier.

The homes of the fashionable and wealthy are in the Upper East side of the city, 47th to 56th streets. Here wealthy New Yorkers maintain apartments. But the area around 49th to 60th streets is notable for its contrasts of wealth and poverty. Park Avenue is the impressive main artery of the region. It was here that men like Carnegie and Vanderbuilt erected mansions.

Another item of attractive sight-seeing is the Central Park. This large area of woods lies between 5th and 8th Avenues. It offers a variety of recreation to New York goers. Items of interest here are the huge Receiving Reservoir—a part of city's water-supply system, conservatory pond, Belvedere Tower and Cleopatra's Needle.

Among New York's many cultural centres which are open to every one, the Metropolitan Museum of Arts is outstanding. The Museum contains works encompassing almost every known school and nationality. Among permanent collections of art may be mentioned such notable ones as those of Degas, Braque, Benton and Calder.

I became greatly interested in the Museum of Natural History. It is a vast world of natural science with 58 exhibit-filled halls occupying 13 acres of the floor space. 60 million old dinosaur eggs, the 76-foot long sulphur bottom whale, the world's largest frog, are some of the wonderful exhibits. Equally wonderful are the specimens of African animal life in natural settings, elephants, lions, gorillas, etc. It would probably require months to look round the exhibits. It appears that there are forty four museums in New York.

The Hayden Planetarium was of the greatest interest to me. I visited this planetarium with Dr. Havemann by about 12 p.m. and witnessed the show. Hayden Planetarium presents dramatic displays of the Heavens as they are today, were before the Age of Man, and presumably will be a thousand years hence. A student of astrology has here several items of great instruction such as a model of the solar system; and models of the Russian sputniks and American satellites encircling the earth.

Perhaps a brief description of this astronomical marvel would be of interest to my readers. Planetarium is the name given to arrangement for producing an artificial sky. By optical methods, images of the Sun, Moon, planets and stars are projected on a large hemispherical dome and by mechanical and electrical means the apparatus can be revolved so as to show the principal motions. You feel the illusion of reality as the apparatus is set going. I saw the 'heavens' as it would appear at 9 p.m. at New York on the day of my visit. With the planetarium one can clearly see in an hour or so motions which can be seen in the heavens only by years of watching. When a year is compressed into a minute or two, the planets can be seen chasing one another about the sky, advancing retrograding, describing loops, just as they do slowly in the natural heavens. I wish some enterprising Indian would construct a small planetarium in Bangalore or Mysore. Even from an astrological point of view, such an arrangement of the heavens would be of great practical and research value. There are planetaria in different parts of U.S.A. Besides the Hayden Planetarium at New York, I visited the Alder Planetarium at Chicago. In the Hayden, there is a collection of 300 meteorites from outer space.

I visited also the Greenwich village, once characterised by intellectual radicalism. It was here that Paine and Whitman lived. Though it is now part and parcel of New York, some of the early charm of the village remains in its rambling streets, chain shops and old houses with gable roofs and chimney pots. At the Washington Square section of the village, you have the 86-foot high Washington Arch, built in honour of Washington's first inaugural.

The Time Square—I resided in this area—is a clutter of sky-scrapers and souvenir shops. But at dusk it changes into a swirl of animated signs flashing neon advertising noisy hawkers, news-spelled out on the Times Building, and tens of thousands of people rushing. The Times Square is in the heart of the amusement centre—theatres, movies and night life. The only 'amusements' I witnessed were a show at the Metropolitan Opera and a visit to a movie cinema.

New York is not without its dark side. While Upper East side is noted for its fashion and wealth, a part of Lower East side is a district of tenement slums and congested streets. Underprivileged children play on docks and dead-end neighbourhoods—China Town where the Chinese are predominant, Mulberry street which is almost a little Italy; and the Jewish quarter with tiny shops, synagogues and chain stores.

Harlem represents the highest and the lowest status attained by the Blacks in the North of the U.S.A. There are some successful Blacks who live with dignity. But there are also lower class Blacks huddled in over-crowded tenements with attendant vice, disease and delinquency. I went round the Negro Harlem and felt that our 'untouchables', despite the persecution they are supposed to have been subject to, lead a more contented and happy life.

Sight-seeing in New York can be almost an endless pastime for those who can afford the time and I do not wish to tire my readers further: If one has a receptive mind, one's visit to the great city of New York will be filled with rich and never-to-be-forgotten experiences.

5 Washington

I arrived at Washington on the evening of 12th October and had to immediately rush to the dinner meeting at Hotel Hamilton, held under the auspices of the Washington Astrological Association by my esteemed friends Mr. and Mrs. Earnest Grant. The distinguished gathering at the meeting drawn from different walks of life included Dr. Gant, noted astronomer and medical man, Dr. Russel Fields, a noted physician, Dr. Granville Longley, a famous surgeon of the Pacific Coast ; Mr. John S. Csepely Electronics Engineer ; Mr. Richard P. Germann, Mr. Dal Lee, Editor and Publisher of three noted American astrological periodicals ; Mrs. Pearl Ornoroff, Mrs. Bernandette Du Bose, and Mrs. Victoria Tucker. There were also several well-known persons present, whom I cannot now recollect. I was told that some ladies and gentlemen had come from places as distant as 80 miles, to the meeting to hear me. At the main tables sat, on either side of me, Drs. Gant and Russel Fields and I had an interesting discussion with Dr. Gant about recent astronomical studies. Dr. Gant is a noted astronomer and has made special studies of the Moon. I was told that the British Astronomical Association had named one of the crators on the Moon after Dr. Gant. The doctor showed keen interest in Hindu astronomy, especially in its cosmological aspect.

After dinner, I spoke on the "Significance of Astrology in Indian Social Life". Introducing me to the audi-

ence, Mr. Ernest Gant said. "When I, along with friends
was waiting this afternoon at the Washington Railway
Station to receive Prof. Raman, I met an Indian gentle-
man wearing a turban and asked him whether he was
Prof. Raman. He said that he was not the gentleman I was
looking for, that he came from the home-town of Prof.
Raman, that he knew him well and that in India Prof.
Raman was held in great esteem. This tribute, paid by an
Indian gentleman, further strengthened my esteem for
Prof. Raman whom it is my privilege to introduce to
Washington citizens tonight." After describing my humble
astrological activities, Mr. Gant concluded his introduction thus: "I have been in correspondence with Prof.
Raman for over twenty years. Today I have the good
fortune of meeting him in person. He comes here as a
representative of the ancient culture of India and the audience is impatient to hear his lecture and message". Later
on I learnt that the "gentleman wearing a turban" was
my esteemed friend Mr. P. Shivashanker, Principal,
Government Law College, Bangalore. Mr. Shivashanker
happened to visit the United States at the same time that
I did.

In my lecture, I dealt with the antiquity of ancient
Indian Culture, the place of astrology in the general
scheme of Indian social life, the profoundity of Hindu
astrology, the relation between Karma and astrology,
how the horoscope merely indicated the resultant of past
Karma and how with effort it was possible to overcome
some of the evil indications present in the horoscope.
Incidentally I also touched on *Varanashrama Dharma*, the
ashrama aspect of Hindu life, etc. Immediately after the
lecture, Dr. Gant congratulated me on what he called
"your wonderful exposition". The lecture was followed
by a number of questions put by members of the audience

In most of the places I visited in America, two typical questions used to be invariably put to me. They were : (1) The Napalese astrologers expected extinction of humanity in 1962. (2) They and some Americans predicted that a part of America would be destroyed or submerged. Did I endorse these predictions? I replied that there would be no extinction of humanity in 1962, but as the conjunction of eight planets in Capricorn involved concentration of force in one part of the heavens, world affairs were bound to be affected significantly. Nor was there any indication of either life being obliterated on earth or any part of America being submerged under water or destroyed by natural calamities*.

The next morning my hosts Mr. and Mrs. Gant took me out for sight-seeing with Dr. Longley and the evening was spent at the residence of Mr. Gant. An interesting discussion took place on different aspects of astrology. I visited the headquarters of the American Federation of Astrologers and the National Astrological Library. The Federation is perhaps the most important representative astrological organisation in America with which are affiliated a number of state-organisations. Founded in 1938, for the purpose of promoting astrology "through research and education" and establishing "a high standard of professional ethics for legitimate astrologers", the organisation has been doing splendid work. Its official organ is the AFA Bulletin published each lunar month. The National Astrological Library has a fine collection of books on Western Astrology and some on the Indian

---

* The 1962 combination has been over and most of the events anticipated by me—death of Kennedy and Nehru, removal of Khrushchev, the Chinese invasion of India, etc.—have all happened.

systems too. It has published some rare and out-of-print editions of books written by ancient European authors. I think a fine tribute is due to the Gants not only for the interest they evinced in my visit to Washington but also for the work they have done unostentatiously for the cause of astrology in America. Mr. Gant is a keen student of astrology and Indian Culture and his belief in the theory of Karma is as strong as that of any Indian. He is averse to personal publicity and his own interests have merged with the interests of the leading astrological association of America. Mr. Gant told me that he became interested in astrology in 1920's with a view to prove it to be an "erroneous belief and absolutely untrue", but he found it to be "the most wonderful road map of life, God has given man". Since his retirement from the administrative work in American Federation of Astrologers, he is devoting his efforts to astro-pathological research, working with physicians, electronic scientists, etc., "in order to advance astrology to the place it belongs", as a means of preventing and curbing diseases of mankind. Mrs. Catherine Gant is said to possess considerable "predictive sense". She has actively supported her husband Mr. Gant in all of his astrological activities. It was a pleasure to meet the Gants, and the fine evening I spent at their residence is bound to remain ever fresh in my memory.

Dr. Granville Longley, who also accompanied us in our sight-seeing excursions, is a leading surgeon on the Pacific Coast. He said that his interest in astrology was only recent but genuine. He was convinced that astrology was a science and could be of great use to mankind. I was told that he was thinking of making a substantial financial grant for research in medical astrology. Dr.

Longley's observation that an astrological diagnosis of a disease can be more reliable than even a physician's diagnosis made within the four walls of a consulting room is signficant.

In the evening I addressed a select gathering on "Yoga and Psychology" at Hotel Houston where I had been put up. I explained the correlation between certain thought-patterns and planetary positions and how by having recourse to certain asanas or postures the thought vibrations could be directed creatively.

Washington, in the District of Columbia, is the capital of U.S.A. Every American is emotionally attracted to his nation's capital. In this city are national shrines, stately public buildings, foreign embassies, and historic tree-lined avenues. Washington is considered to be the world's "largest one-industry town". And that industry is Government. Washington is the city where America's history has been made, and is in the making. There are lots of things to see here. A drive under leafy arches of Washington's wide avenues and through its numerous parks emphasises the Capital's reputation as the city of trees and statues.

I visited as many places of interest as was possible within the time at my disposal. Situated on a hill and surrounded by a 120-acre park the 'CAPITOL' a huge domed building dominates the city. Its corner-stone was laid in 1793. Seventy years later the Statue of Freedom was placed atop the dome. The building is 750 feet long and 350 feet wide. Legislators have been making laws here since 1800 and within the halls can be seen works of art and statuary depicting American History. The White House, the residential place of the United States' President, is an unassuming building. Compared to the palaces of some of our Maharajas, the White House is unimpressive.

It was the Lincoln Memorial that was of great interest to me. This classic Grecian structure with 36 Doric columns—one for each state at the time of Lincoln's death–stands on a 1000-foot circular terrace reflected in the large pool in front of the entrance. The monument is sombre yet inspiring. The colossal statue of the Civil War President Abraham Lincoln presides over the 70-foot main hall in the walls of which are inscribed Lincoln's famed Gettysburg and second inaugural address.

The Library of Congress, which I could only pay a hurried visit to, is considered to be the largest library in the world with over thirty million items—maps, first editions, orchestral scores, rare books, documents, etc.— and the three-storey building, in the Italian Renaissance style, occupies nearly four acres of ground.

Jefferson Memorial is equally interesting. It is located across the Tidal Basin from Washington monument. It is designed after Jefferson's own tastes. The bronze statue of Jefferson stands 19 feet on a pedestal six feet above the floor.

I visited Alexandria also. This city is reminiscent of pre-revolutionary days. Alexandria's historic Christ Church is also worth seeing.

There are other items of interest such as the Supreme Court, National Archives, Federal Bureau of Investigation, Mount Vernon, National Zoological Park, the Botanical Gardens, The Smithsonian Institution and The National Gallery of Art all of which are worth seeing. There is no doubt that Washington is one of the world's most beautiful cities and offers to the eye of a visitor who comes from New York, the City of sky-scrapers, great relief.

During my stay in Washington, I visited the Indian Embassy also. In the absence of our ambassador who was away at the Hague. I was received by the First Secretary, Dr. Dwarakanath Chattarjee. I found him quite friendly and sincere in his job. He made enquiries about my programmes in America and wished me success in my work. At the Embassy I met some of the staff-members also. An air of coldness and self-importance marked their conduct. I wanted to consult some Indian newspapers to keep myself informed about Indian news. The concerned clerk—an Indian lady—did not know whether or not the newspapers wanted by me had been received. She was just busy chit-chatting with another official. She could not find time to attend to my require-ments. But ultimately she was good enough to assure me that the paper had been received but the copy—obviously belonging to the Embassy Library—had been taken home by some member of the staff—she did not know who it was. But it might have been taken by a certain member who was absent on that day.

This is a small matter for I could get the paper from another Indian friend resident in Washington. But it shows the irresponsible attitude characteerising some of the staff-members of our Embassy. It is their duty to treat Indians who go there from India properly and give them the assistance they need. But, facts appear to be different.

On the 15th morning a number of visitors called on me at my hotel. Suddenly there was a change of weather. It was raining heavily in the forenoon when I left Washington by air for Boston.

6 Boston

At the Washington Air Port, I met Mr. Vincent, a businessman who was on his way to Montreal and we spent half an hour together in the Air Port lounge. He said he was a broker and had business connections all over Canada and the States. He showed keen interest in Indian Philosophy and claimed to possess a good knowledge of Western astrology. Of course he had heard my name. According to Mr. Vincent, genuine astrologers were very few in Canada, but interest in astrology was growing. He extended an invitation to me to visit Canada and assured me of a warm welcome.

It was heavily raining when the plane to Boston I was to travel in, took off from Washington. We were flying above a carpet of rain cloud until we landed at La Guardia Air Port at New York. It was very cold at the Air Port and several through passengers did not wish to get down lest they might catch cold. The flight from New York to Boston was of course most pleasant but for occasional bumps. Sitting back on my seat and looking out on the clouds I felt detached from the world below. The changing pattern of clouds as the aircraft cruised at an altitude of about 10,000 feet, presented a beautiful appearance, and reminded me of Varahamihira's observations in *Brihat Samhita*, that the changing shapes of clouds too are sure weather indicators.

Modern meteorologists are now realising that various types of clouds loft are clues to various kinds of air-mass movements. They also indicate closeness to cold or warm fronts, to thundering weather or to smooth flying conditions. The captain of the aircraft told me that clouds formed into lines may serve a kind of what he called "celestial weather wane". A sharp leaning over the top of a "cumulus cloud often indicates a marked vertical wind sheer, which in turn suggests very strong winds at high altitudes". It was somewhat foggy when the plane touched Boston.

Several phone calls and messages were awaiting my attention when I reached Hotel Avery where I was to put up during my stay at Boston. In most places I visited in U.S.A. meeting press reporters became a part of my daily routine.

But in Boston, Mr. Robert Taylor of the *Boston Herald*, who interviewed me as soon as I arrived at the Hotel, made a special impression upon me. He was sympathetic towards astrology. He knew astrology was a serious science. Even though the generality of newspapers were after "sensationalism" even in matters astrological, Mr. Taylor put me only serious questions such as how astrology was used in India, what were Nadi Granthas, what was the attitude of Pandit Nehru, etc. Though I tried my best to explain to him the philosophical and scientific basis of Hindu astrology, it was a bit difficult for him as I could later on find from the published report of his interview with me, to catch the spirit of our culture correctly.

The *Boston Herald* report said :

" 'Astrology', said Prof. Bangalore Venkata Raman, a cheery Hindu gentleman, whose greying hair was neatly parted in the center and whose powder blue tunic was buttoned on an axis to his throat, 'in my country is a fully developed science.'

"Prof. Raman, in town the other day to give a lecture as a part of his first American visit, is an Indian astrologer. He edits a magazine devoted to his subject; he is the author of some thirty books on Hindu astrology and astronomy; he is a general practitioner and a student of the national culture. He paused before proceeding in a precise, high voice.

" 'Astrology in my country,' he said, 'is in a different position than in the West. Here you will find it regarded often with scepticism and ridicule. But in India it is a daily affair of life. The politician, the head of Government, the medical man, each consults his horoscope. Mr. Nehru? He appears to be indifferent. I know, however, the members of his cabinet consult.''

" 'As for me,' continued Prof. Raman, 'my interest in astrology concerns its philosophical aspect and its place in our traditions. You will find quacks casting horoscopes in India, but I am not speaking of astrology on that level. For us Indians the subject has a fundamentally serious purpose. Doctors make use of horoscopes in diagnosing diseases, statesmen study the planets. Editorials in the leading newspapers are devoted to it.' Here is one from *The Hindu* published in Madras:

"We studied the clipping Prof. Raman had given us. Under comments devoted to the local political situation, *The Hindu* had editorialized: 'Astrology does forecast definite trends in an individual's life, and that it is not always able to foretell all events in detail, certainly does not mean that it is incapable of fulfilling its objectives.''

" 'As an astrologer,' continued the 'Professor, 'one is subject to important disciplines in India. One must conform to strict codes of behaviour. We are vegetarians, for example. If an astrologer is not a vegetarian or uses alcohol or tobacco he is not respected. Above all, the profit motive must be absent from his dealings. A customer pays according to his needs; a poor man may receive my services free."

"The ancient Hindus, after ages of experiment, divided the year into 3,600 parts (I had referred to the Zodiac being divided into 1,800 parts—author) 'I establish the latitude and longitude and such factors as the type of birth, the nature of the birth chamber, the quality and kind of the person's education, etc. In a few hours I am able to fix a definite pattern of destiny."

" 'Here' said Prof. Raman, passing over a faded oblong stack covered with Sanskrit characters, 'are palm leaves on which have been written horoscopes hundreds of years old. Each leaflet contains one and half dozen horoscopes. You will probaly find the destinies of many living Americans here. I have corresponded with the psychiatrist, Carl Gustav Jung, who has written me that in complicated case of diagnosis he finds it useful to consult the patient's horoscope. In my magazine I have predicted many international developments correctly for the most part : Hitler's fall, Indian Independence, etc. The Chinese incursions into India were no surprise to me."

The above is a sample of American reporting on matters pertaining to Hindu astrology.

In the evening, I was escorted by Mr. Oscar Weber to Hotel Lenox where I addressed the New England Astrological Association on "Astrology and Indian Culture". Mrs. Dorothea Lynde, Vice-President of the Association, was in the chair. Introducing me to the audience Mrs.

Lynde said. "I had the pleasure of hearing Prof. B. V. Raman at New York when he addressed the Special Conference organised by the Astrologers' Guild of America on 10th October and I was much impressed by the case he made for Hindu astrology. We were eager that he should speak for us that we did not mind changing the date of our regular meeting to accommodate his convenience. Prof. Raman who is the leader of astrology in his country has impressed all those who heard or meet him after his coming to America. It is a great pleasure and pride for us all to have him as the guest speaker this evening."

In my lecture which lasted for over an hour, I dealt with the evolution of Hindu astrological thought and its intimate bearing on Indian Culture, and pointed out where Hindu astrology has scored over Western system and how, according to the ancient sages, astrology did not endorse absolute fatalism, but gave a certain scope for the exercise of what "we call free will". The audience were highly appreciative of the lecture and the President, Mrs. Clara V. Cotta, paid tributes to what she called "an excellent exposition of Hindu approach to astrology". Before the lecture, I was treated to dinner and music and the whole programme was thoroughly enjoyable.

The New England Astrological Association is an organisation devoted to the study of astrology on scientific lines and has membership drawn from the New England States—Maine, New Hampshire, Vermont, Massachusetts, Rhode Island and Connecticut. It has also a group of "analytical researchers"—astrologers who are doing careful study correlating horoscopes that show tendencies of a similar nature towards certain diseases. The programme of the Association includes holding of regular meetings and discussions. Both the President, Mrs. Cotta, and the Vice-President, Mrs. Dorothea, appeared to me to be sincere students of astrology. Another astrologer who impressed me was Mr. Oscar Weber. He is now the President of the American Federation of Astrologers. During the brief time we spent together, I could feel that Mr. Weber had certain original ideas bearing astrological interpretations He told me about what he termed "Weber Potential"—a new theory of his own. Briefly stated, the theory is as follows :

"The Sun is symbolic of the 'evolving spirit' (developing in the future). The Moon is the symbol of the 'soul', the sum-total of the past—be it past incarnations (from a metaphysical point of view) or the genes and the chromosomes inherited from our forebears (from a genetic point of view). Therefore if the present is the meeting point between the past (the Moon) and the future (the Sun), then when the transiting Moon makes the exact conjunction, by sign, degree, and minute (in geocentric longitude) of the birth Sun, a horoscope, calculated for this time, should show the present potentialities."

I have to thank the office-bearers of the N.E.A.A., for the warm welcome extended to me.

Boston, the capital city of the State of Massachussetts, ranks tenth in population and eighth in value of retail trade in the United States. It is a port and an industrial city—noisy, dirty and bustling. It is also noted for its famous "crooked streets" in the north and west ends of the city. The 'Post Office' costing about six million dollars (about Rs. 4 crores) in 22 storeys high and houses not only the Post Office but also the sub-treasury and the Federal Courts. Boston abounds in a number of ancient landmarks, which include public buildings, residences, old graveyards, and the Boston Common. Boston is the centre of a large district in which are situated many notable educational institutions. Across the Charles river stands Cambridge where the cultural history of America has developed side by side with the history of the Harvard University, which is supposed to be the world's richest. Named after John Harvard, a clergyman who at his death in 1638 left the institution a few hundred books and half his estate, Harvard is said to have an endowment today of more than three hundred and fifty million dollars and its library has over five million volumes. Other famous centres of learning are the Radcliffe College for Women and the Massachussetts Institute of Technology, famous for scientific training and research.

The Boston Public Library is one of the most famous libraries in the world. It is housed in a building, simple and striking, and constructed in the Italian Renaissance Style. The Library is said to contain about two million volumes. Of course, Boston is not lacking in theatres and motion picture houses of which the most pretentious and by far the handsomest is the Metropolitan. According to Americans, in this area are buried the "Tap roots" of America's spiritual family. I saw as much of Boston as was possible and I did feel that historically Boston is one of the richest spots in America. Some of the narrow and twisting lanes, old residences, open markets and dead-end streets reminded me of places like Belgaum and Poona. As I was about to leave my hotel for the Air Port, my host said: "Boston is neither ancient nor modern, rich nor poor, beautiful nor ugly. It is not, in short, a single entity, but a composite of many eras, cultures and peoples." And I nodded my head in assent.

7 Cleveland

I left Boston for Cleveland on 15th October 1959 at 7 a.m. The previous evening I had missed my usual fruit-meal. After the lecture at the New England Astrological Association, as some friends stayed on with me till late in the night carrying on discussions I could go to bed only about 2 a.m. and sleep for just three hours, as in the morning I had to be at the air port by 6-30 a.m. Therefore when the plane took off at Boston I was somewhat famished and became my normal self again only after the morning breakfast milk and corn flakes—served in the plane. The four-hour flight to Cleveland was pleasant and the weather—I was told—usually more bumpy—was kind. As we took off from Boston, the sun was gradually rising. A sort of golden-crimson spread. It was a relief to stretch comfortably in the pressurised cabin of the aircraft experiencing the chilling dampness of Boston weather. As the aircraft neared Cleveland, I could get a pleasant view of the City 'perched' as it was on a plateau, along the Lake Erie at the mouth of the Cuyahoga river. We landed at Cleveland at 11 a.m. and it was getting warmer. It took nearly 2 hours for the limoisine to bring me to Hotel Hollenden, a fine hotel by all standards, where I took up residence during my stay at Cleveland.

My first visitors were a couple—students of Hindu astrology—and they had brought two of my books with

them for autographing, which I did with great pleasure.
Casually I complained to the visitors that ever since I left
Bangalore I had not tasted good coffee and that in New
York, Washington, etc., the 'coffee' supplied to me looked
like a decoction of tamarind seeds. They invited me to a
nearby restaurant—supposed to serve the best coffee—and
as the weather was good, I accompanied them in the usual
South-Indian *dhoti*, shirt and *uttariyam*. I was the object
of special attention at the restaurant. The dress I was
wearing was unusual in a place like Cleveland. Several
passers by smiled at me and I heard some of them saying
"wonderful dress".

Before leaving India, I had been cautioned by a
friend, that in Western countries one appearing in public
places with *dhoti* would be ridiculed. I had told him that
it was my feeling that instead of being ridiculed, one
sticking to national attire and national habits would be
respected. My experience has amply confirmed this belief.
"Excellent" coffee, my friends assured, would be served
in the restaurant I was taken to. Though I found the
brown–coloured liquid fairly palatable, it was at best an
apology for coffee one is used to in a place like Bangalore.
As I and my hosts walked back to the Hotel, after passing
through a few streets, a little Negro girl, who crossed us
on the road, bowed to me and yelled, "Yeh! Come from
India !" I reciprocated the courtesy with a *namaste*, the
significance of which formed the subject-matter of my
conversation with the other two friends until they left me
at the Hotel. The elevator–boys, the bearers, and the
hotel staff showed curiosity in my dress. They had never
seen an "Indian gentleman" or for that matter anybody
else appearing in such a "fine attire".

In the evening, Mrs. Joanna Guthrie called on me
along with some of her friends. They were all interested

in "Indian Astrology, Karma and Yoga". Mrs. Guthrie had heard me speak at New York and she and her friends wanted to discuss with me how "culturally India and America could be brought nearer" as they were convinced that ancient India had much to offer them. At 6 p.m. Mrs. Louis Mc Bean, President of the Ohio Astrological Association with other office-bearers, gave a dinner to me at the same hotel. The guests showed keen interest in what I had to say on various aspects of India's social and cultural life.

Under the auspices of the Ohio Astrological Association, I delivered a lecture on 'Saturn in Hindu Astrology' at Hotel Olmstead. Mrs. Mc Bean presided. After briefly describing the great attainments of ancient Indians in science, culture and philosophy, I said : "When Ptolemy was refuting the diurnal motion of the earth giving as his principal reason that if the earth turned, the objects that were not fixed to its surface would appear to move in a contrary direction and that a body shot into the air would fall back to the west of the starting-point, the earth having turned from west to east, his Hindu predecessor Aryabhatta was emphatic that the rotation of the earth round its axis caused the rising and setting of planets and stars." After elaborating the principles common to Hindu and Western astrology and pointing out "certain features which are peculiar to the Hindu system", I dealt with the importance of Saturn, as making or marring one's destiny, illustrating my points by a number of example horoscopes. I concluded my lecture thus : "The effects of Saturn are not always evil. Saturn is also productive of what are called Raja Yogas—indicating power. position and attainments—and these become fully manifest during his main and sub-periods. But bye and large Saturn seems to have a constructive role to play in the long runs for after making the native pass through various phases of difficulties and troubles, he will also enable the person to spiritually progress. But in cases where Saturn joins 'poisonous parts' of constellations along with Mars or the Nodes without any other counteracting influences, life throughout will be marked by misery, struggle and mis-understanding. In the horoscopes of several criminals, Saturn–Rahu–Mars afflictions will be clearly visible. The situation of Saturn in Aquarius favours true philanthropy. development of mystic power and quiet persistence where-as the reverse position is an index of a hypocrite, a social snob and a pimp.

"Hindu astrology does not ignore the transit effects of Saturn, Only they are of secondary importance, as transits should always be interpreted in the light of directional influences. When Saturn is in the 9th or 10th house, in association with Mars Sun or Rahu or in the constellation of any of these planets or in that of a 3rd or 7th lord, and the native has the chance of enjoying the main period of either Saturn or the other associates, the person gets a wide stage on which to act his part. He will be actuated by a lust for power and possession. He will get what he wants but he will be obliged to disgorge his entire acquisitions when Saturn transits the said 9th or 10th place. Saturn-Rahu association especially in certain destructive parts of the different constellations gives also suicidal tendencies. For example, Saturn-Rahu association with the Moon in the asterism ruled by the Ascendant is an indication of suicidal tendencies especially during the main period of Rahu and the sub-period of Saturn. Dozens of cases can be produced in support of these theories. But in all these cases, the affliction planets should secure a certain optimum value of affliction which can be measured by the point–system of judging planetary strength. The Hindus conceived the lunar nodes as the cross-roads of magnetic influences full of potency and gave them the status of planets in so far as their effects are concerned, and their being joined by Saturn has always been considered as a great affliction.

"Most of what I have said just now is not mere text-book stuff. It is based on the experiences of thousands of years and hence they are to be considered as tested formulae. I am sure, with the spirit of enquiry and research, so evident in the attitude of astrologers in this country, it should be possible for you to test some of the salient features of Hindu astrology with a view to convincing yourselves, how far they are reliable and to what extent they can be incorporated into your own methods of prediction.

'Such a vast and important subject as the role of Saturn cannot be compressed into the brief period of a single lecture. Nor could I give any definite suggestions or exact procedures. Therefore I have confined this lecture to give you just a few hints on a certain aspect of Hindu astrology that is unique in its own way and that has stood the test of time and experience for several thousand years. More than the sign positions it is the house and constellational positions that are really important.

"I think by adapting some of these principles to suit the social and cultural conditions in this part of the world, Western astrology can be greatly enriched."

After the question-hour which extended till about 11 p.m., Mrs. Mc Bean thanked me profusely for what she called "an able exposition of an aspect of astrology in

which American astrologers are deeply interested but the
true significance of which is not correctly known".

The whole of next day was devoted to sight-seeing.
Mrs. Joanna Guthrie took me round the town in her car
and I was able to visit a number of places of interest
including some rural parts.

Cleveland is a great industrial city in the State of
Ohio which is considered to be the only area of the world
where there is "a remarkable concentration and balance
of agricultural and industrial wealth". Cleveland is the
seventh largest city in the United States and the population is about a million. One peculiarity I found in this
city is that the streets are not only of unusual width but
well-shaded. Lower Euclid avenue is the centre of retail
trade. Those of the residential areas are in the outlying
sections of the city—Lakewood, Cleveland Heights, Shekar
Heights, Brooklyn, etc. The court house and the city
hall, separated by a mall, are on the edge of the plateau.
The city has numerous fine buildings, the Union Terminal
Building with its tower 720 feet high being visible for
many miles from the city. The Rockefeller Park with 20
"cultural gardens" and busts of national leaders is well
worth a visit. There are innumerable items of interest
for a visitor—the Museum of Art, the Museum of Natural
History, the Zoological Park, Western Reserve Historical
Museum, the Aquarium, Cultural Gardens, the James
Garfield Monument, etc. I became particularly interested
in the Museum of Art. The collections include paintings,
sculpture, metal works, etc. The most cherished items are
the 'nine objects' from the famous tenth century Guelph
Treasure. Among the collections, there is a very fine idol
of goddess Saraswathi. The Garfield Monument situated
on a commanding site in the Lake View cemetry is worthwhile a visit. It is a memorial to James A. Garfield, 20th

President of the United States. A number of fine bas-
reliefs and sculptural works depicting the life of Garfield
are used throughout the Monument. At the base of the
tower in Memorial Hall is a statue of Garfield in Italian
marble. Directly below the Hall is the crypt with caskets
of Garfield and his wife. Of special interest are some of
the fine murals added to the interior by nationally known
artists such as Paul Riba, Michael Sarisky, etc. I had a
delightful view of the Lake from a spot 75 feet above.
The neighbourhood affords delightful walks. I visited
some of the departmental stores where generally the
American housewife makes all her purchases and I got
back to the hotel late in the evening after a sumptuous
fruit dinner given to me by an enterprising couple. The
lady of the house, whose name I do not now recollect, is
an astrologer herself and showed keen interest in my work.

The next day after visiting some friends I left for
Toledo. Mrs. Joanna Guthrie drove me in her beautiful
limoisine and we covered the distance of 140 miles within
three hours, after a brief halt for a few minutes in a roadside gas station for refuelling. We passed through industrial and agricultural areas and the natural scenery at
some places was most lovely. Mrs. Guthrie who was at
the wheel showed herself to be a very good driver and in
deference to my wishes did not exceed the speed-limit
over 60 miles an hour. During the three-hour trip, we
talked on Indian Culture, American history, the race-
problem in America and the East–West tension, etc., and
I was particularly struck by the understanding the lady
revealed in her estimate of the uniqueness of Indian social
life and Indian Culture.

We reached Toledo at 4 p.m. and were warmly welcomed by Mr. and Mrs. Darr. Arrangements had been

made for me to stay with the Darrs in their house in Broadway but I preferred Hotel Commodore Perry, perhaps one of the best hotels in the United States. Mrs. Guthrie dropped me at the hotel and immediately left back for her place. I was scheduled to speak the same evening and as I was about to leave for my lecture, I discovered, to my great discomfiture, that I had lost my brief-case containing my passport, health certificate, American Express dollar cheques and other essential documents.

8 Toledo

The discovery of the loss of my hand-bag containing important documents, passport, America Express Dollar cheques, etc.—as soon as I reached Hotel Commodore at Toledo, upset me for a while and all sorts of thoughts began to cross my mind. The prospect of being stranded in U.S.A. indefinitely, until a new passport was secured from India worried me most as this would upset all my future itinerary not only in America but in Europe. However, I immediately recovered from this temporary aberration. After helping myself with a cup of milk, I prepared a horary chart, the question being, whether the lost article would be recovered. The ascendant at the time was Taurus. Here, the lost article contained travel documents—communications—and therefore the significator is the lord of the 3rd house. The Moon who happened to be such a lord was in Aries—a movable sign, a trikona (trine) from Venus, lord of the ascendant. Therfore, I concluded that the article would be secured, before the Moon entered his own Navamsa, which would be the case by about midnight. The astrological indications were favourable and allayed my fears greatly.

At 7 p.m. Mrs. Darr and her brother-in-law drove me to the Y.M.C.A., where I spoke on "Indian and Western Astrology". Mrs. Clara M. Darr presided. Dealing with the background of Indian Culture I said : "The political subjugation of India in the recent past not only eclipsed her national genius in its multifarious forms but also made an unprejudiced and impartial appreciation of her lofty cultural attainments in the remote past more and more difficult. But if a thorough study of the indigenous sources of history is made by a dispassionate scholar, he is compelled to conclude that the ancient Hindus have evolved a distinct civilisation from which has emanated a continuous cultural stream the flow of which has been uninterrupted even today in spite of the impacts of modern technological and industrial civilisation, although perhaps a few minor ruffles might have been formed on the surface owing to the periodical onslaughts from external agencies. Sometimes it is painful to come across the casual way in which the development of Hindu astronomy and astrology is dealt with by modern historians of astronomy. The best way of getting at truth is to resort to a study of the original and indigenous sources."

After tracing the evolution of astrological thought in India, I dealt with the principles common to the two systems emphasizing the factors where Hindu astrology has definitely scored over the Western system. I further observed : "I can assure you on behalf of my Indian colleagues that the Indian system of astrology is a magnificent edifice with a deep and strong foundation. Some of the unhealthy accretions that may have gathered round it are being clipped. In our systems, there is a wealth of amassed knowledge and it seems to be a waste of one's efforts to do research work into aspects of astrology which have already Been covered so well by Hindu astrologers". I wound up my lecture expressing the hope that 'America' which is in the forefront of scientific development, will also be in the forefront of astrological studies assimilating what is the best in the Indian system and thus forging ahead in the furtherance of astrological knowledge".

After the lecture there were lively questions put by members of the audience ranging from Ayanamsa to the 1962 combination. A number of questions pertained to the part played by astrology in Indian marriages. I impressed on the questioners that in India, marriage was still regarded as a sacrament and not merely an institution for sex satisfaction and that marriage comprehended the equality of the partner in respect of Dharma (right conduct), Artha (financial matters), Kama (sex relations), and Moksha (spiritual life) and that the universality of marriage constituted one of the most striking differences between the Hindus and other races. I also explained the significance of Kutas and how by proper consideration of these factors, a clear idea of the psychological, sexual and temperamental compatibilities could be obtained and how the Hindus have devised an astrological means of judging marriage compatibility whereby relations between the couple might stand the strain of maladjustments. Mrs. Darr, the President, paid a glowing tribute to what she called "my achievements in astrology" and hoped that the Toledo citizens would have an opportunity of listening to my discourses at "not too distant a future". Mrs. Clara Darr has been an active worker in the field of astrology for a long time. She is a keen student of Hindu astrology and has made a good study of the extant literature on the subject. She is convinced that Hindu astrology has made certain definite advances over the Western system in regard to certain aspects of prediction.

After my return to India, I received a letter from Mrs. Darr telling me that "everyone here was so grateful and inspired by your lecture and are eagerly looking forward to meet you again".

I got back to the hotel by about midnight and a pleasant surprise awaited me. And it was a telegram from Mrs. Guthrie to the effect that she had found my hand-bag in her car and that she would herself deliver it to me the next morning by about 11 o'clock. This was a most welcome news and I thanked myself for the fulfilment of my astrological anticipation. The result was I fell into deep and undisturbed sleep immediately I stretched myself on my bed.

The next morning we went round Toledo sight-seeing. The city of Toledo lies on both sides of the Maimme river and the population is about half a million. I visited a number of places of interest including the University, which has a campus of 160 acres. The streets are shaded and wide and clean and some of the streets reminded me of Bangalore. There are also an open-air amphitheatre, a Museum of Natural Science, and Egyptian antiquities. I was told there are nearly 300 churches and one or two mosques in the city. Toledo is also famous for the manufacture of glassware, automobile parts and machine tools. I also visited some important historical sights including the scene of "Toledo War" about ten miles from the city. Toledo is a city of great commercial importance and its charming environs deeply impressed me.

When I was having my lunch about mid-day Mrs. Guthrie called on me to deliver my hand-bag. It was immediately decided that we should visit Detroit and especially the Henry Ford Museum. We reached Dearborn in the State of Michigan by about 2 p.m. It is the home of Henry Ford who was born on a farm in the city. Ford restored the 'Farm' to its early appearance and built the famous "Henry Ford Museum". In this 14–acre Museum, American history comes to life. It contains vast and varied collections which portray the major aspects in the growth and development of what is known as the "American Nation" from pioneer days to the present time. The front buildings of this large structure are architectural reproductions of Independence Hall and the old city Hall of Philadelphia. The Museum is divided into three main sections : the Fine Arts Galleries, the Street of early American shops and the Mechanical Arts Hall. I became particularly interested in the second and third sections. In the second section, there are 22 diverse and completely equipped shops as they existed two hundred years ago, such as Carpenter, Violin-maker, Milliner, Tinsmith, etc. The third section is divided into seven major sections such as Agriculture, Crafts, Industrial Machinery, Steam and Electric Power, Communication, Illumination and Transportation. The evolution of the Ford Motor car from its first ramshacle model. the evolution of the aeroplane beginning from that of Wright Brothers, the evolution of the steam engine, etc., can all be seen in this magnificent museum. Here can also be found objects ranging from precision electronics equipment to the multi-engine airplane which carried Byrd across the soutb pole.

I also paid a flying visit to Greenfield village nearby. There are about 100 buildings representing the different phases of national life as lived by the forefathers of the present Americans. The houses of such men as Luther Burbank and Wright Brothers have been restored. In these two places the Ford Museum and the Greenfield village, one can get a vivid and nostalgic picture of America's rich past. Of all the historical structures standing as monuments to their departed owners, I took keen interest looking round the birthplace of the shed where the first Ford Car was made and the laboratory where Edison completed many of his famous inventions.

We started our journey back to Toledo at 5-30 p.m.
It was drizzling a little as we boarded the car but the
sky cleared up and the weather became quite pleasant.
The sixty mile drive back was pleasant. The Sun was
slowly sinking down the western horizon, and by the
time we reached Toledo, the Sun had disappeared. Trip
by car from Toledo to Cleveland and Toledo to Detroit
and back provided me with an opportunity to see the
countryside. The Midwest covering Detroit, Cleveland,
Toledo and Chicago seems to have its own variety of
topography and climate. It has an infinite variety of life
and culture. It appeared to me to be a land of great
beauty, of springs and streams and lakes of birch and the
pine trees.

When I got back to the hotel I could not help feeling
what a variety of people and places I had already come
across in my travels in the brief period I had so far spent
in U.S.A. America is a nation made up of people of many
nations. And even then sub-national differences become
quite evident to any intelligent man, who keenly observes
the people and places.

On arrival at the hotel, I phoned the "room service"
for a cup of coffee. Draped in a dhoti and a towel I was
glancing through a newspaper. A Negro bearer with the
tray of coffee entered my room and yelled : "Sir what is
that white thread around your neck ? How did it stick to
you?" I said, "It is a sacred thread which I have been
wearing since my 9th year. It is generally worn by most
Hindus and is a symbol of spirituality."

The Negro boy could not follow my explanation but
showed curiosity. "Don't you wear a cross as we Chris-
tions do ?" I retorted : "Hindus are not Christians.
Their religion is older than Christianity." The Negro
continued : "Are the Hindus then Pagans ?" I replied :

"No, Hindus are more civilized, more ancient and cultured than most of the Christians." The Negro said he had studied up to the High School. He looked intelligent. I talked with him for another ten minutes and he departed remarking : "I know you are not a pagan Sir, but excuse me if I have talked any impertinence".

In the night I was treated to a dinner by Mr. and Mrs. Darr. I was introduced to all the members of their family—sons, daughters, daughters-in-law, fiancees of their sons, etc. I was asked to speak on family life in India. They all heard what I had to say with great interest. It was difficult for them to believe that boys and girls in India do not freely mix with each other, that divorce is still unpopular and that vegetarianism is an article of faith with millions of Hindus.

The next morning I left for Chicago by train.

9 Chicago

The railway journey from Toledo to Chicago was pleasant. There are generally two types of accommodation in the trains, the coach and the pullman. The former type of accommodation may be compared to the former first class (now abolished) in Indian railways but with infinitely better comforts and more courteous service. On the pullman we have the 'roomette' and the 'bed room'. Every room has its own private lavatory, radio and shower bath. An easily operated premade bed lowers from the wall to replace a wide daytime sofa seat. I occupied a cosy and comfortable roomette. With its richly upholstered furniture, and heating, lighting and airconditioning controls which can be regulated to one's individual preference, and panoramic windows, it was a new experience to travel in an American train.

When I was reading a newspaper in the club-lounge near the centre of the train, I made the acquaintance of a sociologist. We moved on to the observation lounge at the rear and were relaxing on a sofa sipping coffee.

The sociologist said that a number of Indians were studying in the Institute be was employed in and that most of them were very intelligent and came out successful in competitive examinations. I felt very happy when my countrymen were referred to in such complimentary terms. As we were talking, two children, aged 10 and 8 were playing hide and seek, the parents looking on unconcernedly and our conversation switched on to the problem of youth and juvenile delinquency.

The sociologist said, the problem of teenagers had been causing considerable concern to the parents and the authorities. "How about the teenagers in India", questioned the friend. "They do not yet stand comparison with their opposites in America, but juvenile delinquency somehow seems to be related to a weakening of the old Indian family pattern", I replied. "It is exactly the case here too" retorted the sociologist. The remedies? He had of course plenty of them in his mind but "none of them would work under the present conditions in America".

But our coversation had to be cut down because of the 'delinquency' of the two children in causing noise and running about the lounge. As we were finishing our coffee the train was steaming into the Chicago Union station, and I took leave of the sociologist and got back to my 'roomette' to get ready to detrain.

At the railway station I was looking round to get a porter to carry my baggage. No porter turned up. I saw every passenger carrying his or her own baggage. Used in India to being "invaded" by "coolies" even before the train stopped, it was a bit difficult for me to realise that it was just a matter of one doing it oneself. I asked one of the railway officials whether a porter could be secured to transfer my luggage to a taxi. No, unless the pullman porter places an identification on each piece of the luggage, giving the passenger a duplicate receipt before the train arrives at the station. I carried my luggage to the taxi stand and arrived at Hotel Morrison.

Within hardly an hour of my arrival at Chicago, I was entertained to a dinner at a Chinese restaurant "The Bamboo Inn", by Miss Gloria Barrett, President of the

"Friends of Astrology". Among the select gathering of guests were Dr. Gustav Ekstrom who had come from Minneapolis to hear me speak, Mr. Sucher of the Landvidi Institute and Mrs. Julie Bam.

After the dinner, we walked to the headquarters of 'Friends of Astrology' about two furlongs from the Bamboo Inn and I delivered a lecture on "Astrology and Remedial Measures". There was a good gathering of Chicago astrologers. Miss Barrett was in the chair.

After thanking Miss Barret "for having enabled me to meet you all this evening and to tell you something about a very important aspect of Indian culture, viz., Astrology, in which I know that many of you are much interested", I said.

"I have been in the United States for about two weeks and have had the good fortune of meeting quite a number of astrologers and those interested in astrology. I feel convinced that American friends are very eager to know more about India, her people and her ancient culture. I can now visualise a period of fruitful co-operation between American and Indian astrologers to bring about the development of astrology on sound lines and also initiate researches into the vast and unexplored field of ancient Indian astrology".

After explaining the indigenous nature of Hindu astrology, I dealt at length with the theory of Karma. "The relationship between the planets and Karma," I went on, "may roughly be compared to the relationship between a thermometer and one's body temperature. The thermometer just records the temperature. It does not bring about the fever. Similarly planets do not cause the events to happen even though they just show the burden one has to bear in life's pilgrimage due to causes generated by him in his previous lives, *i.e.,* his past karma. Suppose one has caused the death of somebody's child in his previous life. The consequence of this is he will lose his children. And this is shown in the horoscope by Mars and the Moon's ascending Node (Rahu) occupying the 5th house. Similarly if Venus is afflicted by his conjunction with Saturn, Rahu or Mars, the interpretation that would be put on this combination will be that the karma of the person in his past lives was such as to call for punishment in the direction of want of happiness in married life, and this is indicated by the position of Venus. Of course in these cases. we say that the influence of Rahu in 5th is to cause death of children; and that the affliction of Venus is the cause of loss of wife, etc.

"An old sage sums up the doctrine of karma thus : Sow a thought, reap a character, sow a character and reap a destiny. According to the sages, the truth of karma theory has been based upon direct experience of the sages, a proposition I know, that many modern thinkers will not easily endorse. But that is no reason why the doctrine of karma cannot be accepted."

I further said : "The proof of the pudding lies in its eating. The truth of remedial astrology is a fact of experience. But it may not fit into the current theories of science. That is a different matter. But I would like to refer to concrete cases. Resorting to remedial measures to overcome the adverse indications in the horoscope is a common feature in India, as common as the American citizen visiting a physician for ill-health or a psychiatrist for mental ill-health.

"A middle aged merchant, a victim of advanced tuberculosis and discharged by a sanatorium, after three to four months of treatment as an incurable case, got complete relief within a year from the date of discharge.

The patient's family astrologer, learned and experienced in the traditional lore, was emphatic that the patient's horoscope showed good longevity and that he was only passing through a very serious crisis which would be tided over by astrological remedies, which consisted in the application of the energies of Saturn and the Moon's ascending Node on to the patient, for a period of forty days. The patient, who was unable even to walk, began to show signs of improvement and within three months he was on his legs. His recovery was gradual and he is now declared by the medical men to be above danger.

"The wife of an eminent Scientist, who was the head of a leading Institute of Science who now occupies a very prominent position in the field of science in India, fell seriously ill and the leading doctors advised surgical treatment, involving one lung. In accordance with the prevailing practice of consulting astrologers before agreeing to such drastic medical treatments, the lady's horoscope was shown to a well-known astrologer. His finding was that no surgical operation was necessary and that the defects noticed in the lung would be automatically set right if remedial measures were performed in resyect of the afflicted planets. The astrologer's advice was heeded to and within three months the lady came to normal health.

"Perhaps remedial astrology is still not much known in the Western system. But in Hindu astrology, this has been well developed and widely put into use so as to have attained considerable perfection. Years ago, one of your esteemed countrymen Mr. John O'Neil, Science Editor of the *New York Herald Tribune*, who was deeply interested in astrology, wrote to me on the same subject. According to him prediction of future, even if correctly done, would not be useful unless man could overcome or minimise the adverse indications. He suggested that it might be possible for science to design certain contrivances which could offset the afflicted rays of planets. When I brought to his notice that remedial measures were an important feature of Hindu astrology and that Hindu sages had developed certain processes involving the use of sound vibrations, etc., he was not only amazed but showed great interest in understanding these techniques.

"I am happy to see that astrologers in U.S.A. are brimming with enthusiasm not only to place the science of astrology in its proper elevated place but also to learn more and more about Hindu astrology. I feel that if the scientific spirit so evident amongst American astrologers could be blended with the vast mines of knowledge we have in the Hindu system, substantial progress in predictive methods can be made. There is a variety of spheres in which my people and your people are currently co-operating to the mutual benefit of mankind. Let us try to widen this sphere by including joint research in astrology also."

After paying a handsome compliment to my "work in the field of astrology" the President commended the doctrines of Indian systems to the attention of American astrologers. Miss Gloria Barrett is an active worker in the cause of astrology. Besides being President of "Friends of Astrology" she is also recording secretary of American Federation of Astrologers.

After the lecture, I walked back to my hotel with one Mr. Calvin Hanes, a keen student of Astrology. He has been developing an interesting theory on the lines of Uranian astrology to help timing events on the basis of

5

secondary directions. As we neared the hotel, roaring blizzards made walking very uncomfortable.

The next morning I addressed a select group of Chicago astrologers on "Progressions" at my place of residence. After dealing briefly with the various methods of progressions in vogue in the West, I explained the superiority of Indian Vimshottari Dasa system and how by proper assessment of the significations and strengths of the lords, events could be anticipated with a great degree of accuracy.

Incidentally I also referred to the part played by Gochara or transits in interpreting the Dasas and emphasising at the same time that transits are only secondary in importance.

Before I began my address, some of the astrologers narrated their own experiences with the methods in vogue in America and particularly one lady astrologer was dogmatic in asserting that transits can overpower even directional indications. Just a day before, she said, a client of hers broke his leg, because Mars was transiting a certain position from the radical Sun. Another client lodged divorce proceedings against her husband because Uranus was squaring her radical Venus!

I had to emphatically declare that undue importance should not be given to transits and that an event not shown in the horoscope cannot happen because of a transit and that at best their role would be similar to the role of the force of gravitation in affecting the course of a bullet expelled by a rifle. I tried to convince the group that Indian astrology offers a fertile field for research and that the Hindu Dasa system could be adopted by them with suitable modifications befitting their social and cultural conditions. There is no doubt that an influential section of thinking astrologers in America have begun to feel that Hindu astrology merits serious attention.

Declining with gratitude a beautiful limousine placed at my disposal by a Chicago businessman, I decided to go sight-seeing, all myself, in the local transport service and by foot as I wished to see how the bus conductors behaved towards the passengers and *vice versa* and how the transport system functioned in Chicago, as compared to Indian cities. The experience was most interesting and in a way thrilling because I was able to see not only all the interesting places but also to meet and talk to several common people.

The City of Chicago, the second largest in the United States with a population of nearly four millions, sprawling along the South-western shore of Lake Michigan is the Central Terminal of the United States. As you travel by train you can see the large fertile farm lands surrounding the city. It is supposed to be the greatest railroad hub in the world. The driver of the transport—an air-conditioned bus with comfortable seats—showed himself to be an expert guide and narrator. Interspersing his description of the city with sarcastic references to some of the big capitalists, he said : "Chicago was not raised, it grew. Bitter labour wars, race riots, boomtimes and depressions forged into it a bold hardiness. From detective Allen Pinkerton, reaper inventor Cyrus Mc Cornie, meat packer P. D. Armour, railroad magnate George Mortiner Pullman, merchant Marshall Field and social worker Jane Addams, Chicago gained a strident, vital confidence."

A century ago, Chicago was an unincorporated village of fifty people and today it is one of the largest cities in the world. With its suburbs, Chicago occupies a crescent shaped area the concave side of which is the shore of

Lake Michigan. There are a number of buildings notable, for architectural boldness such as the Chicago temple, the Wrigley building, the Auditorium, the La Selle, and the Blackstone and Sharaman Hotels. The Art Institute of Chicago, the Museum of Science and Industry and the Chicago Natural History Museum are also noteworthy. It is said that in Chicago the most intensive modern industrialism and commercial activities have been harmonised with beauty, social welfare and cultural centres.

There are a number of fine parks in the city—nearly 300—some of them are of great size and beauty. The peculiarity is, the park in each district usually located near a school, is all inclusive in its provision for all comers "from boyhood to maturity" and is open all day. I particularly visited the Lincoln Park near the lake shore, with its zoological gardens, the Jackson Park, the Humboldt which has a fine rose garden, and the Grant Park containing the Art Institute, the Adler Planetarium and Natural History Museum. The Adler Planetarium interested me much. It is like the Hayden planetarium in New York which I have described earlier. I paid a visit to the University of Chicago. The campus of 110 acres has about 85 buildings, most of which are "Gothic in architectural style and grouped in quadrangles". The importance of this University becomes evident if we note that expenditures under the University regular budget for 1949-50 comprising continuing educational research activities were 16,566,019 dollars and for auxiliary enterprises (residence, dining halls, International House, etc) 3,960,397 dollars. The consolidated budget expenditure totalled 42,425,735 dollars.

The financial district is situated in La Selle Street but it stands no comparison to New York's Wall Street. Chicago is no unblemished gem. No doubt in many ways it is a beautiful city, but packed into 23 of its 212 square miles are some of the worst slums. The Loop with its ancient, elevated and surface street cars is noisy and a test of the visitor's patience. The Loop is the financial, shopping and amusement centre. Below the stock-yards, middle class residential flats fill up the south side. The west side is famous as the home of a large majority of Chicago's half million foreign born Poles, Germans, Russians, etc.

It was nearing midnight when I got down from the bus in the Michigan Avenue near the Art Institute. I walked for 15 minutes and then took a turn to the left. The street was dimly lit. A hefty person near a drab-looking building accosted me saying : "Won't you come in to witness the show ?" "What show ?" I asked him. "It is an art show, admission free." Curiosity made me step in. But to my utter discomfiture, I discovered that it was a night club. Strip teasing had started. It was a scene of revelry. The atmosphere was nauseating to my sense of decency. I could not stand the "show". I came out within a couple of minutes and walked briskly towards my hotel. I missed my way and a kindly pedestrian took me by my arm and left me near Hotel Morrison, thanking me profusely for the "valuable talk" I had with him on India.

The next morning I again went round places of interest which I had not covered the previous day. I drove to Chicago Heights, an important industrial centre about 28 miles south of Chicago, in a latest Cheverolet and my industrialist-friend took me round a glass-manufacturing concern with which he was connected. By 11 a.m. we were back at the Midway Airport. I took off by a TWA plane to my next destination—Los Angeles.

10 Los Angeles

As the aircraft I flew in into Los Angeles gained altitude and speed, I looked back at the city of Chicago with its modern buildings. The midday sun was blazing, and the sky was clear with scattered clouds down below the aircraft. The cloud-framed view of Chicago, especially the blue waters of Lake Michigan, presented to me an imposing scene. I settled down in my seat and stretched myself comfortably. We were already flying over vast farm lands. Los Angeles was nearly 10 hours flight and I was thinking as to how to spend the time when a copy of the day's *New York Herald Tribune* and some other periodicals were handed over to me by the air hostess. As I was glancing through the last pages of the newspaper, it was lunch time, 1 p.m., and the hostess was standing behind me with the lunch tray. Perhaps due to remissness, the authorities had not advised the hostess that I was a strict vegetarian. She had nothing else to offer me. I was feeling hungry because, after the morning's sight-seeing at Chicago, I had driven direct to the airport. After some consultations with her colleague, she gave me some biscuits, milk and coffee.

I had entirely forgotten that as an emergency measure Mrs. Rajeswari Raman had placed some beaten-rice in my air bag just before my departure from Bangalore and she had also reminded me about this when I was about to reach Chicago. I immediately searched my bag and there lay the food adequate to sustain me till the evening. I gave a sample of the beaten-rice soaked in milk and sugar to the air hostess and she said it was very delicious. I was the only Indian passenger in the plane attired in my national dress and naturally an object of some attention to other passengers most of whom were Americans.

An elderly gentleman, sitting two or three rows away, smiled at me when I looked at him and after the food episode, he walked up to my seat and introduced himself as a physician. I shall call him a Dr. Rogers. He was returning to Phoenix where he was practising medicine. We talked on a number of subjects. By then another passenger, a friend of Rogers, who was also on his way to Phoenix, joined us, in our talks. He was a businessman, but was greatly interested in psychology. He had once seen an Indian Yogi "drink acids and swallow nails" in Los Angeles. He was also a student of Jung and therefore believed that Yoga was something higher than just drinking acids or poisons. Astrology! Both Rogers and his friend were confirmed believers. But Rogers would not own his belief in public lest the official medical association he was a member of, would frown upon him. We had plenty of time at our disposal and while we talked on every subject, modern psychology and yoga received special attention. Both of them it occurred to me, had a firm grip over modern psychological trends. We talked of Freud, Adler, Jung, Pierre and Janet and we switched on to psycho-analysis. Mr. Rogers said : "Freud began to study symptoms of neurotics in connection with their mode of life." According to Freud, mental and nervous troubles, said my friend, belong to the unconscious part of the mind. In the course of evolution a number of tendencies, which were once part of our conscious life, have been repressed by the conscious life and therefore detached from the ego. If a thing happens to us, it may be due to something 'in ourselves'. "According to Adler," Mr. Rogers went on, "the nervous constitution is the cause of neurosis. Some individuals exist who contain in their ego complex a specially well developed feeling of inferiority. It is in these unfortunates who possess the nervous character and who repress their instincts to a far greater extent than self-preservation demands that nervous diseases take root. Such individuals not only repress sex but also all those instincts that adapt them to reality". Mr. Rogers further continued "According to Janet, all the mental distress and agitation is secondary and conceals other and deeper troubles. These other troubles, which are invariable and fundamental, are of the nature of incapacity for adequate and active response to the present situation ; the anxieties and distress are derived complications. The obsessive retains all his mental capacities but has lost the feeling the rest of us always have rightly or wrongly that we constitute an actual part of reality of the present world."

The talks went on the above lines for nearly two hours. Somehow as a student of Yoga the jargon of psychologists does not appeal to me much. At best it is of academic interest. To me it appears that the approach of the Western psychologist reduces psychic happenings to a kind of activity of the glands and thoughts are just secretions of the brain. It was then my turn to talk, I told my friends that Western psychologists were still speculating on the structure of the mind. The ancient Hindus had gone far deeper in these matters. They recognized the fact that there is but one law that governs a single force—call it life or atman—and this operates in all conditions of life, manifest and unmanifest. It is the invisible force that unites spirit and matter and brings all things into being. The real objective of Yoga is spiritual This apart, Yoga enables one to secure mental peace, poise and health and of course spiritual satisfaction. Yoga consists in bringing under control, and purifying the three vehicles of man, *viz.*, the body, the mind and the spiritual self. The immediate use for ordinary mortals is that if properly practised Yoga enables one to regulate his thoughts, his feelings and his conduct and in conquering jealousy, hatred and vice. Yoga unites man with man, man with society and man with God.

The tea time had arrived and the friends departed to their seats. The hostess handed to me a cup of tea— diluted decoction. I did not relish the beverage. I turned my attention to the western sky. There were dark clouds. And crimson rays of the sun penetrated some of them and the scenery was grand. I fell into sleep. When the Hostess woke me up, it was 4 p.m. and the plane had already landed at Phoenix. I got down and had with these two friends a cup of coffee at the airport restaurant. As the time of departure of the plane was delayed by about 40 minutes, I took the opportunity to drive round about the airport in Mr. Roger' car and saw a little of the countryside of Phoenix. The plane again took off at about 4-50 p.m. The flight was smooth and I landed at Los Angeles by about 5-50 p.m. I was disappointed that my hosts were not there. I hailed a taxi. The cabman twisted his face, when I asked him to drive to Hotel George Manor. He could not simply catch what I said. I wrote down the name on a slip of paper and by 6-30 p.m. I reached the hotel. I had become disgusted with

staying in sky-scraper hotels with their air conditioning,
temperature controls, etc , and 'George Manor' was a
contrast. It was more or less a cottage with not more
than half-a-dozen rooms. I was greeted by the proprie-
tors—an aged lady and her husband—and was shown into
my well-furnished room. After a bath I had a stroll for
an hour and got my first impression of the city of Los-
Angeles. By the time I was back at my hotel, a message
had been waiting for me from Mr. and Mrs. Jones that
they had been to the airport expecting my arrival by the
6 o'clock plane, but that the airport officer said that
"some Indian gentleman" had arrived by the earlier plane
and they thought that I was the person. They called on me
at 9 p.m. and the programme for the next day was fixed.

The landlady of the hotel, an elderly woman, was
kind and obliging. It was a lodging place only. I was
sitting in the lounge with a few others talking to the
landlady. She said that no breakfast would be served in
the morning but "as a special case" she would prepare
coffee for me because I was from India. Her husband,
son and daughter-in-law were all very kind and helpful.
"By the way" the lady queried, "you speak such fine
English, better than we do here. Is it your mother-
tongue?" I replied : 'No. English is not our mother.
tongue. I picked it up in my school and college." She
continued : "Your accent is not difficult to follow, and
you speak more grammatically and precisely."

It was 10-30 p.m. I was not interested in any further
talk. I was feeling tired and went to bed. The next
morning, as I was awakening from bed, the sun was
already shining through the shades of the window blinds.

Precisely at 8-30 a.m. Mr. and Mrs. Jones were ready
at the hotel to pick me up. After a brief conversation,

we started in their beautiful limousine to go round Los Angeles, a city that is spread over nearly 40 miles between San Gabriel mountains and the Pacific Ocean.

We drove straight to the Disneyland often called a 'Magic Kingdom'. It is the creation of Walt Disney and combines fantasy and history, an adventure and learning, together with every variety of recreation designed to appeal to everyone. According to Walt Disney, Disneyland is dedicated to the ideals, dreams and the hard facts which have created America with the hope that "it will be a source of joy and inspiration to all the world". It was opened in 1955. The attractions are so many that it will be impossible to describe all of them. As one steps into the "Land" there is the "Main Street, U.S.A." representing the typical "Small town" and the way of life at the turn of this century. It is the America of 1890–1910, the gas lamp being replaced by the electric lamp, the plodding horse-drawn street car giving way to the "chugging horseless carriage". For the younger visitors it "turns back the clock to the days of grand-father's youth". There are the apothecary, the icecream parlour, the market house, etc., realistically recreated from a bygone era. I enjoyed a ride in a horse-drawn street car and also in an old-fashioned double-decked omnibus, in the Main Street. After the ride, we went to the Main Street's Plaza, a '1890 restaurant' and had some corn flakes and coffee. The next attraction was the Fantasyland. Here the classic stories of childhood have become actual realities. We journeyed through the "dark forests to the home of the seven dwarfs". I raced with Mr. Toad in his wild autoride through old London Town and this was some sort of a hilarious adventure. The "nonsensical" world of Alice in Wonderland has been made a reality. Aboard gay canal boats I was a visitor to story-book land and saw many "famous scenes" including "Pinochlinos village nestled below the Swiss Alps". From Fantasyland, our next sojourn was to the Frontier land. This has a number of attractions. Here we journeyed round the rivers of America aboard a "sternwheel" steamboat for a glimpse of Mark Twain's America. We "booked passage" for a voyage aboard the three-masted sailing ship the "Columbia"—a replica of the original ship that made maritime history as the first American vessel to sail round the world. A "voyage of discovery" awaited us. As we cruised in this vessel, we saw in "Indian" raid, etc., all episodes in recent American history.

My next attraction was the Tomorrowland. You can experience what men of science and industry have predicted for the world of tomorrow. I enjoyed with my hosts my trip in the submarine "Nautilus" viewing the "lost Continent of Atlantis". I travelled beneath the "Polar Ice Cap" and voyaged into "liquid space". I had the most wonderful experience of my life when I boarded a "rocket ship" and "blasted off" into outer space on my way to the Moon leaving the earth far below. Imagine my surprise when I saw America from a space platform as it orbited around our globe. Our "adventures" in space were short-lived. Of course it was just an illusion created by Disney. And the illusion was quite realistic. We next went inside "snow–capped" Matterhorn Mountain, again an artificial creation, over a coral lagoon in a skyway 'career'.

Nor did we miss the Adventureland, a land filled with "wild animals", and native "savages" who often display their hostility to your "invasion" of their jungle privacy. We enjoyed all this, on an explorer boat cruise. Our "adventure" took us to the misty Amazon with its tropical rain forest, the Murky Mekong River of Indochina, the dangerous hippopotamus filled waters of the Belgian Congo and the swirling rapids of the Nile. As we steamed towards cascading Schweutzer Falls, a bull elephant, his ivory white tusks gleaming in the sunlight, trumpetted at us, while further on "native head-hunters" chanted their war cries as the boat approached them. A boy of eight who was with us became so frightened at the sight of these "head-hunters" that he closed his eyes until we got back to the starting point. Everything was so realistic that I got a bit upset when Mr. Jones played a joke with me by drawing my attention to the gaping mouth of an attacking hippo and the boat guide fired a point-blank pistol at the animal. There are so many other items of attraction, informative and entertaining, that it will be impossible to describe them all. Many other "attractions" are still in the "dreaming" stages and as we were leaving the wonderful Disneyland my hosts said that some of these items may be ready for "me and my family to enjoy in my next visit".

By the time I returned to my hotel it was already 3 p.m. There were some visitors who were anxious to meet me. They knew about my arrival at Los Angeles and they were all students of my books. Their visit was in the nature of a courtesy call. Discussions with them went on for an hour and again I started sight-seeing with them to other places of interest nearby. It was hardly ten minutes that I had returned from my 2nd sight-seeing trip, when my hosts were again ready to remind me of my lecture at 8 p.m.

I was scheduled to lecture on "Nadi Astrology" but my kind host suggested a talk on the general aspect of Hindu astrology as she expected a "cosmopolitan auidence". Under the auspices of the First Temple and College of Astrology, I spoke on "Astrology and Indian Life". Mrs. Thyrza Escobar was in the chair. There was a large and distinguished gathering and the hall was full. I dealt with the place of astrology in Indian Culture and how Hindu astrology had been developed to considerable perfection even as early as 3000 B.C. I also explained the salient features of Hindu astrology, and the scope it provided for further researches. I suggested that American astrologers should pay greater attention to the Indian system and try to absorb, aspects of astrology which are peculiar to the Hindu and which have never been studied or understood in the West. The question-hour was lively. The concluding remarks of Mrs. Jones about me were flattering.

Prominent amongst those who attended the lecture were : Mesdames : Lois C. Gould, Margaret Mc Alister, Veera Lee, Liola Hurd, Lilliah Gregory, Daisy Durall, Dora Chandler, Carole Manver, Elinor, A. Augst, Ruth Jones, Mrs. Aynes S Finch, Mac Basch, Marie Bishop, Blanche Clarke, Grace Finaly Son, Adelaide Forbush, Ilda Hanchette, Ruth I, Houlton, Ruth Johnson, Juno Johnson, Gladys King Agnes Oxley, Roderna Peiree, Lena Pritichard, Kiyo Cuddy Roth, Wanda Strauss, Messrs. Richard Alder, John Bradford, Whitney, E. Greene, Vincent Gregory, Joseph Jones, Edwin Lee, Gilbert Obson, and Rex Taylor and Mr. and Mrs. John Horrath. Then there was Dr. Judith Tyberg, head of the East-West Cultural Centre, the noted photographers, Mr. and Mrs. Fahs, Dr. Bruce Gordon Kingsley, internationally famed musician and lecturer, and a friend of late Alan Leo of astrological fame ; Mr. Dick Juline, the head of Llewellyn Publications, Ltd., the well-known publisher of astrological books, and Charlotte Johnson (Joyzelle), the painter. Amongst the audience I was able to recognise only two Indians, Mrs. Bode, wife of Prof. Bode, visiting professor at the California University, who said she had met me in 1940 or so at Bangalore ; another Indian gentleman who, I learnt later on, was a professor at Delhi University. There were some cine artistes from Hollywood. One of the actresses came to the dais after the lecture and invited me for lunch in "Vedantha Centre" of which she was a member.

I think special mention must be made of my hosts the Joneses and their interest in astrology. Mr. Joseph A. Jones, an Engineer by profession, is keenly interested in astrology and has published several tables bearing on mathematical astrology and his book *Will the Price of Gold be Raised this Year ?* is not only thought-provoking but bears testimony to the methodical way of his work. He has devoted much time and effort to the study of the stock-market and economics. He is almost a specialist in the study of gold. His good wife, Mrs. Thyrza Escobar Jones, has been an active worker in the field of astrology for several years. She is the spirit behind the First Temple and College of Astrology, an entirely non-sectarain institution devoted to the study and dissemination of astrological knowledge. The college has one of the best astrological libraries. Astrological classes are held each Tuesday and instruction is free. Diplomas are issued to students who pass in a written examination. Three courses of study are suggested : Beginners, Intermediate and Advance. She has a sound knowledge of the Western system. Since 1932 she has been associated with the First Temple and College of Astrology in some responsible position or other.

After my return to India, Mrs. Jones was kind enough to write: "Thank you, Prof. Raman, for re-opening the door, so to speak, to Hindu astrology and culture which I have so lightly skimmed although it offers a whole 'new' universe. Your visit was such a pleasure to both my husband and myself."

After the lecture it was nearly 11 p.m. I wanted to return to my hotel as I felt very exhausted. But my hosts said: "No, we will take you round the town so that you could see how Los Angeles and Hollywood look in the night."

We drove to different parts of the twin cities of Los Angeles and Hollywood and the extravagant illumination of the cities coupled with the flashing neon advertising of variegated hues, looked like a fairy land when viewed from the Beverly Hills. It was past midnight when my hosts took leave of me at my hotel.

I had a very busy day on 23rd October 1959. It was a fine morning. By the time the first rays of the Sun began penetrating through the window blinds of my room I had finished my ablutions and was about to leave the hotel for further sight-seeing. I wanted to visit some parts of Los-Angeles by local transport before my hosts came to pick me up, when the arrival of a small group of people to meet me was announced by the bearer. As I walked into the lounge I was greeted by the group.

It seems word had gone round that 'a Hindu Mystic' was staying in this hotel. The visitors took me for the 'mystic'. They said they wanted certain clarifications on Hindu mysticism, reincarnation, etc., as they were "all students of these subjects". I protested that I was not the 'mystic' they were after and that I was merely on a visit to the United States on a lecturing tour as some sort of an unofficial ambassador, anxious to spread the message of Indian Culture and Astrology. They would not listen to my protests. They persisted that I was the person—"the Hindu mystic", who spoke the previous night at First Temple of Astrology—they were after because their friends who had attended the lecture had suggested that they should meet me. I had no alternative but to yield to their persuasion, as I did not wish to disappoint them.

A sense of seriousness marked their questions. I gave a brief outline of Hinduism and Hindu philosophy and explained how there has never been a conflict between science and philosophy in India because Hinduism unlike other religions did not owe its origin to any personality but was based on certain eternal values—human and moral—universal in application. I said Hinduism is not exactly a religion in the sense in which the term is generally understood in the West, but is based on what is called *Dharma* or a certain moral order.

A member of the group queried : "What is the attitude of Hindus towards the Bible?" I replied that consistent with the tolerant nature of Hinduism, the propounders of biblical teachings are at liberty to preach whatever they like. I went on. "As a Christian religious book, we hold the Bible in esteem. But the role of the Bible in the hands of the majority of missionaries, especially when the British power was being consolidated in India, was indeed ignoble. The Bible followed the bayonet. The average missionary felt—and some of them seem to feel even today—that Christianity is a superior religion intended by Providence to civilise us. The missionaries opened hospitals and educational institutions but there was always the sinister objective of proselytism and denationalising

6

the Hindu. It is this negative role of the Bible that thoughtful Hindus have always resented. I do not think that except as a piece of literature the Bible could appeal to a thoughtful Hindu, nurtured as he has been on the doctrines of the sages—where emphasis is always laid on personal purity, personal morality and personal improvement as leading to Divine Grace. There is a moral law and everyone must move in conformity with this moral law." My visitors seemed satisfied and took leave of me with protestations of gratefulness.

I got into a bus and rode as far as it went in the downtown area of Los Angeles and got back to my hotel by 9 a.m. to be picked up by my hosts.

We drove to the Philosophical Research Society. The Founder-President Dr. Manly P. Hall received us warmly and took us round the Library. It is one of the finest Libraries that I have ever come across. Dr. Manly Hall, a great savant and philosopher, has built this Library and the collection which includes 45 to 50 thousand separate items is indeed impressive especially in regard to ancient manuscripts and early printed works in their original editions. I was happy to find a number of manuscripts —some palm-leaves—written in Sanskrit and some in Sinhalese. In this Library, one can find sections pertaining to the period from 3000 B.C. to the beginning of Christian era, Chinese inscriptions and Maya and Aztec cultures. Then there are original manuscripts and rare facsimiles published by learned societies and private scholars. Facsimiles of all the known Maya codices are also available. There are quite a number of manuscripts and printed works of the early date bearing on Asian cultures—India, China, Siam, Arabia, etc. Of particular interest was a Buddhist Sutra written entirely in human blood. There was no dearth for books on European schools of thought. There is a broad coverage of sacred books and commentaries and the Christian Bible is available in rare versions and printings in several languages. Modern psychology section is well represented. I was particularly struck by the collection of books on astrology—mostly Western—especially rare and early printed works. On Hindu Astrology, collections include some works of my revered grandfather late Prof. B. Suryanarain Rao, some of my own books and *Jinendramala*, English translation by late Mr. Chidambara Iyer. The Library owes its existence to the vision of Dr. Manly P. Hall. I found the doctor well-informed, cultured and friendly.

I next visited the East–West centre. The previous evening Dr. Judith Tyberg, who had attended my lecture, had extended a cordial invitation to me. I had an interesting discussion with Dr. Tyberg with whom, she reminded me, I had some correspondence in 1947 or so when she was in Varanasi preparing for her doctorate in philosophy. The atmosphere in the Centre was thoroughly Indian with photos of all Hindu gods and goddesses prominently displayed and with books on Indian Culture and Philosophy neatly arranged. I spoke briefly on the greatness of Sanskrit language. Dr. Judith M. Tyberg is a Professor of Sanskrit. She had travelled all over India and met Sri Ramana Maharshi and Sri Aurobindo. She is also an author of books on Indian religions. The East–West centre is said to be of a non-sectarian and non-political character. Its aim is to give "greater expression in life to that spiritual unity, God power and God wisdom which universalises, transforms and leads to an integral divine flowering in man".

After my lecture at the First Temple of Astrology, the previous evening, I had been invited for lunch at a cultural organisation by a Hollywood actress, a member of the institute. As I was busy signing autographs, I had asked the actress to fix up details about my food, etc., with my hosts. Whether or not the actress understood my hosts correctly, a comedy of errors was enacted when I drove to the organisation the next morning from the East–West centre with my hosts. We were received by a Swami—an American—and taken round the premises and the garden. Books on Vedanta adorned the Library. There were pictures of Rama and Krishna and other Indian saints. We spent some time in general conversation. I was taken to the Pooja Hall where I found half-a-dozen Americans, draped in Salem dhothies in the style of uttariyam, in meditation. I was happy to see all this. The lunch hour was approaching. I requested Mr. and Mrs. Jones to ascertain the "menu". The Swami said: "Today's speciality is beef." I was shocked as also Mr. and Mrs. Jones. There was some misunderstanding somewhere. Probably the actress did not understand the matter correctly. My hosts felt embarrassed. I declined to participate in the lunch. Instead I gave a brief discourse on "food" and explained the advantages both from spiritual and health points of view of vegetarian food. According to Hindu sages *satwtic* type of food is the best for those who, like the members of the organisation whom I was addressing, were interested in spiritual development. I went on : "Especially as followers of Vedanta, animal food must be eschewed. In India, millions of people have been vegetarians for thousands of years by tradition as well as by religious behalf. Since you all claim to be students of *Bhagavad Gita*, it is essential that before you study the

Gita, you should be able to avoid animal food." The American Swami felt sorry for the 'misunderstanding' and confessed that it would be difficult for people like them whose habits have included flesh-eating for generations past to change their habits suddenly, and that they would try their utmost to eschew at least 'beef' though it would be their endeavour to become vegetarians.

Mr. Jones regretted for this comedy of errors and said that we should have our lunch at the vegetarian restaurant in Hollywood run by the S.R.E. Centre. Here I was treated to puris (wheat dough prepared in milk), potato chips (fried in olive oil) and plenty of fruits served by American ladies dressed in Indian sarees. I was told that this restaurant, the only one of its type where only vegetarian dishes are served, is frequented by a large number of patrons.

After a brief rest at my hotel, we again went out sight-seeing. Los Angeles is considered to be the "most exciting city in America". Here the mountains, the desert and the sea meet in a thrilling scenic beauty. Situated in the southern part of the State of California, between the mountains and the sea, the location of the city is attractive. Sunshine, citrus groves, oil wells and a tremendous expansion in industry has boomed Los Angeles to the third largest city in the United States in population and perhaps first in the world in area 450 square miles. The streets generally run at right angles. There are broad boulevards giving access to the ocean, valleys and mountain wilderness. Compared to Chicago or New York, the buildings are not imposing. There are several buildings resembling bungalows in India but now most of these bungalows are being replaced by ultramodern houses. Several streets in Hollywood reminded me of my own hometown of Bangalore. Los Angeles has a number of

parks—about 108, with an aggregate area of 7,921 acres.
The Museum of History, Science and Art has a spacious
building in Exposition Park. It exhibits mounted skeletons of sabre-toothed tigers, "Imperial elephants",
American mastodons, etc. The South–West Museum is
housed in a building ornamented with cement casts from
Mayan sculpture. There are a large number of Libraries
also but Huntington Library and Art Gallery at San
Marino are rich in rare books and manuscripts.

Hollywood is not a compact package of glamour.
The movie and radio studios, the homes of the stars are
all widely separated. I visited one or two studios, saw
the radio city and drove through the Hollywood Boulevard, passed the residences of several cine artistes, entered
the Hollywood Avenue and after a look at the 'Bowl'
reached the "sunset strip" where are located theatrical
agencies, designers' shops and famous night clubs. It was
past 4 in the evening. We had tea in a fine restaurant and
my hosts dropped me at the Llewellyn Publications on
National Boulevard. Mr. Richard W. Juline extended a
most warm welcome to me. He took me round his book-
shop, printing press and office and we had an interesting
talk concerning astrological books. Llewellyn Publications
are perhaps the largest publishers of astrological books in
America. From here we again went round other parts of
the city. Through the Ocean Avenue we entered "right
into the Pacific Ocean" up the hill to Inspiration Point.
From here we had a beautiful view of the Pacific Ocean.
The weather was not bad. And the sunset was glorious. It
looked as though for a few minutes, the flaming crimson
orb assumed myriad wondrous shapes until the orb was
actually "dripped" in the roaring waters of the magnificent Pacific. The effect on my mind was marvellous. I

became contemplative and completely absorbed in the appreciation of this most glorious phenomenon. All kinds of thoughts crossed my mind. Even the glorious Sun, the creator and sustainer of life, fades away, may be temporarily, from our view. What of the puny and proud creature called man?

My host tapped on my back. I opened my eyes. The Sun had already set and as we wended our way through Sunset Boulevard, Santa Maria, etc., back to the hotel it was a sight to see the illumination of the twin cities. I took leave of my hosts Mr. and Mrs. Jones thanking them profusely for their hospitality. They made my visit to Los Angeles pleasant, useful and thoroughly enjoyable.

I must also thank Phil and Anita Fahs for the excellent pictures of me they took in Los Angeles. They have presented me with a number of very fine enlargements of these pictures which I cherish as a memento of my visit to Los Angeles. This charming couple are noted photographers and have photographed many celebrities. Anita Fahs is also a keen student of astrology.

The same night I left for New York, *via* Chicago.

11 The United Nations

Travel has its own fascination. It brings one into contact with strange faces and stranger circumstances. It provides one with the opportunity of meeting people whom otherwise one could never meet : and of knowing things first hand and of gathering interesting impressions. My travels in America enabled me to come into contact with different types of people. On my way back to New York from Los Angeles, I spent a couple of hours at Chicago. Rail journey from Chicago to New York was quite pleasant. I travelled in a "room" and the Negro porter in charge of our compartment was all attention to me. What he could not understand was my "aloofness" and absence from the dining car at the lunch hour.

He took pains to teach me how to bring down the bed, how to "tune in" the radio and how to turn the hot and cold water taps. He said that I could make myself comfortable and that his services were always available. I should just press the button of the electric buzzer and he would present himself before me. When he first got into my room I was wearing dhoti. He must have felt that I was a boor, ignorant of even "turning the tap" and much less of "tuning in" the radio. "Which country you come from Sir?," was the first question he put to me. "India," I said, "the land of ancient culture and civilisation." "Gyandi's (Gandhi's) land, he was a great man Sir. I like his non-violence. But Neru (Nehru) is different.

He always talks in favour of communist countries,"
harangued my friend in this strain. He said that he was
a regular reader of newspapers and that he was quite
up-to-date in his understanding of world affairs. He
found it difficult to follow my accent as I did to follow
his American English in which there was a liberal interspersing of slang expressions. It required considerable
effort on my part to convince him that Mr. Nehru was not
anti-American and that we are a free nation, as free as
America. After all, the Negro porter is no entity and
what he thinks of India or her foreign policy may mean
nothing. But what is important to note is that many an
American admirer of ancient Indian culture and generally
friendly to the aspirations of modern India, seemed to me
to be perplexed. A German scientist friend, who stayed
in India for a couple of years, who is now resident in
America and is sympathetically disposed towards India,
told me plainly : "The average American seems to feel
that India is following a double standard—professing
neutrality but adopting a pro-communist policy, despite
the fact that America is extending significant economic
aid to India." I tried in my own humble way to convince
these friends who were critical of India's conduct in the
U.N., that we are a neutral nation and I think I was
successful to a large extent.

I was back at New York on 26th October 1959. I
went round the city, calling on friends and visiting places
of interest that I had missed before. I drove about the
city in the afternoon and called on Mrs. Joanne Clancy,
Editor of *American Astrology*, with whom I spent an hour.
Our discussions covered a wide range of subjects including of course Hindu astrology. Mrs. Clancy is an admirer
of the Indian system and her journal generally adopts a
sympathetic attitude towards Hindu astrology. She took

me round her offices and I was glad to meet members of
her staff. Founded in 1932 and largely due to the efforts
of that indefatigable worker late Mr. Paul G. Clancy,
American Astrology became one of the leading exponents
of astrology in the West, and it is indeed creditable that,
after the death of her husband, Mrs. Clancy has been
continuing the journal and maintaining its usefulness and
standard.

I should say that my visit to the United Nations was
memorable. I watched the proceedings from the distinguished gallery when the Russian delegate was speaking.
My good friend, Mr. K. Balaraman of *The Hindu*, took
me round the entire building and introduced me to a
number of diplomats. Some of the diplomats showed
themselves interested in astrology and many of them were
keen to know how the international situation would shape
itself within the next few years. According to one of the
diplomats—he said he was a student of mundane astrology
for over 20 years—a good many delegates participating in
the deliberations of the U.N. are astrologically minded.
I also met some of the members of the Indian deligatlon
to the United Nations. I spent some time with some
Indian personnel of the United Nations. In an informal
chat I had with them and with a few Indian journalists,
there was free comment that many of the members of the
Indian delegation sent to the U.N. at considerable expense
to the Indian Exchequer, did no useful job. I was told
that excepting the leader and one or two others the rest of
the members whiled away their time in the U.N. lounge or
in sight-seeing. It is for our Government to find out
whether any useful work is being done by all the members
of the big delegation they send to the U.N. Among others
I met at the U.N. were Mr. Gopala Menon, the Indian

Consular-General at New York, Major Vasist and Mr. Dayal, the then Indian ambassador to Nepal.

The United Nations is housed in a 39 storey building flanking East River from 42nd to 48th streets. It is a top tourist attraction. Actually there are four buildings in the Headquarters group. The most conspicuous is however the Secretariat Building which houses the offices of the United Nations. Dominating the group, it stands 544 feet high with glass walls on two sides and solid marble ends. At its foot stands the Conference Building where the day by day work of the U.N. delegates is conducted in Conference rooms, lounges and restaurants. The Conference Building connects the Secretariat building and the General Assembly building, which with its flaty dome, curving morble side and front wall of solid glass, contains the most dramatic assembly hall in the world. The inside is a real wonder : the daring functional decort the striking association of colour and design, the electronic arrangement by which visitors, by turning a button, can hear a speech delivered in Russian for instance, translated into four languages— English, Chinese, German and French. You can see here men and women of all nationalities. Delegates from nearly 90 nations, scurry about in a hurry on affairs that can influence destinies of millions of people. You can buy souvenirs from all the world in a U.N. shop. There is an international rose garden through which one can stroll. I was told that the number of visitors to the U.N. are so many that nearly Rs. 3,500,000 worth of luxurious rugs are wearing out years ahead of schedule causing a minor budgetary crisis among the United Nations officials.

Over a cup of coffee in a U.N. Lounge, an interesting discussion ensued on the astrological set-up of the United

Nations. I was of course the main speaker. Those who participated were a diplomat from a European country who is also a keen student of mundane astrology and three of his friends, an Indian, an Egyptian and a South American. It was an informal discussion and they were all keen on knowing what the future of the U.N. would be according to Hindu Astrology. The diplomat astrologer showed me some sort of a curve of tension, a graphic representation of periods of international tension and comparative peace following a certain sequence of Uranus–Saturn–Jupiter movements. I explained that the U.N. was brought into existence under unpropitious influence. In the U.N. horoscope, the Moon, representing human nature, is in conjunction with Rahu, an incendiary planet while the 10th is aspected by Mars and Saturn. Therefore the U.N. would once again thwart the human instincts which are nothing less than the outward sign of growth on the part of nations. The horoscope mirrors the distrust and intolerance of the nations composing the body. The Saturn–Mars conjunction which is at the base of power-politics between the western democracies and the communist countries will further increase the ever–darkening fog of distrust. The U.N. is bound to go the way of League of Nations.

Some of these high pressure diplomats, who generally function in a make-believe world of their own, showed a very intelligent grasp of astrological knowledge, that I began to wonder why in public they pretended ignorance of astrology and even showed hostility while believing it in private. Perhaps this attitude is perfectly in line with their diplomatic professions !

I was interviewed by the *Life–time* newspaper at their Studios. I presented the case for Indian Astrology and explained the place it occupied in the social and cultural life of an average Indian. Mr. Charles Jayne was also present at the interview.

Later on in the evening Mr. Jayne had arranged for a meeting at his residence and amongst those present were Dr. Ryberg, Dr. Wagner, Mr. Ralph Schitter, Mr. Alfred Emerson and Mr. Hans Niggeman. The meeting was in the nature of leave-taking. I expressed my grateful thanks to all these friends for the co-operation and friendliness extended to me.

I visited the Indian Consulate office as I wanted to get some clarification as regards what articles I could take back with me to India duty-free. The concerned official was not available. The Receptionist did not know where this assistant had gone. But he was expected any moment. I wasted nearly one hour waiting to meet this august official. He did not turn up. Some other official of the Consulate offered to help me. He gave me a copy of the latest exchange rules and gave me details of articles I could take with me back to India as personal baggage without incurring any duty. He was emphatic that the information he gave me was quite correct. When I returned to India and presented a list of articles I had brought to the Customs at the Bombay Air Port, I discovered to my amazement that I had been wrongly advised by the official at the Indian Consulate at New York. I must confess from the experience I had at Washington and New York that Indian nationals do not seem to receive the assistance they have a right to receive from their own official representatives abroad. Some of them seem to suffer from the dead weight of bureaucracy. It looked as though they functioned care-free aping their western colleagues in manners and habits. Some of them are amazingly ignorant about Indian culture and our own problems. There may be honourable exceptions. This view of mine is shared by other Indian friends who have had similar experiences, and whom I happened to meet.

The *next morning I was with Mr. V. K. Krishna Menon for nearly three hours. Just then China was knocking at our doors and we were getting a very good demonstration of *Pancha Sheela* from our great neighbour.

On 28th October, I sailed for Europe by the Luxury Liner "S.S. QUEEN MARY". I went on board the ship at 12 noon and I was shown my 'room' by the steward. The room was fully furnished and the amenities provided were the last word in comfort. A New York friend had warned me that I might suffer from sea sickness. But

----

*Mr. V. Krishna Menon privately expressed a desire to have my astrological advice in regard to some personal problems then agitating his mind. We spent over three hours at his hotel. The discussions ranged over several topics. He had then a rub with lateGeneral Thimmayya and was feeling uneasy that he might be required to quit. After examining his horoscope I told Mr. Menon that he would not be required to resign from the Indian cabinet, but that his Waterloo would come only in 1962, when, according to me, as a consequence of the eight–planet combination China was likely to commit aggression against India. My forecast about him relieved his anxiety but he said that my prediction about China might not turn out correct as he would never expect a "socialist country" to commit aggression.

After China invaded India in 1962, and Mr. Menon resigned, we had a chance to meet at Bangalore and he congratulated me on the fulfilment of both the predictions. The last time we met was at Bangalore Air Port in April 1972. I was on my way to Lucknow for a Conference and we flew to Delhi together. He was all praise for astrology but deprecated the role of some "professional astrologers who brought discredit to the science by sensation-mongering predictions". He was a great man in his own way—frank, fearless and patriotic.

I was confident that just as I did not suffer from any air sickness throughout my air travel extending over fifteen thousand miles, a voyage of just 5 days, would not cause any sea sickness. I went up the deck at 1–30 p.m. At 2 p.m. the ship weighed anchor and "Queen Mary" serenely moved out to open water. Fifteen minutes later we were passing the Statue of Liberty. The great sky-scrapers of New York were quickly receding. As the city of New York was disappearing from my view, I bade good bye to the United States of America, the land of Lincoln and Emerson. I came down to my cabin and my first act was to thank the all-merciful Providence for enabling me to complete my mission successfully.

12 S.S. "Queen Mary"

This was my first sea voyage and I had been looking forward to this new experience ever since I had planned my trip to the United States. The maximum distance I had ever gone on the sea was about 12 miles from Bombay— Elephanta caves and the islands round about. For a few hours after S.S. "Queen Mary" sailed from New York, I was feeling a bit uncomfortable because of the thought that I had to spend five days in the ship without any friends or acquaintances. As soon as I came into my cabin, the steward handed over to me a list of passengers and I found that I was the only Indian passenger in the first class. I walked up and down the 'Sun Deck', 'A Deck' and 'B Deck' and got back to my cabin. The cabin steward reminded me that it was time for lunch. Then I went to the dining hall, and sat at my table for a couple of minutes. It was the first time I saw meat, etc., served openly. Bottles of wine were being liberally uncorked. I could not stand the sight. I got back to my cabin. I told the head steward that I would like my food—raw vegetables, fruits, milk and corn-flakes—to be served to me at my cabin. He showed some surprise at my request but gave the necessary instructions to the cabin steward Mr. Massey. Indeed I found the crew—mostly British—very polite and courteous. Massey suggested that I eat plenty of boiled peas. Of course he could not understand why I would insist on eating only raw peas. His other suggestion was that I should take Horlicks instead of milk, as fresh milk could not be had. I accepted his suggestion. He asserted that I was the only passenger that he had ever come across in the whole of his service with the Cunard Line, who was so scrupulous about food and drinks.

After lunch I was just relaxing, glancing through newspaper-clippings containing reports of my lectures in America, given to me by a friend on the eve of my departure from New York and the bell rang. Ten minutes later, Massey entered my cabin and said : "Hurry up sir, to the 'Sun Deck' for rehearsal." On the first day every passenger should undergo rehearsal on the use of life-belts. I got dressed and went up to the 'Sun Deck'. That was my third experience the other two being when I boarded the Air India Constellation at Bombay and the Pan American Boeing at London. Of course there was difference in the use of belts. In the first two instances, the use of the life-belt was contingent upon the force-landing of the plane on the sea. Here we were actually on the sea. If the ship met with an accident, the passengers must know how to save themselves. We were assured there was no prospect of any such imminent danger to the ship. Characteristic of British thoroughness we were taught in detail how to use life-belts.

While this practice was going on, I became friendly with an Englishman—I will call him Mr. John, and a Malayan couple Mr. and Mrs. Wang.—By the time I was back in my cabin the ubiquitous Massey was ready with the question "what would you like to have, sir ? coffee, tea, sandwiches ?" I said : "either coffee or tea whichever is good." "Both are good, sir, I will have special coffee prepared for you," he went on. I said : "bring special coffee and special tea. I will select whichever is better." Within ten minutes, he came with two trays. The tea was light and tasteless and coffee was much better. I preferred the latter beverage, though it was nothing but an apology for what one is used to in South India.

After the strenuous programme I had in America, I had decided to take complete rest in the steamer. I had instructed Massey to wake me up at 7 a.m. Exactly at this hour he would greet me with "good morning sir, had sound sleep" and place the coffee tray on the table. My room in the ship was quite big and furnished with two sofas, two comfortable beds and chairs and full-length mirrors, with two attached bathrooms provided with facilities for hot and cold salt-water and hot and cold fresh-water baths. I had ample time and convenience for reading and meditation.

The "Queen Mary" is said to be 'a giant of the sea'. I was told that her bow would extend "nearly 40 feet beyond the 884 feet Eiffel Tower of Paris. She would fall short of the 1,046 feet Chrysler Building in New York by less than 30 feet and she would extend nearly three times the height of St. Paul's Cathedral". The "Queen Mary" (83,238 tons) and the "Queen Elizabeth" (85,000 tons) are supposed to be the largest and the fastest liners afloat. They have all the qualities of a floating hotel : private bathrooms to all the first class cabins, gymnasia, swimming pool, a long range of public rooms and a restaurant for those who are not satisfied with the menu provided in the first class dining room. The overall length of "Queen Mary" is 1,019 feet and breadth 118 feet. It was launched on 26-9-1934 and made her first voyage to New York on 27-5-1936.

I thoroughly enjoyed and I think I was also benefited from the health point of view by the bracing Atlantic breezes on the vast open 'Sports deck'.

I used to spend several hours on the 'Promenade deck' relaxing on a chair and Mr. John kept company with me discussing astrology and allied subjects. He said he was a 'tropicalist', *i.e.*, an advocate of the Sayana system. He was emphatic that astrology originated in Chaldea and that we copied the Hindu system from the Greeks. Of course I hold very strong views that astrology origi- nated in India and that it spread to the West *via* Arabia. Despite the fact we held antagonistic view in the matter of the origin of Hindu astrology, we had very interesting discussions. He had with him a copy of the *Greek Horo- scopes* edited by O. Neugebauer and H. B. Van Hoesen and published by the American Philosophical Society. The intention of the authors, in publishing this book, was not to serve the cause of astrology but to make available for study Greek horoscopes which could be expected to reflect at least some of the current techniques of Greek astronomy. In the introduction, the word Apoklima is defined as a sign which precedes, in the order of the signs of the zodiac, a centre; thus Aries is Apoklima if midheaven is Taurus. Mr. John said that Varahamihira has used the Greek term 'Apoklima' and hence Hindu astrology was indebted to the Greeks. I conceded there might have been exchange of astrological ideas between India on the one hand and Greece and other European countries on the other; but that was no proof of Hindu astrology having been derived from the West. I quoted a few slokas from Parasara to show that Hindu astrology was absolutely original.

Leaving aside the controversy whether or not Hindu astrology is original, I found the book in possession of

Mr. John a valuable one. It contains discussions of horoscopes by ancient Greek astrologers taken from *Vettium Valens* (2nd Century A.D.) and the *Catalogus Codicum Astrologorum Graecorum*. To my surprise I found that the "Terms" or sections of signs associated with planets, *e.g.*, "Jupiter rules the first 6 degrees of Aries, Venus the next 6 degrees", etc., were identical with *Hadda Chakra* given by Tajaka writers. The Tajaka system is said to have been perfected by Yavanacharya. Who is this Yavanacharya? A great astrological scholar in Mysore, who met me recently to get a foreword for his book in Kannada on Tajaka, had the following to say about Yavanacharya. He was the son of a Brahmin father and a low caste woman born somewhere near Ujjain. The father having died very early in life and the mother ostracised by the society, he was obliged to leave the place of his birth. He went to Banaras and learned astrology from great masters. On a lucky day, when he was asleep the Sun God appeared in a dream, revealed to him the secrets of Tajaka and asked him to spread the science not only in India but also in Yavana and Mlechha countries. He went to Greece and introduced the system of Tajaka and he came to be known as Yavanacharya. The story may lack historic authenticity but a Hindu astrologer getting disgusted with the treatment meted out to him by his own community and going away to a foreign land cannot be ruled out. The "lots of fame, daimon, eros", etc., given in this book correspond to the Sahams of the Tajaka system.

On the second day of my voyage, when I was having my evening coffee, Massey was talking to me about his career on the ship. Incidentally he remarked : "Sir, you are a first class passenger. Your ticket includes finest American and continental cuisine, morning bouilion, dancing to Harry Taylor orchestra, cinema, play-room, cock tails, library and the world's choicest wines and liqours. If you wish, there are extras—barber shop, laundry, shopping centre, etc. But I find you do not make use of these facilities." I could not answer his questions. But I said that I would visit the cinema, which I did for the next 3 days. As Massey said, for those who can participate, there are any number of events taking place on the ship, a programme of which is made available to each passenger at 7 a.m. everyday. My difficulty was, I could not reconcile my conception of relaxation and enjoyment with most items provided in the ship. "Eat, drink and dance" appeared to be the slogan of many of the passengers. The westerners are used to certain habits of life which are totally repugnant to our sense of values and morals. It is indeed a shame that many of our countrymen are falling an easy prey to the temptations of cheap gaeity.

When Massey learnt that I was an astrologer of some fame, he came to me one night and said: "Sir, I understand you are a seer. I want to know whether the dispute I have with my wife will be resolved amicably or will lead to serious complications. I can pay you one pound as your fee."

I smiled and asked him to meet me the next day. When the question was put, Taurus was rising, Jupiter was in the 7th and the lord of Lagna was in the 4th. The Sun, the Moon and Mars were in the 6th and Saturn in the 8th. The 7th house was subject to Papakartari Yoga and the 5th was afflicted. The ascendant and the 7th lords were mutually in the 3rd and the 11th. Jupiter's aspect on 11th and his situation in the 7th favoured resolution of the the dispute. I therefore told him that within 8 months— Jupiter would then be transiting Capricorn—his relations

with the wife would become normal though in the meanwhile things would continue to look bleak. I told him:
"Look here, the outcome will be favourable ; don't worry
and don't think of any litigation." It looked as though
he was pleased. When he offered £ 1/- as my fee, I
declined. From that day onwards we became good friends
and he started paying more attention to my needs. Often
we would spend an hour with one chit-chatting and
narrating in his own colloquial style the happenings on
the ship.

On the third day of the voyage, I again met in the
library a Malayan couple—the Wangs. I had become
acquainted with them on the first day of the voyage,
when we were taught how to use life-belts. Mr. Wang
was a professor in a college in Singapore. He had to fly
to Washington *via* Tokyo, along with his wife to attend
some official conference. That was his first flight in an
aeroplane. As he put it, "due probably to fear" he
got a mild heart attack and the doctors had advised him
not to fly again but to return to his country by ship.
He expressed surprise that he did not see me either at
the dining hall or at the ballroom. I explained to him
my difficulties. He said he was himself a teetotaller and
did not like the western way of life but just for the sake
of curiosity, he had no objection to sit and watch others
dancing or drinking and I should also see how they spend
their time. The same evening after attending the cinema
we went together to the 'Observation Lounge', where
several passengers were helping themselves to large dozes
of liquor. At 9-45 p.m. we went to the Main Lounge
and watched the 'Bingo'. I was told it was some sort of
a gambling. At 10-45, we went to the 'Long Gallery'
where 'Get-together Dance' was already on. The notice
board said : "Come along and join in the fun and meet

your fellow passengers." We watched the dance for a few minutes and I noticed that several couples were in different stages of inebriation. The whole atmosphere was so stinking that I could not stand the scene. I told the Malayan friend that the 'fun' that was being indulged in before us was no fun but sin and that such fun was against Indian sentiment and culture. He agreed with me and we left the place. And as we got back to our respective cabins, my Malayan friend remarked that seeds for divorce, separation and breaking-up of the family life were generally sown first in the ballroom where the most important of the "ten commandments" of Christ were deliberately set at naught by the very people professing the Christian way of life.

On 2nd November at about 2 a.m. the steamer reached Charborough, a port of call on the soil of France. Passengers were allowed to go on shore. I along with the Malayam friend and another American passenger went round the city, saw the important thoroughfares, the market place, the church of La Tririte, the *hotel de ville* and the statue of J. F. Millet. Charborough is a naval station and is situated at the mouth of the Divette. This town is supposed to occupy the site of the Roman station of Coviallum. William the conqueror is said to have provided this town with a hospital and church. The streets are narrow and untidy. The American suggested that we should have some coffee as French coffee was supposed to be noted for its flavour. After some searching we selected a small coffee shop. English is not understood, but the word 'coffee' was enough to make the servers understand our requirement. We were made to wait for twenty minutes and in broken English, a server announced that she had brought "fresh coffee" in filters, the decoction still trickling down into an attached container. In the meanwhile, the maid had brought her neighbour to explain to us in English that sugar and milk should be added to the decoction to make it tasty. Of course the warm liquid tasted like coffee! We got back hastily to the ship which set sail at 12 noon. By 11 p.m. we were in Southampton.

Disembarkation began the next morning at 7 a.m. I took leave of Massey and he showed complete satisfaction when I gave him one pound as a tip. The customs formalities were over within half an hour. The officials were thorough in their examination of baggage but quite courteous. As there was still time for the train to leave for London, I entrusted my baggage to my travel agent and went round Southampton. The harbour is said to be one of the finest natural harbours. Southampton is not only an ancient historical seaport but also a country borough with a population of about two lakhs. It was from here that Henry V sailed for France and Agincourt in 1415. And again it was from here that the *May-flower* and the *Speedwell* sailed in 1620. A considerable portion of the old town walls still remains. St. Michael's church and the chapel of St. Julian are worth seeing. The town suffered severely from the air raids of the last world war.

The train left Southampton at about 9 a.m. and the 80-mile journey to London was pleasant. The journey by train enabled me to have a glimpse of the countryside. A Jewish businessman, who travelled with me, pointed out what he called 'the New Forest' of 93,000 acres, reserved for himself by William the Conqueror for hunting purposes and now belonging to the Crown. I arrived at London by noon, engaged a taxi and drove straight to Strand Palace Hotel.

13 London

The first to call on me at my London residence was
Mr. Ronald C. Davison. We spent some time together
discussing astrological matters. Before I had left India,
Mr. Davison had extended to me a cordial invitation on
behalf of the Astrological Lodge of London to address its
members. I was to have spoken on "Nadi Astrology"
but the engagement could not be fulfilled because I could
not reach London in time. Mr. Davison suggested that I
address the Lodge the next Monday. That was also not
possible because I had to be in Paris on that day. Mr.
Davison is not only the President of the Astrological
Lodge and the editor of *Astrology*, but is also author of a
book *The Technique of Prediction* in which there is a
clear presentation of western astrology. We had a
pleasant discussion and I found Mr. Davison courteous,
and well-informed in astrology. Mr. Davison also appeared to me to be quite fair in his assessment of Indian
astrology.

Other prominent astrologers who met me at my hotel
were Dr. William J. Tucker and Mr. George Cecil Nixon.
Dr. Tucker is a prolific writer on astrology and has nearly
20 books to his credit. He has presented in his books
certain novel theories of interpretation which do not seem
to have found favour with many British astrologers. I
had known Dr. Tucker by correspondence for over 25
years. I think it was in 1935 or so that we first began to

exchange communications. He was then bringing out *Science and Astrology*, a high class monthly journal. Warm-heartad, friendly and frank, Dr. Tucker impressed me as one genuinely interested in the study of astrology on scientific lines.

Though his writings in THE ASTROLOGICAL MAGAZINE are seemingly critical of Hindu astrology, Mr. Nixon, throughout his talks with me, showed himself to be an admirer of Indian Culture and Hindu astrology and hinted that his criticisms were well meant and were only intended to provoke healthy discussion. Mr. Nixon is not only a keen student of Hindu astrology but is a 'siderealist'. I will have to say more about 'siderealists' and 'tropicalists', in the concluding chapter of this book. But suffice it to say now that Mr. Nixon has been doing useful work for Hindu astrology and some of his attacks on what he calls 'the tropicalists' in the British astrological press are sharp and lively.

Apart from a number of admirers and students of Hindu astrology who met me at my hotel I think I should make particular mention of Dr. Rogister, Mr. Douglas Hunt and Dr. Kedar Nath Prasad. Dr. Rogister is an international lawyer. His interest in astrology is academic, but he is a great admirer of Indian Culture and Vedanta. He is perhaps one of the very few thinkers who is of the view that books on Indian history written by European scholars are not quite unprejudiced and that Indian civilisation and culture are not only ancient but are full of vitality. Dr. Rogister feels that Indian values of life are of perennial significance. He is a keen student of Mantra Sastra and when he was in India in 1957–58 he visited some important pilgrim-centres including remote villages. He also met great religious personalities. He shares my own humble view that ancient Indian history must be written by scholars who are proud of their ancient culture and not by those who have still been deriving their inspiration solely from western oriental scholars and who think that it is below their dignity to differ from accepted western views.

In his excellent book *Indian IST An Ders*, Dr. Rogister refers to his several meetings with me at my residence, and the discussions we had on astrology, Hindu philosophy, our ancient history, spirituality, etc. On page 112 of this work he says: "Prof. B. V. Raman is a great upholder of the universal truth and today is the greatest prophet of the time immemorial spirit of India. He is a 100% Indian and is never adversely influenced by the west. One can feel the Indian spirit in every word he speaks."

At another place Dr. Rogister observes: "Whatever prediction Prof. Raman makes is indeed mostly accurate. For example, his prediction about the Indo-China relations is amazingly true to the point, right from the beginning of August of 1954 till the breaking of India's relationship with China in November 1962. One can see how prophetic Prof. Raman was towards this international question. In June 1960, Prof. Raman wrote in his journal, warning Mr. Nehru of the immense danger that threatened his approach to China. Prof. Raman had said: 'The time now for Pandit Nehru is very good to take into confidence other neutral nations for a common front against Chinese aggression. Our Prime Minister is always shy to seek defence support from the western side to face the aggressive attitude of the Asiatic nations. But he should know that no support would come from these nations. As such our foreign policy should be realistic and in our own interest."

"In June 1962, realising that his warnings were not heeded, Prof. Raman declared: 'Chinese attack on India is to be expected. In this connection if we do not take a firm stand, there is no other alternative than facing the aggressions from our eastern neighbour'."

"The expected happened on 20th October 1962.

"Just at the time when Prof Raman made these statements I met some Indian friends. They bewailed 'if only we had known these predictions earlier'. I showed them what Prof. Raman had actually written in this situation. To them it was a surprise and wonder and they agreed with all the suggestions Prof. Raman made."

I spent quite an enjoyable time with Mr. Hunt discussing matters of common interest. Mr. Hunt had been a regular contributor to THE ASTROLOGICAL MAGAZINE for several years. Though brief and to the point Mr. Hunt's survey of the astrological and occult world in the West under the feature "Around the World" had been realistic, interesting and thought-provoking. A friend of India and Indian culture, Mr. Hunt impressed me as sincere and well-informed.

*Dr. Prasad who hails from Patna is a keen student of astrology and yoga He was doing his doctorate at Cambridge. At the invitation of Dr. Prasad I visited Cambridge and delivered a lecture on astrology before a select gathering of science teachers, medical men, etc. A report of my visit to Cambridge is given as Appendix I in this book. By the time I arrived in London, winter had already set in and the cold was biting. For one used to the salubrious and temperate climate of Bangalore, it was difficult to bear the cold in London. Snow was already

---

*He was for some years Vice-Chancellor of Patna University and is now the head of The Department of the Economics there.

falling and I think London Airport had been practically
closed for 2 or 3 days. On the day I went to Cambridge,
the snowfall was heavy and the cold biting. After com-
pleting my engagements at Cambridge—a dinner given to
me by the President of the Cambridge University Majlis
and a brief talk at the King's College—I left the city back
to London by the 9 p.m. train. Due to heavy snowfall,
the train moved so slow that it reached London round
about 1 a.m. There were no taxis at the railway station.
I walked for a while when an Iranian couple who had also
arrived from Cambridge in the same train hailed a taxi.
They offered to drop me at my place and I felt greatly
relieved. I paid my share of the fare—Sh. 16—and got
down at my hotel by about 1-30 a.m.

Dr. Prasad's report of my visit to Cambridge has
been published as Appendix II in this book.

On 5th November, I visited the office of *New World
Astrology* at Ludgate Hill and spent some time with the
editor Mr. Edward Whitman. Later on accompanied by
Dr. W. J. Tucker, and Mr. T. J. N. Rowell, a student of
Hindu astrology, we drove to the Alliance Hall, Westminster, where at a special meeting arranged by Dr.
Tucker under the auspices of the Federation of British
astrologers I spoke on "Astrology in India". There was
a large gathering which included a number of British
astrologers. Mr. A. Ward presided. Introducing me to
the audience Dr. Tucker, a past president of the Federation, said : "We have gathered here this evening to listen
to the address of India's most distinguished astrologer,
Prof. Bangalore Venkat Raman, Editor of one of the
world's greatest astrological monthlies THE ASTROLOGICAL
MAGAZINE and author of many astrological text-books.
Before coming here Prof. Raman had been touring the

United States of America lecturing to crowded audiences. He attended the International Congress of Astro–Science held in New York.

"Prof. Raman is, of course, one of the foremost of world's astrologers and to my mind he must also be accounted the greatest living authority on Hindu astrology.

"Comparisons are invidious and I am not going to tell you that THE ASTROLOGICAL MAGAZINE is the world's finest and best astrological publication. But I can say that it is a remarkably strong challenger for that coverted honor. To my mind and I speak completely objectively— judging against a very realistic standard of comparison— there are only three really outstanding astrological jour- nals which are at one and the same instructional, infor- mative, entertaining, non-sensationaly, authoritative and progressive; these being *Horoscope* and *American Astrology* of U.S.A. and THE ASTROLOGICAL MAGAZINE of India. At present these periodicals are running neck to neck in the race; and the only thing which prevents Prof. Raman's magazine from taking the lead is the reason that so many western readers lack an elementary knowledge of the basis of Hindu astrology and remain baffled by the relatively few Indian nouns which are naturally used by many of the writers. Yet despite this rather severe handi- cap, it does strike me that Prof. Raman's magazine bids fair to pass from the status of challenger to that of the winner, unless the American editors remain alert and become more discerning.

"This happens to be the first occasion on which I have had the great and enormous pleasure of meeting Prof. Raman personally. For this is the first time he has visited our country."

After dealing extensively with the differences between the zodiacs employed by Hindu and Western Astrology

Dr. Tucker concluded thus : "By this time the audience must be impatient to hear our principal speaker of this evening, whom I have had the honour of presenting to you and I will now vacate the rostrum in order that this great astrologer may address you."

In the course of my lecture, I explained the antiquity of Indian Culture and the significant role played by astrology in the life of an average Indian from his birth to death. I also gave a brief exposition of the essential features of Hindu astrology and how it differs from the western system. I concluded my lecture with an appeal to British astrologers to take a more lively and sustained interest in this ancient system, so that western astrology could be further enriched.

In his closing remarks Mr. Ward paid me suitable compliments for what he called my "thought-provoking address" and endorsed my suggestion for a more liberal attitude towards Hindu astrology. The question hour was equally lively except for a brush with an elderly gentleman who gave a religious twist to the theory of Karma.

Prominent astrologers present were : Mrs. Beatrice Blackstaff, President of the British Federation of Astrologers, Mr. W. G. Gilby, Mr. B. C. Gordon Reuter. Mr. R. H Burgess, Baroness Lippit, Mr. Irvine Dove, Mr. T. J. N. Rowell, Miss Gerson, Mrs. Marshall, Mr. J. C. Jones, Mr. Edward Whitman, Mr. E. H. Bailey and Mr. Gandhi. Many of the readers of THE ASTROLOGICAL MAGAZINE should be familiar with the name of Mr. Bailey. He was the doyen of British astrologers. His contribution to the cause of astrology through his books and the now defunct *British Journal of Astrology* is indeed considerable. My first contacts with Mr. Bailey were made as early as 1932 In those years I contributed to his journal a series of articles on "Kalatra Bhava". Mr. Bailey had always shown a sympathetic attitude towards Hindu astrology and had been fair in his appraisal of the uniqueness of the Hindu system. It was a great pleasure to meet him in person. He passed away in 1960.

I was able to do a lot of sight-seeing in London. As far as possible I tried to explore this city on foot and linger among its historical interests. There may be several readers of THE ASTROLOGICAL MAGAZINE who have seen London and I am sure most of them will endorse my impression about this great city. For one who has seen New York, London is a city with narrow streets and buildings of all ages and styles. Once the hub of the British Empire, London does not seem to have lost any importance though Britain has divested herself of most of her empire. London seems to extend as far as the eye can see.

As one of my British friends remarked one needs a sense of history to understand the present state of London. The city has a history dating back to 64 A.D. According to Tacitus it was then "a place much frequented by merchants". In 61 A.D., after the Roman Governor Suetonis retired, Bondiccas Hordes sacked London and inflicted a crushing victory over the British restoring Roman authority which thereafter lasted for nearly 4 centuries. Modern London contains many of the survivals of its ancient past. Massive fragments of the wall built by the Romans still remain; so does the castle that William the Conqueror built, a thousand years later. Just as there were several Delhis beginning from Hastinapura of the Pandavas, there have been Roman London, Saxon London, Norman London, Tudor London. Stuart London, etc., until we come to modern London. The accumulation of history does not seem to have interfered with the march of progress. London is nothing if not up-to-date, and living cheek by jowl with the monuments of the past are the mammoth conceptions of a living and ambitious present. The ancient city has been rebuilt again and again. But here and there, there are interesting survivals of original buildings. Mayfair and Bloomsbury remind one of the 18th and 19th century aristocracy and professional classes respectively. North and south of Hyde Park and Kensington Gardens are residential districts "typifying, though poorly, the last stand of style".

The area of greater London is estimated to be about 690 sq. miles and the population is nearly nine millions. The traffic problem in London seems to give a lot of headache to the authorities concerned. It is a source of wonder how the police have been dealing with their work of traffic control. Trafalgar Square, Marble Arch, Piccadily Circus, Chatham Palace and Victoria Station are perhaps the centres of heaviest traffic.

One evening while driving with a British friend our car was held up at the Ludgate Circus for nearly 20 minutes. My friend said that such hold-ups were a common feature in London. According to him, an intersection like the Ludgate Circus or Hyde Park corner carries about 9 to 10 thousand vehicles in a period of 12 hours. This figure could give one an idea of the volume of traffic. The passing of streams of vehicles is a sight to see. My own observation is, compared to Bombay or Calcutta, the congestion in the narrow streets of London is exceedingly severe.

London has so many attractions that it is impossible to see them all unless one lives in the city for months together. Among the important places of interest in London I visited were the Westminster Abbey, Buckingham Palace, Dicken's House, Hyde Park, Houses of Parliament, The

Tower of London, Trafalgar Square, The White Hall, Zoological Gardens and the British Museum.

The Buckingham Palace is the London residence of English sovereigns since 1837, when Queen Victoria first took up residence there. Compared to the Palace of the Maharaja at mysore, it is an unassuming and unattractive building. The only attractive items are the wrought iron gates. I witnessed the "Guard Mounting Ceremony", a relic of the 18th century and much is made of the ceremony of the changing of guards.

On the day I visited Westminster Abbey, some memorial service was being held with the usual paraphernalia of some big political guns participating. The English, just like the Hindus, are conservative by nature. They will "fight tooth and claw to retain it". It was in Westminster Abbey, a superb example of 13th century architecture, that Norman William was crowned in 1066 and it was in the same place that Queen Elizabeth II was also crowned, based on the ritual prescribed in the Liber Regalis, prepared in 1399 for the coronation of Henry IV and still in the Library of the Abbey. Originally a Saxon Abbey, it was rebuilt by Edward the Confessor in the 11th century and again by Henry III in the 13th century in which form, it is said to exist today. Among the Abbey's treasures are the magnificent Chapel of Henry VII, the Coronation chair and the Stone of Scone, the helmet which Henry V wore at the battle of Agincourt.

The first authentic records place its foundation in 1042 A.D. by Edward the Confessor and since that time it has been the traditional setting of historical ceremonies.

14 London—2

High on the summit of Ludgate Hill, stands magnificently, the great St. Paul's Cathedral. Within this Cathedral are the memorials of many famous men. The building is said to be the "crowning achievement of England's greatest architect Christopher Wren". In its present form it replaces the Cathedral burnt in the Great Fire of London in 1686 and clearly predicted in advance by the great English astrologer William Lily. The tombs of Wellington who vanquished Napoleon at Waterloo and Nelson the hero of Trafalgar are worth a visit. The richer politicians live in streets at the back of the Abbey and very near to the Houses of Parliament. It is again in this same locality that you will find headquarters of missionary societies including that of Church of England.

I spent considerable time going round the Tower of London. Situated on the north bank of the river Thames, it appeared to me to be a grim-looking castle with a haunted appearance. My guide explained that according to tradition, Julius Caesar was the founder of the Tower, and this reminded me of Shakespeare's Richard III (III. I). The Tower is surrounded by a ditch, formerly fed by the Thames, but now dry. In the White Tower or Keep may be seen collection of old armour and instruments of torture and the rooms said to have been Sir Walter Raleigh's prison. There is also here St. John's Chapel, "a superb miniature Norman Church". I saw with much interest the crown jewels, among which are the largest diamonds in the world, kept in Wakefield Tower. It seems that it was in this particular chamber that Henry VI met with his death while at prayers. On the south is the famous Traitors' Gate by which prisoners of high rank were admitted. The main historical interest of the Tower lies in its association with such prisoners.

As a High School student, I was generally scoring high marks in English History. I am supposed to possess a little bit of historical sense and hence I was very curious to see the spot where Henry VIII's queens were beheaded. Tower Green is the sight of the scaffold where Anne Boleyne, Catherine Howard, Lady Jane Grey and her husband Dudley and the Duke of Monmouth were executed. There is a belief or superstition that the British Empire will come to an end when the ravens, which may be seen on Tower Green, leave the tower. Hence their wings are clipped. There was also a royal palace within the Tower which was demolished by order of Cromwell. Another interesting feature is, the attendant staff "Yeoman warders of Her Majesty's Tower of London" familiarly called "Beef-eaters" still wear Tudor Costume.

An English friend who is proprietor of a publishing concern took me round the Piccadily Circus and the Houses of Parliament. As I have already said Piccadily Circus presents the West End of London with one of its worst traffic problems. At the centre of the Circus stands the famous statue of Eros and from it radiate some of London's best known streets—Piccadily, Regent Street Haymarket and Shaftesbury Avenue. Regent Street is one of the busiest in London and is the capital's fashionable centre.

The Houses of Parliament, officially the Westminster Palace were once a royal residence. Built in late Gothic

style they are said to contain over 1,000 rooms and 100
staircases. They are now the seat of Government and the
"heart of the Commonwealth". In 1834, they were destroyed by fire and rebuilt by Sir Charles Barry. Again in 1941,
they were destroyed by Hitler's bombs and were subsequently rebuilt by Gilbert Scott. In these houses were
fought innumerable political battles—for the beheading of
Charles I, for making India the "brightest jewel" of the
British Empire and for the ultimate liquidation of the
Empire itself.

In the evenings I used to roam about Trafalgar Square
with an English friend. This is the London's best known
landmark. The north side of the Trafalgar Square is
occupied by the National Gallery and the National Portrait
Gallery. In the centre are the Nelson's Column, some
elegant fountains and a great many overfed pigeons.

My stay in London coincided with Guy Fawks Day
on 5th November. Some of the streets had been littered
with burnt fireworks. The anniversary of the discovery
of the gun powder plot is celebrated on this day by bon-
fires, fireworks, and the carrying of "guys" through the
streets. I was told it was not safe to move about in the
narrow streets because of fear of crackers being thrown
at passers-by, by teddy boys. I watched the fun, near
the East End of London. It was like our Deepavali but
with greater abandon. Who has not heard of the gun-
powder plot involving Guy Fawks? Fawks was known for
his exceptional courage and coolness. It is said he had
actively associated himself with the plot to blow up King
James I and Parliament on 5th November, 1605, as a reply
to the anti-Roman Catholic laws initiated vigorously by
James. Guy Fawks with some of his associates was hauled
by, severely tortured, confession extracted and being
drawn on a hurdle from the Tower to the Parliament

House; was put to death with Thomas Winter, Rosewood and Keyes. The trial of Guy Fawks was held in Westminster Hall. It has a beautiful hammer beam roof. This hall has echoed to the solemnity of state trials and has seen the dethronement of Edward II, Richard II, Henry VI and Charles I who were sentenced to death in the hall. It has served as a tilting hall, and has housed the law courts, as well as book stalls and booths.

Of equal interest is the Whitehall, the broad thorouhfare which runs from the Houses of Parliament to the Trafalgar Square. Here flourishes the existing machinery of Government, the Home Office, the Treasury, the War Office, the Admiralty and other Government Departments, each one housed in its own imposing palace. There is also the Cenotaph opposite the Home Office, which commemorates the fallen, in two world wars. The famous Downing Street is an unpretentious little street on the west side of the Whitehall. Here, at No. 10 resides the Prime Minister of the day. It was in this place that Winston Churchill during war years shouldered a load of responsibilities which would have crushed any other man. It was again in this house that the same Mr. Churchill thundered that he would not be His Majesty's first Prime Minister to liquidate the British Empire. At the northern end of the Whitehall, is the equestrain statue of Charles I erected on the spot where rejecides were executed.

While in London I called on Dr. Shelvanker of *The Hindu* and was with him for some time. I also visited some newspaper and magazine offices in the Fleet Street which is the publishing centre of London.

I had long walks in Hyde Park which together with Kensington Gardens combined are not as big as Central Park, New York. But they seem to have a greater sense

of size probably because they have not been enclosed by
tall buildings. Hyde Park, like Trafalgar Square, is often
the scene of political and other popular demonstrations.
You can see budding politicians haranguing at all hours
of the day. The neighbourhood of Marble Arch is the
resort of orators on social and religious topics. Other
landmarks of the Hyde Park are the Serpentine, an extensive boating lake, and Rotten Row, a track of riding and
the corner on the southern side. In the west-end of
London, Hyde Park is perhaps the largest open space.

I visited the Zoological Gardens. They occupy 34
acres. Originally opened in 1828, they contain very fine,
comprehensive and best housed collection of animals from
all parts of the world, perhaps ever brought together.

15 London—3

An elderly Englishman told me that "in the good old days" of Queen Victoria and King Edward, "when a man's income was more than half his own," the London season with its gaieties and festivities was sharply demarcated. Today, in this utilltarian age. there exists no clearly defined demarcation. Nevertheless, outdoor events such as horse shows, flower shows, exhibition of paintings by the Royal Academy, the Lord Mayor's show, etc., still take place at the same time of the year. With November comes the return of pageantry, especially the state opening of Parliament by the Queen. For this event, as well as for the Lord Mayor's show the streets are sanded and lined with troops and at the end of the day they are supposed to be lined with "orange peel, lost children, stray dogs and paper flags".

I was not much interested in these events. I mechanically listened to the description given by my English friend. As a tennis fan I was particular to visit the famous Wimbeldon. The lawn tennis championships held here in June are the most famous international lawn tennis events of the year and draw thousands of spectators and players from all over the world. I spent some time in the Wimbledon Courts watching amateur players' practice.

I think few cities in the world can compare with London as a museum centre, except perhaps New York. In the brief period of my stay in London, I could visit only the British Museum. Even at the risk of being prolix, I would like to give my readers a detailed account of this famous museum. It is situated in Great Russel Street, and comprises the National Library. To gain even a summary impression of the British Museum one should be prepared to spend at least half-a-day in its galleries. To me it appeared that the contents of the Museum cover man's activities throughout the ages and perhaps throughout the world. The living beauty and drama of the thousands of priceless exhibits defy an adequate description by my humble pen. The British Museum advances learning by the provision of materials and facilities for research, and by the encouragement of the study of literature, history archaeology and art. Public use of the collections, which illustrate every aspect of the progress of civilisation is afforded by the Reading Rooms and services in the library departments ; by Students' Rooms in other Departments; by exhibition of select material in the Public Galleries; by public lecture-tours ; by the publication of catalogues, guide books and reproductions ; by photographic services; by the supply of casts; and by information given in response to personal enquiry.

The history of the Museum is interesting. I think it came into existence in 1753, as a gift (against payment of £ 20,000) from Sir Hans Sloane who bequeathed his library, natural history collections, antiquities and works of art. The Parliament appointed a body of Trustees to take charge of these collections. Later on the collections were enriched by gifts by Royalty and public-spirited men and by purchases. These collections originally placed in Cotton House, Westminster, were moved to the present premises in Bloomsberry in 1755 or so.

Broadly speaking, two main divisions can be recognised—the library and the Departments of Antiquities. Somehow I have a liking for books—especially those of ancient authors and I spent most of my time in the

Museum looking up manuscripts and printed books. My
second interest concerned the antiquities—especially so-
called pre-historic. The Library of printed books is said
to be the largest in the world. Every branch of literature,
ancient and modern, is represented. The total number of
printed books in the Library is said to be about six million
volumes. The Department of Manuscripts includes outstanding treasures such as the Codex Alexandrianus of the
Greek Bible, the Lindisfarne Gospels of A. D. 700, and
the last collection of Greek Papyrus from Egypt and vast
quantities of medieval and modern historical papers and
literary autographs.

In the collections of the Department of Oriental
Printed Books and Manuscripts "the countries of the Far,
Middle and Near East, with their many and diverse languages and scripts are strongly represented both in manuscripts and printed productions of different ages. Of
particular importance are the unrivalled collections of
early Hebrew and Syriac manuscripts of the Old Testa-
ment; the Chinese Library, which includes the collection
of more than 6,000 rolls which had been walled up for
about 1,000 years in Tun-Huang (North China) until discovered by Sir Aurel Stein in 1907"; and the collections
of books and manuscripts of Hindu and Islamic worlds.

I was thrilled to read the original of the famous
Magna Carta issued by King John in 1215, of course
under compulsion from his barons. The history of the
Charter is well known to need mention. The clauses of the
Charter were regarded with veneration long after they
were out of date and it seems men read into them meaning
which would have surprised their original drafters. 17th
century lawyers "ignorant of the law of the early 13th
century, knowing nothing of the conditions of the time,
saw in the Charter, a solemn grant to the people of Eng-

land of rights which the Stuart Kings were withholding".
It seems modern historians have done much to put Magna
Carta in its proper perspective though even the 19th century historians thought that trial by Jury, the principal
of *habeas corpus* and the right of Parliament to control
taxation were secured by Magna Carta. Another principal
exhibit in the same room which attracted my attention
was a deed bearing the signature of William Shakespeare.
In the 'King's Library', amongst other valuable collections I noticed two cases showing the first folio of Shakespeare, the first edition of Milton's *Paradise Lost* and a
number of other famous books.

The gallery of oriental art should be specially interesting to an Indian because you could see there special
exhibits showing the great ancient civilisation of not only
India but also Greater India. I saw beautiful images of
Ganesa, Saraswati, Vishnu and Siva.

Egyptian antiquity is equally well represented. The
great collection of Egyptian sculptures, the numerous
objects of art and ornament and articles of domestic life,
the series of mummies and antiquities connected with the
burial of the dead, the inscriptions and other written
documents, which are brought together in the museum,
afford an unrivalled means of estimating the knowledge
and powers, the thought and religion, the art, and the
daily life of this ancient people.

In the Egyptian sculpture gallery are arranged
sculptures in order of date, beginning from the V Dynasty
(2000 B.C.). The colossal red granite head of Thothmes
III (1400 B.C.) and statues of Ramses II are all interesting
exhibits giving us a picture of the great past of Egypt.

When I was closely examining the mummies I chanced
to meet a Swiss gentleman, who was all praise for ancient

Egyptian and Babylonian civilisations.   After mutual
introductions, he said that he was an egyptologist and
had made a special study of Egyptian planetary texts.
We together went round the Department of Antiquities
where Greek sculpture stands conspicuous, particularly
the remains of the temples of Ephesus and Phigalia and
the Babylonian Room housing the principal objects discovered during the excavations at Ur of Chaldeans.   The
Swiss friend explained to me the various scenes of war
and peace engraved on the "Mossaic Standard" a Sume-
rian object of about 2500 B.C.   We got into a taxi, drove
to a nearby coffee house and spent an hour discussing
ancient astronomy.   Somehow, many of these scholars
appeared to me to entertain the strange and untenable
view that the civilisation of Egypt was more ancient than
that of India.   I have strong convictions in the matter of
antiquity of Indian Culture. With due deference to the findings of historians, it must be noted that Egypt was after
all originally a colony of the Hindus.   This theory can be
supported not only by historical evidence but also on
ethnological grounds.   Thanks to the researches of late
Mr. Harbilas Sarda, evidence is now available to show
that Egpptians were only Hindus who migrated to Egypt
about 8 thousand years ago.   The Swiss friend had his
own objections to endorse my view, but appeared to me to
be open-minded also.   He gave me an interesting account
of Egyptian astronomy.   It seems the Egyptians used two
types of Calendars—one using the year of 365 days and
the other based on intercalation—adding one day at the
end of every four years.   This is clear evidence, according to this Swiss gentleman, that the origin of the zodiac
related to some fixed star, just as in Hindu astronomy,
disregarding precession.   In calculating the positions of
planets, latitudes were ignored.   It is well known that

ancient Egyptians, like the ancient Hindus, were great astrologers and that their study of astronomy was only intended to help them in their astrological pursuits. O. Neugebauer, said my Swiss friend, was of the opinion that astrological purposes of these ancient astronomical texts should be excluded. I think it is safe to leave the question to be solved by my good friend Mr. Cyril Fagan, whose original researches bearing on Egyptian and Chaldean astronomy are a matter of great admiration.

It was not possible for me to visit all the Museums in London, but I did not miss the Dickens' House and Madame Tussads. I went to the Dickens' House with a number of friends. Who has not heard of Charles Dickens the great British novelist and his *Pickwick*, *Oliver Twist* and *Nicholas Nickleby*. I was told that it was at 48, Doughty Street where Dickens' House is situated that the great novelist lived. I saw the Dickens' relics, especially some of the original manuscripts. Some American visitors who were with me were arguing amongst themselves about the merits of Dickens' novels. One of them said that the books of Dickens were full of bores. The Second one said that his characters were often fantastic caricatures, while the third felt that genius of Dickens consisted in seeing in somebody, "whom others might call merely prosaic the germ of a sort of a prose-poem". The fourth one felt that Dickens was a wild satirist, but he had a sensible view of life. I am no literateur. But I have enjoyed reading *Nicholas Nickleby*. Therefore I am too humble to pass any remarks on such a great writer as Dicknes. But I concurred with the final opinion of the half-a-dozen American tourists who were with me that just as in the case of Cervantes, Dickens has outlived his descendants as well as his contemporaries and that the importance of Dickens as a human event in history is more than assumed. Dickens was born on 7th February 1812 and died on 9th June 1870. In addition to novel writing, Dickens edited some magazines and gave public readings of his works both in the United Kingdom and America.

I was much impressed by what I saw at Madame Tussads. The Museum is well known all over the world for its wax works of famous and infamous people. To a casual visitor like me it is the variety of models that proves the importance of the Museum. They are all so well done that one may be tempted to mistake them for real personalities. The wax model of Gandhi is tolerably good. That of Nehru is grotesque. You can only see a sickly haggard and despirited Nehru. There are also models of many of the prominent leaders and victims of French Revolution. As I was about to get down into the "Chamber of Horrors" I was requested by a German lady who had brought her young son with her, to hold his hand as he was getting terror-stricken at the sight of a model showing the beheading of a revolutionary. I assured him that it was only a figure. But he could not be convinced. He was closing his eyes until we left the chamber. One should admire the imagination of Madame Tussad, for having established such an exhibition. Marie Tussad born at Berne in 1760 was taught modelling by her uncle J. C. Curtins who established a wax cabinet in the Paleis Royal, Paris. She married in 1794 and "in 1802 transferred the wax work Museum to London establishing it first in the Strand. It was transferred to Marylebone Road, the present place, in 1884".

During my stay in London, I attended one or two plays in a famous theatre and saw a current film also. Nor did I miss the Petticoat Lane (corresponding to our ghuzli) where a wide selection of new and second-hand items are hawked. I found fascinating antiques, China and brick-a-brick for sale, in the Caledonian Market in Bermondsey. This is supposed to be London's most famous open-air market. In the Petticoat lane, I found several Indians hawking sandal-sticks and other Indian products.

Few cities in the world exercise such fascination upon the visitor as does London : Why ? Other great cities have their own distinctive features ; New York for its sky-scrapers and Paris for its beauty and Geneva for its splendid health-giving climate. But the charm of London! It is more subtle. London has seen great changes after the second world war. Despite these changes it has retained its charm. The ebb and flow of life on the busy high-ways, the picturesque blending of medieval and modern archi-tecture and the essentially international character of its population—all combined have made the city of London exercise a peculiar fascination over the minds of people.

I returned to my hotel rather late in the night exhaus-ted and within a few minutes of going to bed, I fell into deep sleep. Just before daybreak the next morning, all kinds of thoughts about London, about my family, about astrology, etc., began to cross my mind.

Just then the maid entered my room greeting me with a "good morning, Sir" and bringing my morning coffee. I had just taken a sip of coffee and the telephone bell rang. And the wonder was—Mrs Rajeswari Raman was at the other end in Bangalore wanting to talk to me. It was 12 noon in Bangalore she having already taken her food and it was 6–30 a.m. in London, I just then helping myself with coffee. Thanks to Marconi's genius, we could talk to each other intimately though separated by a distance of 6,000 miles. It was a thrill to listen to the voice of Mrs. Raman and my children. The human in me was feeling

my family members did not want me to prolong my stayout
of India. I began to feel homesick, curtailed visits to
Brussels and Amsterdam and within 24 hours was on my
way back to India.

When I boarded an Air India International Plane, it
was raining at the London Airport. I became friendly
with an Englishman who was on his way to Calcutta. We
boarded the plane together. Just before take-off, the
Englishman remarked that the weather being bad, flying
on that day might be a hazard. I nodded assent. The
plane took off at about mid-day. Soon we were above the
clouds and could not get even a glimpse of receding
London. The changing pattern of clouds below presented a very picturesque appearance. My mind had been
absorbed in the contemplation of this fascinating scenery
when my English friend reminded me that we were above
the Alps. Because of cloudy weather and rain, it was not
possible to differentiate between a mountain peak or
cloud formation and he was feeling uneasy that the plane
might accidentally hit a hillock and get blown off. I
found from the faces of some passengers that they were
also uneasy. I was no exception. But I kept my composure
and as I was explaining the Englishman that astrologically
there was no chance of any such mishap happening, we
were above the Lake of Geneva and within a few minutes
the plane had safely landed and we were at the Airport
restaurant sipping excellent coffee.

The flight from Geneva to Cairo was quite smooth
and enjoyable. At Geneva we were joined by a big
compliment of passengers and all the seats in the First
Class were full. The passenger next to me was a boy of
about 22. He told me later on that he was the son of a
millowner at Coimbatore. He was on his first visit to
Europe on some sort of an inspection tour, to negotiate—

purchase of textile machinery. He had been deputed by his father on this work. He was proudly narrating that he stayed only in First Class hotels—Dorchester in London for instance. He asked me why I stayed in Strand Palace and not in Dorchester. I told him that I had no millionaire father to spend money on inspection tours. The teenager had already become addicted to certain vices. I was shocked to find that during the flight from Geneva to Cairo, he helped himself with Champagne —about half-a-dozen times.

It is a pity that such inexperienced boys are sent out by their parents. What sort of machinery this boy could select, is a matter of guess. I wonder how they are able to secure foreign exchange for such pleasure trips, when for more useful and serious purposes, the authorities have no foreign exchange to spare !

After a halt of 30 minutes at Cairo, where we had excellent fresh lemon juice, the plane took off at about 2 a.m. I did not get sleep and went on reading *Primum Mobile* of Titus a copy of which I had secured in London. I had finished the introduction and I was feeling drowsy. The air-hostess drew a blanket over me as chill winds were blowing. By the time I was awake, we were within half-an-hour's flight to bombay. I had not had my supper in the night and the hostess was considerate enough to get me a cup of coffee and some cashew nuts. As I exhausted the beverage, I could see the landscape of Bombay. My heart was overjoyed as soon as I set my foot on the soil of India—my motherland.

Just before landing, one of the passengers—Mr. X —who had a tape-recorder with him hinted that if I had brought any articles from Europe and America, I should

9

just put them into my pockets and walk out. I said that it was improper not to declare such imported articles. Mr. X did not agree with me. He warned that honesty would not pay and that I would be harrassed by the Customs.

The Customs examination at the Bombay Airport was really most irksome. I had purchased a pocket-sized transistor radio at Boston and two wrist watches at Geneva, besides some articles for my children and I declared all these articles. One of the clerks showed surprise that I was declaring all the articles! I was also under the impression that if I placed all my cards on the table, the authorities would show appreciation and let me off with a polite warning because I had made the purchases relying on the advice of Indian authorities in New York. I could not imagine that I had been wrongly advised. However the authorities took a different view and insisted that articles worth and above Rs. 500 would not be allowed. The radio and the watches were seized. After months of prolonged correspondence, the articles were returned to me against payment of fine and duty. When I came out of the Customs and was about to board a taxi, another Customs official took me into confidence and said that had I not declared the articles, I would not have been harrassed at all!

Later on after a few weeks, I chanced to meet Mr. X at Bangalore. He was proud that without paying any duty he was able to bring his tape-recorder. I asked him how? He said that "everything is prearranged. There is a way of greasing palms and getting things done. We just walk into the Customs and after the formal inspection we walk out". I retorted, "You do an improper thing and get out without any trouble." He burst into peels of laughter. I also laughed but had the satisfaction that what I did at the Airport was proper despite all the annoyance I had to meet with.

On the evening of 12th November, I was back at home.

131

daughter. I also laughed but had the satisfaction that

16   Astrology In America

Though during my brief stay in the States, I met
number of astrologers and the astrologically interested, it
was not possible to contact all the groups and individuals
connected with astrology either as exponents, practitioners, or investigators.   Therefore, my observation as
to how astrology and astrological studies have been thriv-
ing in U.S.A., are subject to this limitation.

In this so called creative age of science, interest in
the study of astrology in America appears to be growing
by leaps and bounds.   Paradoxically there are some
persons there belonging to the caste of scientists as we
have in India belonging to the caste of professional
politicians, who look down upon astrology, because they
think it is fashionable to do so.   According to a newspaper correspondent, who interviewed me at New York,
the United States, to, what he called "the horror of some
so-called rational people", has been caught up in the
biggest astrological maze.   I asked the correspondent as
to why some of these rationalists should not consider
such astrological revival as a healthy sign of the times
unlike in the past decades, when men calling themselves
educated "turned a blind eye to the science of astrology".
He merely repeated that the revival of interest in astrology
is looked upon by some of "these rationalists" as a
symptom of the state of "widespread intellectual desti-

tution," but quickly added that even some of these "rationalists" privately consulted astrologers.

Broadly speaking, there appear to be three categories of people in America connected in some way or other with astrology. I would classify them as : (a) professional astrologers, (b) men of science interested in astrology and (c) astrological scholars and adepts. Of course, category (c) has also several astrological practioners. Among the professional astrologers, there are experts well versed in the subject, and quacks who call themselves as astrologers, though really speaking, they belong to the circle of "numerologists, palmists, and hypnotists". The professional astrologers are said to be nearly 5,000 in number catering to the needs of thousands of consultors drawn from all walks of life ; and such customers turn out to be nearly 10 million people a year. Nearly 10 or 15 percent out of this large section of consultors regulate their daily lives on the "celestial schedule" furnished by their astrological advisers. The *fee is said to range from ten dollars (Rs. 70) to 100 dollars (Rs. 700) for a consultation. Human nature is the same wherever you go. It is no wonder that even in the materially advanced America there should be people who consult their favourite astrologers even on such matters as what to eat, what to wear and what to see.

In India, almost every newspaper has an astrological column. Even 'National' Newspapers, whose columns are daily filled to capacity with the stale rigmarole of ministerial utterances and who cannot spare even half a column space for a serious astrological discussion or article, dole out weekly and daily forecasts. The same

---

* This has reference to 1959. But today (1984) the fees range from 100 dollars, (Rs. 1000/-) to 1000 dollars (Rs. 10000/-)

phenomenon with a little variation can be seen in U.S.A. also, where nearly 100 newspapers with a daily circulation of nearly 40 millions have "what the stars foretell" columns. There are readers who hardly miss a glance at these daily and weekly forecasts. Mostly run on a commercial basis and having nothing to do with higher reaches of astrology, there are, I was told, a dozen or so institutions, whose business is to "popularise" astrology in the sense of exploiting man's lure for the unknown.

One day as I emerged out of a meeting in New York, a meticulously dressed young man introduced himself as a "psychologist, astrologer and thought-reader" and handed over to me a copy of *Your Daily Astrological Guide*, He said it was brought out regularly by a publishing firm in the midwest and that he was connected with several such firms which manufacture such stuff as 'Dream Interpretations", "Hollywood Horoscopes", "Stellar Diatetics" and so on. He said that he was a qualified astrologer and knew how to cast horoscopes. His knowledge of predictive astrology was of course confined to preparing Sun-sign readings. He went on : In order to create serious interest in astrology, in the minds of the common public, it was necessary to give them something light and non-technical. While I could appreciate his point of view about popularising astrology, I could not easily reconcile myself to the proposition that an unqualified astrologer could ever promote the cause of true astrology.

I think it was in Washington that I casually walked into a "palmist and an astrological consultant". There were two ladies on aged about 60 and another about 25. Her fee for answering five questions was just one dollar. She asked my date of birth and then 'examined' my palm. She said she was also a 'sensitive'. She gave me "sincere help and advice on health, future, marriage" and took "great pleasure in helping me". Again her performance was no better than that of 'fortune tellars' we are familiar with. Again at Chicago, I met a 'natural clairvoyant and astrologer". Each consultation would not require more than 10 minutes and within this time he would deal with "business, marriage, health, love affairs and emotional unrest". Because perhaps of my pigment I had the "privilege" of spending nearly 30 minutes with this "clairvoyant". He said that he learnt clairvoyance from an "Indian gentleman" and that he was now learning "Hindu mysticism" and "Hindu astrology". I asked him who was his teacher in Hindu astrology. He said: "Raman, the Hindu mystic. I am studying his *Hindu Predictive Astrology*." He showed me a copy of this book. I told him that I had met Raman and that he was not a mystic. I also told him of course without revealing my identity that if he wanted to apply Hindu astrology to his client's problems, he should devote at least one or two hours for each customer. "That is right, Sir," he said, "but this is business and I use a lot of human psychology to deal with customers." Later on in the night I telephoned to him from my hotel that I was the author of *Hindu Predictive Astrology*. Within half an hour he met me with protestations of admiration for Hindu astrology and apologised for what he called the "professional treatment" extended to me earlier in the day.

I am narrating these instances to show that there are a large number of exploiters in America, who calling themselves as astrologers, exploit the creduious people. Refinements of astrological calculations and interpretation are far beyond the meagre powers of most of these "working astrologers".

In America the depth of belief may range from occasional interest to fanaticism. It is impossible to doubt that astrology is a considerable iufluence in determining decisions of many private lives. I must caution my readers, that whether in Europe or in U.S.A., it is a great mistake to judge astrology solely by the professional astrologer.

There are also persons in America who are concerned with the application of astrology to such odd things as fashions in women's costumes. One such person whom I happened to meet assured me that investigation based on planetary cycles have revealed that the "bell-shaped skirts used by women today would give place to a bustle type of skirts by 1970 or so'. According to him, changes in fashion are not capricious but they follow a 36-year cycle corresponding to the movement of the Nodes and Jupiter. He also claimed to foretell—he incidentally referred to a theory of Prof. Roxford Hersy—when next, one will be dancing in air convinced that life is wonderful or one will be on his or her way to the nearest psychiatrist to be treated for extreme depression !

Coming to category 2, I was pleasantly surprised when some psychologists, astronomers and medical men were introduced to me as persons greatly interested in astrology. Most of them are men of science and not astrologers in the literal sense of the term. They are convinced that astrology works. These men seem to feel that scientists should not refuse to give attention to astrology. They are anxious to see that "astrology is built up as a new science on a demonstrable basis of facts and statistics.", but they do not want that their names should be publicly known for fear of being "frowned upon by orthodox scientific bodies" to which they happen to belong. Prominent researchers are working on ways of "measuring planetary influences on earthly happenings". The positions of these men appeared to me to be similar to the position of Galileo, *vis-a-vis* the Catholic Church. Just as Galileo's views had vast implications which could not be ignored, so also the views of these men of science, based on their own independent researches, seem to confound the faith of the orthodox scientists. While the discoveries of correlation between certain planetary dispositions and magnetic disturbances made by some American scientists may be an "eye opener" to "men of science" who had hitherto believed that nothing could exist beyond the ken of their pet theories, to Indians nurtured on the traditions of Varahamihira and Gargi such discoveries are like carrying coal to New Castle. There are still some "educated" persons in India to whom the opinion of a Western man of science is gospel truth. Scientist John Nelson of R.C.A. Communications, *New York, has discovered that the most severe ionospheric disturbances will come when the "combined influences of Mars, Mercury and Venus are such that all three will be arranged in positions where there will be a great concentration of planetary influences near Saturn-Jupiter team". In a letter addressed to me Mr. Nelson writes thus: "My own work in the forecasting profession pertains to forecasting the quality of shortwave long distance of radio signals. I use the heliocentric angular separations of the Sun's nine planets as the basis of my systems. Sunspots are related to magnetic storms and magnetic storms to bad radio signals. I have found that certain planetary arrangements are often accompanied by active sunspots which induce magnetic storms here on earth, the methods presently in use employ other angles besides 0–90–180 degrees but in all cases these other angles are sub-harmo

---

*My meeting with Mr. Nelson in 1972 has been described in the chapter xxi of this book.

nies of 90 degrees.   I am not an astrologer myself but I
do hold a healthy interest in all fields of forecasting."
Mr. Nelson finds certain planetary arrangements—which
in the astrological language is called benefic aspects or
Yogas pacifying to the ionosphere while other relationships malefic-aspects disturbing to the ionosphere.

I found that several medical men were also engaged
in a "statistical approach to medical astrology".

17 Science And Astrology

A few months before I left for America, the wife of a European diplomat at Delhi brought to my notice the fact that when she was away in the States, she discovered that the majority of psychoanalysts and psychiatrists there were applied astrologers, *i.e.*, they made liberal use of astrology for diagonising mental ills of their patients and that they did not publicly call themselves as astrologers, because they were afraid they would be excluded from the membership of their respective official organisations. This report of diplomat's wife was amply confirmed during my travels in America. Thanks to the initiative of the great Swiss psychologist Dr. Carl Jung, whose recent death is a great loss to the astrological and medical worlds, astrology appears to be largely made use of to find out what the psychiatrists call the "predisposition of their patients towards certain types of mental and physical illnesses".

Many of these astro–psychologists have been corroborating the astrological theory that certain disorders arising from psychosis and neurosis and certain mental abnormalities—exaggeration of certain traits recognisable nearly in all normal people—are respectively caused by a combination of factors involving certain geometrical dispositions between Moon, Mercury, Mars, Saturn and the Nodes. Another Chicago psychologist, based on statistical research, claims to have discovered a marked correspondence between different types of mental disorders and Mercury's afflictions. Obviously he has upheld the age-old astrological theory of the Hindus that if in a horoscope the Moon and Mercury are in certain mutual dispositions afflicted by Mars, Saturn or the Nodes, it generally indicates mental disorder. In actual practice, such a combination is present mostly in the horoscopes of persons suffering from obsessional neurosis, delusions, dissociation and false beliefs. A false belief which is impervious to logical disproof is a form of dissociation. Where a patient in a mental institution believes himself to be emperor of the world and cannot be made to see that his very restriction in an institution behind bars is sufficient disproof of his omnipotency, he is suffering from dissociation. But if there is jupiterian aspect, the picture is entirely changed. The person will be thoughtful, will have a very understanding mind and good judgment. Remove the Moon and substitute Mars, you have the mechanical aptitude. Without resorting to any intelligence-tests of the psychologist a good astrologer can give a clear picture of one's intelligence or dullness of mind.

An important psychiatrist of Chicago—I shall call him R—told me that he was making use of astrology with much success in his practice. He said the horoscope could give one an idea as to the time–sequence—whether the illness would be permanent or temporary; if temporary, the probable time when the affliction will lift, if permanent whether there would be lessening of the affliction at any time. According to this Doctor, there is a growing body of opinion in America favouring a more serious understanding of not only astrology, Yoga and Vedanta but also certain Indian values of life, by adopting which, he felt, several social ills peculiar to Western pattern of life could be tackled more satisfactorily.

I found that several medical men were also engaged in a "statistical approach to medical astrology". For instance, the experiments of Dr. Edsen J. Andrews have revealed interesting results on the Moon's influence on the outcome of surgery. Dr. Andrews noticed that sometimes all his patients seemed to make good recoveries but that at other times many had haemorrhages and had to be returned to the operating table for emergency treatment. Tabulating the dates of the emergencies on a calendar it became evident that they were indeed "clustered around full-moon periods". Dr. Andrews kept records on all tonsillectory cases for three years. In more than 1000 cases tabulated, 82% of bleeding crises occurred between the Moon's first and third quarters.

Dr. Russel Fields, an M.D., whom I had the pleasure of meeting at Washington, has made a statistical study of "Angioma" in the light of astrology. Having studied 301 cases, the learned doctor seems to have come to the conclusion that individual degree—either on ascendant or the meridian—might play an important factor. Degree distribution, sign distribution, etc., have all received their share of attention. He also found that in 243 of the 301 cases studied, Venus was afflicted.

"Of the 243 charts with Venus afflicted, in 53 cases, Mars was the other planet involved; in 42 additional cases Saturn was in affliction with Venus; Jupiter was next in 35 cases; Uranus in 34 cases; the Moon in 30 cases; Neptune in 26 cases and Pluto in 23 cases.

"In the 46 cases where Jupiter was afflicted by aspect of some other planet, in 21 instances Saturn was involved, while in 8 cases, it was Uranus, in 5 cases, either the Moon or Mars, 4 cases the Sun; 2 cases Pluto and 1 case Neptune.

"In the 12 cases where the Moon was afflicted, and

not Venus or Jupiter, Saturn was involved in 4 cases, Mars in 3 cases, Neptune in 2 cases and the Sun, Uranus and pluto in one case each.

"Considering a composite picture of afflicted Venus', Jupiter's and Moon's, Saturn was the afflicting body in 67 cases, and Mars in 61 cases. In 43 cases Uranus was involved, the Moon in 35 cases, Jupiter in 35 cases, Neptune in 29 cases, Pluto in 26 cases, and the Sun in 5 cases."

Another instance of an European Scientist "wanting to destroy once and for all any suspicion that there could be a relationship between stars and man's character" was brought to my notice after my return to India. In the course of his analysis by means of the most rigorous kind of statistical methods, this particular scientist discovered to his amazement that a fairly large number of authenticated cases revealed correlations between the position of Mars, Jupiter and Saturn in the 4 angles of the horoscope and certain professional types—doctors of medicine and members of the Academy of medicine, military men, painters, priests and Congressmen. Of each category from 500 to 1000 births were considered. According to his discoveries (which are more or less in accord with Hindu astrological principles), Mars "is found predominantly in its zones of influence in the horoscopes of men of sports : it is together with Jupiter in the charts of Generals. Saturn is dominant in the charts of priests. The charts of scientists and medical men reveal Mars, Jupiter and Saturn in zones of activations", etc. These findings have started some scientific people thinking and a wave of interest has been aroused.

*Among the non-astrologers, the contribution of

---

* In a letter written to me, from surrey, England, dated 19th December 1948. Dr. Tomaschek observes:

Dr. Rudolf Tomaschek to the seismological aspect of astrology is indeed praiseworthy. Dr. Tomaschek, with whom I had the privilege of correspondence in 1948, is a former Director of the Institute of Physics, Munich. For the first time in recent times in the West, he sensed that the cause of earthquakes was extra-terrestrial. He arrived at significant conclusions on the correlations between earthquakes and planetary movements. Using 134 severe quakes between 1900 and 1957, Dr. Tomaschek uncovered what Western scientific circles consider an amazing fact concerning the planement of Uranus at the time and epicentre of the disturbance. In nearly 70% of the cases studied, Uranus "was mysteriously near the meridian of the place squaring or trining Jupiter, Saturn or Mars." Researches are being carried on in America on Dr. Tomaschek's theory, and one of the astronomers, who was engaged in this research, said "I must admit, that before I began this investigation I was very sceptical about the effectiveness of these midpoints but they thrust themselves as one in earthquake configurations". However to Dr. Allen Hynak, another astronomer who could not be bothered with any discovery that might embarrass orthodox scientific theories this was just an "astronomical oddity".

After meeting with a number of thinkers who interest in astrology is serious I gained the impression that astrology in America is no more the monopoly of fortune tellers or montebanks and that it has been receiving the attention of serious thinkers. In recent times there appears to be an astrological renaissance in the West. It is not a ghost coming back to haunt the modern mind but a world spirit capable of linking man with the cosmos, a most fascinating intellectual study and a remarkable tool for scrutinising the fringe of future events.

18 Astrology in Europe

Before dealing with some of the problems facing modern Western astrologers, I should like to give my esteemed readers, an idea however inadequate of how astrology flourished in Europe in the past and how it developed there, as it did in India as a quest for verifiable and communicable knowledge pursued by man.

Many European scholars seem to think that astrology sprouted first in Chaldea and Babylonia somewhere during the 2nd or 3rd millennium B.C. I do not think that we Indians can accept this theory as correct or sound. Astrology, just as every other science, had its beginnings in India, the cradle of civilisation, thousands and thousands of years before Christ. If we treat the Puranas and ancient Hindu chronology not as museum piees to be interpreted according to the whims and fancies of the Western educated Hindu who has lost his cultural moorings, but as authoritative and authentic documents made available to us by sages whose intellectual and moral integrity were above board, we can easily fix the age of astrology which will be millennia before the Greeks and the Chaldeans opened their infant eyes to knowledge. I was happy to find that many a scholar in America were more favourably inclined to the theory of Hindu origin of astrology.

Wherever astrology may have originated, it is universally recognised that the ancient Chaldeans, Babylonians, Egyptians and even Greeks were great astrologers and were capable of making correct predictions. These ancient masters had advanced far enough in astrology to elaborate a system of correspondence between celestial movements and terrestrial happenings. The constellations, signs, etc., were allotted to particular divinities. They had realised, like the Hindus, that the universe existed and functioned, not merely because of physical laws, but also because of the operation of moral laws. The theory of of Karma had been woven into the matrix of their lives.

From Chaldea, Astrology is supposed to have made its way into Greece and Rome in the first millennium, B.C. There was no greater Jyotishi (astronomer-*cum*-astrologer) among the Greeks than the great Claudius Ptolemy author of the astronomical work *Almagest* and the equally exhaustive astrological work *Tetrabiblos*. It is the ancient classic that still forms the basis of all modern Western astrological text-books. If a dispassionate scholar goes through Ptolemy's great work, it will not be difficult for him to discover that Greek astrology accepted the entire astrological heritage of India with perhaps such modifications as the local conditions required. The worship of planets—even in this sputnik age, we Hindus, continue to retain *Navagraharadhana*—was a part and parcel of Greek religion and culture. Even Plato referred to the planets as "the greater visible Gods". Perhaps Plato and Pythagoras were more scientific in their conceptions when they talked of planets as 'divine beings' than some of the materialist scientists of today to whom the planetary orbs are just huge masses of matter.

Some of the modern astronomers cannot simply understand how, the Greeks, possessing as they did such exceptional powers of reason, accepted astrology as a science. Even Hipparchus, probably the greatest Greek

10

astronomer, in the words of Ptolemy, "can never be sufficiently praised, no one having done more to prove that man is related to the stars".

In Rome, Augustus and Tiberius were enthusiastic adherents of astrology. The doctrine of neo-pythagoreanism expounded the eternity of the universe and the rule of the celestial bodies over the sub-lunary world. The astrological wave had seeped through to all sections of people—intellectual and common. The adoration of the Sun "became a central feature of the reformed pagan". The belief was firm that since planets and their motions governed all earthly happenings and that since the courses of planets were linked with the Sun, the Sun became the ultimate ruler of the universe. What the twentieth century science has discovered after all the fanfare of its researches—*viz.*, Sun's energy and radiance animate all living organisms on earth—was well known to the ancient Romans, Greeks, and Hindus. Just as in India (ancient and modern), in ancient 'pagan' Rome also, we should like to italicise the world pagan because, Christian theologians gave it a wholly derogatory sense implying one steeped in superstitious beliefs as different from the true beliefs they arrogated to themselves—the Sun-worship (Suryopasana) reached its peak. A Sun-god was "postulated who was an abstract image (Chaitanya) of the Sun and who resided outside the planetary universe and ruled over it. The visible Sun was merely its material expression".

As some of the modern writers are apt to think, it was not merely the sense of wonder and adoration at the sight of the star-studded sky that made the ancients believe in the divine aspect of celestial bodies. It is an honest recognition of the fact that nature is mysterious, that man is humble, that man and nature are mysteriously linked by an inseparable bond, and that the "stars unveil themselves for us" the mysterious future of man and mankind.

Greek astrology is largely, if not entirely, dominated by Ptolemy. He was an astronomer as brilliant as Varahamihira and an astrologer, as skilled as his Indian counterpart. They may have been contemporaries. We do not know. But there is no doubt that they lived very close to each other's periods—Ptolemy in the 2nd century A.D. and Mihira in the 1st century B.C. It was a period full of significance to Greek and Indian thought. Scholars in philosophy, astrology and astronomy must have come to India from the distant lands of Greece and Rome to acquire learning and gain wisdom. Indian scholars must have gone to those lands to impart knowledge to the deserving and to get the benefit of Greek experience. The Greek astrology, as much as the Greek philosophy, was indebted to some extent to Hindu astrology. The resemblance between certain Hindu and Greek astrological terms and methods is too close to be accidental. As the eminent Colebrooks says : "the hindus were in this respect the teachers and not the learners". This did not mean that in those days, the Hindus hesitated to learn from their Greek counterparts. In India, Greek scholars were referred to with great respect as 'Yavanacharyas' and some of their views have been quoted by commentators like Bhattotpala. According to Count Bjornstjarne "the doctrine of transmigration of souls was indigenous to India and was brought into Greece by Pythagoras".

Western tradition ascribes to Pythagoras the geometrical theorem of the 47th proposition, Book I. But if you referred to the *Sulva Sutras*, you will find that this theorem was resolved by the Hindus at least two centuries earlier "thus confirming the conclusion of V. Schneeder that the Greek philosopher Pythagoras owed his inspiration to India". Or take Algebra. According to Elphinstone, "the superiority of the Hindus over the algebraists is scarcely so conspicuous in their discoveries as in the excellence of their method, which is altogether dissimilar to that of Diaphantus and in the perfection of their logarithm". Elphinstone goes on : "their application of algebra to astronomical investigations and geometrical demonstrations is also an invention of their own". In the *Edinburg Review* (Vol. XXI, P. 372) is a striking history of a problem to find x so that $ax^2 - b$ shall be a square number. The first step towards a solution is made by *Diaphantus. It was extended by Fermat, and sent as a defiance to the English algebraists in the seventeenth century, but was only carried to its full extent by the celebrated mathematician Euler, who arrives exactly at the point before attained by **Bhaskaracharya.

These instances are quoted not with any idea of belittling the great astrological and mathematical achievements of Greeks but to point out that the Greeks were not only getting their astrological and mathematical ideas from the Hindus but also there was interchange of thought, each country drawing liberally from the other. Hindu astrology is essentially indigenous and original and was not imported from outside though there may have been subsequent impacts of Western astrological thought which resulted in a new system of astrology—the Tajaka-being

---

* Colebrooks says : "In the whole Science he (Diaphantus) is very far behind the Hindu Writers"—*Essays* p. 438.

** Elphinstone's *India*, p. 131. Bhaskaracharya wrote the celebrated book *Siddhanta Siromani*, and treatises on algebra and arithmetic.

evolved. But the scholars were careful to see that the original system of Parasara remained pure and unsullied.

According to *Brihat Jataka* (I: 19) "the measure of the Rasis from Mesha (Aries) to Kanya (Virgo) inclusive is 5–6–7–8–9 and 10 multiplied by 4, respectively, the other half from Thula (Libra) to Meena (Pisces) in the reverse order". In his notes Prof. B. S. Rao adds that the figures arrived at by multiplication (20, 24. 28, 32. '36 and 40) will give the duration of Rasis (in vighatikas) if further multiplied by 10. Prof. Rao rejects any suggestion that these figures represent the duration of signs. But the figures 20, 24, etc., given here correspond exactly to the figures given in *Vettius Valens* "a system of rising times based on Alexandria" and these figures are also put to certain astrological uses.

In dealing with Hadda Chakra the ancient work *Neelakanti* says thus : "In Aries the first 6° are ruled by Jupiter, the next 6 by Venus, the next 8 by Mercury, subsequents by Mars and the last 5 by Saturn". The Hadda division is an important part of Tajaka astrology. These sections of the signs associated with the planets. known as "terms", are exactly the same as those mentioned by Ptolemy in his *Tetrabiblos*.

The *Thrirasis* mentioned in Tajaka are the same as the 'triangle' given by *Vettius Valens*. Similarly many of the Sahamas extolled by Tajaka writers—Kesava, Yavana and Neelakantha—are similar to the 'lots' or arabic points. These are new points calculated from the longitudes of the Sun, the Moon, the ascendant and planets in the horoscope. All of which suggest that astrological ideas from India seeped into the West and *vice versa*. Many of the ideas might have been absorbed by Tajaka writers : while generally receptive to new scientific thought, the Hindu astrologers were careful to preserve in tact their indige-

nous system of astrology. I give below a sample horoscope as recorded in the ancient [1]*Vettius Valens*, so that
Indian readers can have an idea as to how ancient Greeks
were making predictions.

"Sun, Saturn (and) Mercury in Sagittarius, Moon in
Cancer, Jupiter in Taurus, Mars in Leo, Venus in Capricorn, [2]*Horoscopus* in Virgo, Clima 2. This person began
as Deputy Governor, but falling into the Governor's
disfavour in his 34th year was condemned to the quarry.
For Mars with the Sun ruled the period—of Sun 19 and
Mars 15 are 34. In the 36th year by the aid of greater
(persons) he was released from Confinement as disabled
and at that time the rising time of Leo (location of Mars)
was operative in the 36th year, and 12 of Jupiter in dominant aspect and 24 of Taurus are 36: But also of Capricorn (location of Venus) 28 and of Venus are 8 and 36.
The beneficent (stars) then were strong. In the 39th year
his circumstances were upset through the former enmity
and he was condemned to an oasis. For the stars in Sagittarius ruled the period, of the Sun 19, Mercury 20 make
39 : and take two thirds of 58 (years) which is 38 (years)
8 months. Again of Sun 19, Mercury 20, and Leo, because
(Leo is the location) of Mars in trine, 19, make 58.
(Again) : for Mars (in Leo) 19, and of the [3]Sun 19 and of
Mercury 20 are 58. In the 40th year he lived precariously
and fell ill. However, his wife accompanying him affectio-
nately comforted him and shared her possessions with
him. The 40 years were indicated by the approaching
conjunction of the Moon (in Cancer) with Mars (in Leo)

---

1. *vide* P. 101 : *Greek Horoscopes* by Dr. Neugebaur.

2. Horoscopus means Lagna or Ascendant.

3. Sun 19, Moon 25, Mars 15, Jupiter 12, Mercury 20, Venus
8 and Saturn 30.

—for 25 of the Moon and 15 of Mars are 40—and the triangular position of Jupiter and Venus indicated the same, for 12 of Jupiter, 28 of Venus are 40. And these are the prognostics I myself found.

After acquitting himself of his initial talks of meeting all current criticism of astrology in the first three chapters of his work *Tetrabiblos*, Ptolemy sets out to outline the essence of the science of prediction. According to Ptolemy, "the Sun heats and dries, the Moon moistens and putrifies, though it has some light and heat too, Mars dries and warms ; Jupiter heats and humidifies and produces fertilizing winds :" "Venus warms by virtue of her proximity to the Sun and humidifies because of proximity to the Moon, while Mercury also vacillates rapidly between drying and humidifying." A waxing Moon "is productive of moisture at first and later of heat, while upon waning she radiates dryness in her initial stages and subsequently cold". The fixed stars too have special powers, especially those located within the constellation of the ecliptic, the zodiac. Within each constellation the powers vary. For example, "the stars in the head of Aries (the ram) have an effect like the power of Mars and Saturn, mingled ; those in the mouth like Mercury's power and moderately like Saturn's ; those in the hind foot like that of Mars, and those in tail like that of Venus". The significant events to ascertain are the ascension of the sign of the zodiac which rises at the moment, and the *Syzgy* or the positions of the Moon in opposition, *i.e.*, the full Moon in conjunction or the new Moon preceding birth. The appearance and build of the 'native', as the individual under examination is called, "get due attention and bodily injuries and diseases come in from their respectable share and so do the problems of

the spirit, soul, mind and reason of the native". Few
mental or physical features are neglected. All are fully
and meticulously accounted for "through detailed and
intricate divination". Abnormal psychology, including
epilepsy and insanity, comes in for its share. Signs can
even be read which foretell when mental ailments can be
cured "by medical treatments, a diet or drugs" or not at
all. The configurations of the planets foretell or rather
determine sexual excesses. When "Mars or Venus are
made masculine the males become addicted to natural
sexual intercourse and are adulterous, insatiate, and ready
on every occasion for base and lawless acts of sexual
passion, while the females are lustful for unnatural
congresses, cast inviting glances of the eyes.. and perform
the functions of the males".

Ptolemy's work is not only the culmination of organised astrological thought in Greece but marks the foundation upon which all subsequent astrological literature has
been built up. Subsequent to Ptolemy, there have been a
large number of celebrated astrologers in Europe, who
have kept the flame of astrological knowledge burning
despite theological opposition. Until perhaps the middle
ages or even after, astrological assumptions held firm
sway over the minds of a great majority of naturalists,
physicists, medical men and even biologists.

In the midst of attacks on astrology which were
launched by Christianity after its victory over 'Paganism'
in Rome, there also came on the scene learned Christian
theologians whe defended astrology. Julius Firmicus
Maternus was one such. He made a spirited defence of
astrology. According to him "God created the universe
and man. Prayer is good for the soul and free-will is its
salient attribute." But the stars none-the-less decree and
control man's fate. Morals and free choice are essential

for the good of life and the "human soul is indeed immortal." Yet the stars are part of God's creation and serve as signs in his heaven. The astrologer "must be learned but he must be upright, unselfish, and pious to shine as a model to the rest of mankind". The arguments of Maternus are indeed significant when he says: "the human spirit which conceives religion and other sciences can unravel astrology too. Horoscopes are as nothing by comparison with the really difficult task of mapping the course of planets, which the astrologers have attempted and with such amazing success. All about us we see fate at work. Otherwise how can one explain the fact that good and noble men like Socrates, Plato or Pythagoras met with ill-fate while such men as Aliabibiades and Sulla prospered".

During the 13th century astrology in Europe was as important as are "mesons and neutrons today". According to William of Auregne, a Christian theologican (1249) "the multitude of men lead, it is sorrowful to say, neither moral nor intellectual lives, but rather are their dispositions vile and emotional in the manner of brutes. Hence astrologers may predict with a fair degree of accuracy anything pertaining to mob action and second, to individual fates involving emotional vices, since these do not spring from man's moral sense or his soul but from his physical constitution. Besides, even such causality may be modified by prayer".

It looks as though until the 17th or 18th century astrological studies engaged the attention of some of the most brilliant thinkers of the day. The doctrines of astrology are fully expounded and accepted. The effects of Moon and planets, the detailed action of planetary aspects, exaltations, conjunctions, etc., are given their full credit. The view is propounded that free-will, reason and divine intervention are in no way imposed upon or interfered with by the stars. Exactly the same situation prevails in the case of Albertus Magnus, Thomas Aquinas and Roger Bacon. In his *Suma Philosophia* (19 volumes Grosseteste), Grosseteste a Bishop of London says that "all events and activities in the inferior world are motivated and guided by the motions of the superior bodies. The seven planets are identified with the seven metals; earthly disharmony can be corrected by the application of knowledge of celestial harmony. Astrology cannot only serve to guide activities and predict the future but also to cure diseases and curb passions".

Albert Magnus, regarded by many modern historians as "the father of the method of science in the middle ages, the father of today, etc.," an original and acute observer declares : "There is a man in double spring of action, namely nature and the will; and nature for its part is ruled by the stars, while the will is free; but unless it resists, it is swept along by nature and becomes mechanical. Knowledge of astrology gives the wise man power to modify or annul the effects of the stars." Like many defenders of astrology, Albert has few kind words to say about the practitioners of the art. "It is they who brought the art of science of divination into disrepute" because "almost all men of this class delight in deception and, being poorly educated, they think that what is merely contingent is necessary, and they predict that some event will certainly occur and when it does not, these sciences are cheapened in the sight of unskilled men although the defect is not in the science, but in those who abuse it. For this reason wise Ptolemy says that no judgement should be made except in general terms and with the cautious reservation that the stars act *per alliud et acciden* (subject to other forces and to accidents) and that their significations meet many impediments. More-over, the pursuit of sciences dealing with the future would be idle, if one could not avoid what one foresaw" (*ibid.*, V. 2, P. 285). Aquinas too insists that "Reason and experience, saints and philosophers, have proved over and over again that celestial bodies rule all inferior matter".

Many of the great astrologers of the Middle Ages were doctors of medicine, astronomers and men of science. In fact there is a vast array of giants in the history of science whose attitude towards astrology was sensible and serious. Francis Bacon, father of modern science, was an astrologer. He, of course, chided astrologers for "their abuse of the art" but "looked forward to the day when it would be established on a more scientific basis". Bacon claimed—and I have no doubt his modern counter-parts in this atomic age would simply laugh at this claim —that only "a reformed and scientific astrology would be capable of predicting wars, plagues, famines and revolu-tions". In his *Advancement of Learning* Bacon concluded that "astrology should rather be purged than absolutely rejected". Newton was equally a great astrologer. He never questioned the basic astrological beliefs. It seems Newton's Library was famous for its astrological collec-tions. When Newton's friend and pupil Halley ventured to deprecate his master's excursions into astrology, he was pulled up with the rejoinder, "I have studied these things, you have not". Napier, the inventor of logarithms, was an astrologer and his famous *Bloody Almanac* contained several forecasts.

It was about the same time that Didacus Placidus an Italian monk, an extraordinary mathematician and philo-sopher, published his great work on astrology *Primum Mobile*. Titus addresses his readers thus: "with the regard to the revolutions of the stars and their efficient power, no candid reader will deny that a genuine and true science may exist, though for a man to make a full acquirement in it must doubtless be acknowledged at very easy task". According to Placidus, "the true moment of the day, on which any one is born (laying aside all opinions of predecessors and all his successors of others) is when the foetus becomes independent in its finitmate cause". Placidus, like all his predecessors and all his successors upto Dr. Simmonite, considers the twelve signs, planets Sun to Saturn and the five important aspects—conjunction, trine, sextile, opposition and square. For timing events, he employs what is known as primary directions. It is said that this great astrologer had several successful predictions to his credit. There were other astrologers, equally great and outstanding like William Lily who predicted the plague and fire of London, Guido-Bonatus and Jeran Cardan.

Coming to recent times Dr. Simmonite, Commander Morrison, and A. J. Pearce were not only authors, but successful astrologers also.

The disappearance of astrology from the so-called horizon of science coincided with the beginning of the 19th century.

19 Problems Facing Western Astrologers

My discussions with a number of learned astrologers in America and United Kingdom have led me to feel that modern Western astrologers are faced with two important problems of a controversial nature, *viz.*, (1) House division and (2) Timing events. There is a certain confusion evident when these astrologers are not decided as to which system of house-division they should adopt to cast horoscopes. Some astrologers think that methods of interpretation, casting, and timing now in vogue in the West and applied with great success by celebrated European astrologers like Placidus, William Lily, etc., are not quite reliable and that they have to be improved by further investigations.

In India this problem of house-division does not bother us much. There are only two methods, one based upon Sripathi used by a large number of astrologers and the other, the equal house-divisions employed by the Nadi writers. To give my readers an idea of the confusion prevalent in the West, I propose to deal briefly with some of the methods of house-division in use there.

The Equal House System.—The ascendant is of course the cusp of the first house. The second house is obtained by adding 30' to the first and the other house by successfully adding 30° thereto. The tenth house will not be the M.C. but a point 90° behind the ascendant. I was told that this system is gaining increasing popularity amongst some of the leading astrologers. There are some who calculate the M.C. and take the ascendant as 90° from M.C. This means that the child is supposed to be born at the equator and not at the place of birth. Arguments are advanced in justification of this system also. This method was originally proposed by Zariel.

Porphyry.—Hindu astrologers will be quite familiar with this system. The ascendant (Udaya Lagna) and M.C. (Madhya Lagna) are determined and the intermediate houses are obtained by the trisection of the arc of the ecliptic intercepted between the horizon and meridian. This is the method of Sripathi and is used by the group of astrologers led by Bailey.

Placidus.—The method of Placidus, widely used in America at the present day, is also known as the semi-arc system. The principle involved is the trisection of the semi-arc of each degree of the ecliptic. For instance, when the ascendant point has been calculated, the cusp of the 12th house is obtained by adding one-third of its semi-arc to the R.A. of the M.C. Mr. Colin Evans has pointed out that this system is "based on artificially equalised sub-divisions of the naturally unequal amounts of a time, a degree of the zodiac spends in each quadrant". Some so-called "mathematically minded" astrologers condemn it because according to them it is not "geometrical". Its discovery is attributed to the Italian monk Placidus a great astrologer and mathematician of his time.

Then there are the methods of Campanus and Regiomontanus. The former is now favoured by some U.K. astrologers who reject Placidus while the latter is generally used on the continent. Both these systems make all cusps (except those of the ascendant and M.C,.

points on lines perpendicular to the prime vertical and meeting at the south and north points of the horizon. The difference is that Campanus sets these lines equally wide apart "dividing the prime vertical itself into 12 equal parts between the 12 cusps while Regiomontanus spaces them unequally so as to divide the equator equally". In Campanus the prime vertical is divided into 12 parts whereas in Regiomontanus it is the celestial equator that is divided into 12 parts.

A discussion of the problem of house-division may, no doubt, be of academic interest. But if we try to understand the problem with an open mind, it will be found that it is not of much practical importance. Take for instance the method of Placidus. It was successfully used not only by Placidus but also by a number of English astrologers until someone found that it should be discarded in favour of, say, Campanus of Regiomontanus. The houses in a horoscope are symbolical in character. They may have a certain scientific basis but we do not yet know what it is. Therefore, the division of the heavens into 12 houses is also symbolical. A strictly mathematical approach to this problem of house-division is not called for. But some of the "scientific astrologers" are only concerned with the theory of the matter and they have not produced any practical proofs in support of their theories.

In astrology, what may seem theoretically scientific and sound may not practically work. If the arguments for and against each of the various systems examined carefully, we find that most of the systems 'collapse' at higher latitudes. Between "mathematically sound" systems which fail in higher latitudes and systems such as the equal house-division, based on deep symbolism,

perhaps the latter is more preferable. The experience of
generations of astrologers from Placidus to Zadkiel
should not be ignored by our Western friends.

Another matter that is worrying the Western astrologers is whether they should consider the cusp as the
centre of the house. In this respect Hindu astrology is
more rational because we consider the cusp as the bhava-
madhya or the middle of the house, the influence commencing at the *arambha sandhi* and ending at *virama sandhi*.
This perfectly rational method is not acceptable to some
of the Western astrologers who have begun to attribute
an orb of 10° to the ascendant, 5 to a cadent house and so
on. Suppose Aries 18º is the ascendant. According to
Hindu astrology, the effects of Lagna bhava start from
about 3° of Aries, reach the maximum in 18° and end in
3° of Taurus. But according to Western astrologers,
Aries 18° makes the most powerful part. But if a planet
is in 15° Aries, it is in the 12th house.

The other baffling problem facing our friends in the
West is that of progression. It is perhaps the most
divergent point in Western astrology. If one goes through
the various methods in vogue one is bound to get bewil-
dered. Here also over-scientific and over-astronomical
methods have led to some sort of a fiasco. There are the
primary and secondary directions which are supposed to
be astronomical methods, while the symbolical systems
concern themselves with the concept of an imaginary
movement. According to some, primary directions give
accurate results. I have heard it said by late Prof.
B. Suryanarain Rao, that late Dr. Pearce was able to
predict correctly on the basis of primary directions.
However, today in the West, most astrologers seem to
rely on the secondary directions.

According to this system, one day after birth is equivalent to one year of life. Therefore if we want to know the indications, say for the 35th year of life, we must look to the planetary positions on the 35th day after birth. According to this theory, all the directions to be formed within the life-span of a person who may live for 75 years are formed within $2\frac{1}{2}$ months from the date of birth.

Then there are those who take converse or prenatal secondary directions because they think such directions are powerful factors in producing events. How far this theory is rational, it is not for me to say. But I have heard some friends in the United Kingdom swear by secondary directions. Suppose a person born on 8-8-1912 at 7-35 p.m. wants to know the directions for 1961. The age on the birthday would be 49. Therefore a map must be cast 7-35 p.m., on 49th day after birth. The aspects between the progressed positions of planets, M.C., etc., and the radical ones are then interpreted. I am not competent to pass a judgment to on the reliability of the secondary directions. The number of arcs of direction, due to the number of espects between various planetary bodies, angles, etc., arising from the variety of methods— 'direct', 'converse', etc.—employed in calculating the directions is so formidable that an astrologer is often baffled as to how to sort out most powerful and appropriate ones and how to interpret them in respect of the nativity.

Take for instance the horoscope of King George V. In the year 1928-29 he fell seriously ill. If you calculate the secondary directions by erecting a horoscope for 1-20 a.m. on 5-8-1865—and this indicates the progressed horoscope for 3rd June 1928—the directions for 1928-29 do not at all show any serious illness. The planets in the Western horoscope, for directional purposes, are interpreted more as natural signifiactors of various events and certain factors in the life and in a way can be compared to the idea of the Karaka system in Hindu astrology. For instance, according to Mr. G. C. Nixon, the Sun in the Western horoscope stands for the father, male relatives the profession, the soul, the people in authority and public life. The Moon indicates the mother, the mind from the emotional side, the domestic and personal life, removals, journeys, sea voyages and one's relationship to the public. Mercury is the indicator of business, correspondence, controversy, short journeys and intellectual and scientific activity. Venus is the indicator of the sexual and social life, marriage, birth of children and wealth. Mars is the indicator of business enterprises, physical activity and sports, quarrels, disputes, dangerous illness and accidents. Saturn denotes deaths, chronic illness, poverty, frustration and hardship. The three extra-saturnine planets—Uranus, Neptune and Pluto— which are not recognised by Hindu astrology, have a very impersonal effect upon the life of the individual and denote the disrupting, corrupting and consuming power of political, totalitarian and cosmopolitan factors. Uranus indicates the effect of the state, machinery, scientific invention, speed, and consequently transport and aircraft disasters ; Neptune, the effect of moral degeneracy, perversion, gambling, doping, hallucination and danger from drowning and asphyxiation, while Pluto indicates death by fire, atomic or chemical explosion, strange psychic disorders, as well as a manifestation of occult or psychic powers. On the basis of the directions obtaining in King George's horoscope for 1928–29 could any astrologer have predicted in advance the King's serious illness ? I have may own doubts. But if we switch back to the Hindu system, the indications become crystal clear. Between July 1928 and August 1929, the King was passing through the major period of Saturn and the sub-period of Mars. The major lord is owning the 11th and 12th and hence afflicted in the 6th from the Sun, indicator of the body, retrograde, in his own asterism and in association with Rahu and aspected by the sub-lord Mars, Who is debilitated and who owns a death-dealing house. Rahu was transiting the 8th from the Moon indicating what is called arishta or affliction to the body. These dispositions indicate a crisis in health. Let not my friends in the West think that I am belitlling their directional methods. Nor am I suggesting that our system of predicting events is perfect. Directional astrology is an alluring subject and the Dasa system of predicting events has certain definite advantages, which I think the other methods are lacking.

There are astrologers who consider that symbolism should be the basis for directing. South measures are $2\frac{1}{2}°$ arc or $3°/7$ or $4°/7$ or $4°$ per year are advocated. Despite these symbolic measures, outstanding events cannot generally be anticipated. By speculating on these various symbolic measures, some of the astrologers fondly hope to discover the lost keys of predictions. With the innumerable number of symbolic measures and house-divisions, any event can be proved by the 'passage' by progression of planets to the cusps. A *post-martem* examination of an event is not always the right method. I do not think that astrologers in the West can assert with unanimity the right method of house-division or the right method of progression.

While with a flair for mathematics, we may discover a dozen arcs of direction concerning all the planets which may measure closely to the date of any event, in actual practice, with the aid of the same train of directions a future event such as the birth of a child or marriage or death of a person cannot be anticipated with certainty. Asrologers in America do not appear to have been as much involved in these controversies, as their European counterparts, though some "mathematically-minded astrologers are experimenting with new methods".

In the field of psychological astrology, however, the West has really made certain advances which we have not. The reason for this is not any lapse on the part of ancient sages who propounded astrology. Our attitude to life and the sense of values we have been cherishing are different from those held by Westerners. Our belief in the theory of karma is still so strong that we do not easily succumb to nervous and psychological ills. In the West, psychosis and neurosis have been claiming a large number of victims because of the peculiar social and industrial conditions there. It is therefore understand-able that Western asrologers, in order to take problems peculiar to their civilisation, have been successful, in developing psychological astrology to considerable per-fection. We can with advantage 'import' these findings and adapt them to our own needs.

The American astrologer is more receptive to new astrological ideas and thoughts. He is not dogmatic. He is free from inhibitions. Therefore Hindu astrology appeals to him. I have nothing but admiration for American astrologers. The vast majority of them are sincere, honest and eager to advance the cause of astro-logy by their predictive abilities. Many of them are also conscious of the shortcomings in the Western system of astrology and they do not hesitate to indent on the Hindu system for which they have great regard. I found a number of leading astrologers in America express great reverence for Hindu astrology. They are convinced that we have made greater progress in certain aspects.

Thanks to the work of Mr. Cyril Fagan and Mr. Donald Bradely, the movement for Sidereal astrology has been gaining in number able adherents in the West, particularly America. The contribution of Mrs. Joan Clancy through her fine periodical *American Astrology* to the popularisation of this movement is considerable. She has an open mind and she loses no opportunity of giving Hindu astrology its due. *Horoscope*, another equally popular journal edited by Mr. Wagner, is also sympathetically disposed towards Hindu astrology. *In Search* (now defunct) ably edited by Mr. Charles Jayne is an interesting endeavour. Mr. Jayne himself is a man of promise and is a lover of Indian culture and astrology.

It is in U.K. that 'tropicalists' and 'siderealists' have been crossing swords. There is not much sense in carrying on this battle of the zodiacs. Based on the Sayana Zodiac, certain methods of interpretation have been developed in the West and 'tropicalists' can continue to employ these methods, while 'siderealists' are welcome to pursue their methods of investigation. Unfortunately a certain fanatical attitude is adopted by the extremists on both sides. One of the siderealists— I have no doubt he is quite sincere in what he says—told me that it is his intention to "overthrow once and for all the false tropical astrology which has the entire Western world in its grips". I have a feeling, and it may not be quite justified, that leading Western astrologers are slowly coming over to the sidereal zodiac.

I have already referred in the previous instalments of this series to individual astrologers and institutions in America, who have been doing useful work. I must add once again that astrology and astrologers have been well organised in America, each state having its own association and most associations being affiliated to the American Federation of Astrologers, a national organisation having its headquarters in Washington. Many of these organisations have been doing useful work and some of them are conducting serious research into different aspects of astrology. As is natural, the American astrologers have their own factions and group rivalries. Some of them are individualistic, eager and ambitious to achieve a top dominance in astrology and to put over their theories in a big way and believe they have nothing more to learn. There is no co-operation also between some of these groups, largely promoting who, I was told, were more interested in promoting their own personal interests than the good of astrology. Despite such group rivalries which are inevitable in any sphere of activity whether in America or in India, I am convinced that the astrological student-body in America as a whole is probably the most sincere and the most deeply devoted to the cause of astrology.

I had told the Americans and I repeat here what I said then that Indian astrology offers a fertile field for furnishing additional knowledge and that if they try to understand the Hindu system properly and adapt it with suitable modifications befitting their own social and cultural conditions, I am sure many a gap in astrological knowledge can be bridged over.

A word of caution to some of the Indian astrologers who would like to look "progressive" before the Western world. These remarks are intended for a certain section of astrological upstarts who pose themselves as authorities in the science and whose only qualification appears to be that they cater to popular terms by writing popular predictions in certain obscure daily papers and occasionally indulge in undignified criticism of Hindu astrology and whose knowledge of astrology does not usually extend beyond "trines, squares, and opposition" and not for those research-minded scholars who out of genuine quest for truth or for purposes of comparative studies, take into consideration the three newly discovered planets also. It will be seen that Uranus was discovered by Herschel in 1781. Its period of revolution is about 84 years. Neptune was discovered in 1846, its period of revolution being 164½ years. Of course Pluto is yet a baby, known to us from 1930 only!

Western astrologers have tried to assign rulerships, *etc.*, to these planets, by omitting Saturn from one sign or making Uranus part-ruler of some of the sign, as if such allotments depend upon the whims and fancies of astrologers. When we do not know what their rulerships are, where they are exalted, where they are friendly or inimical etc., they cannot be integrated into a system of prediction that has a set of well-defined rules and principles. Moreover the periods of revolution of these three planets are beyond the normal life-span of an individual. For thousands of years we are aware of the characteristics of the nine planets. Yet their proper interpretation is a difficult matter. When such is the case, how can these 'new' planets be considered, when their very rulerships or astrological characteristics are of doubtful proposition? Outpourings of thoughtless critics who are 'over-anxious' to 'modernise' Hindu astrology may therefore be safely ignored. The nine planets recognised by Hindu astrology comprehend almost every human event and they provide us with an adequate and rational basis for making predictions.

In concluding my remarks on "Astrology in America" I must once again gratefully acknowledge that the American astrologers of all groups and ranks extended to me a most warm, friendly and affectionate welcome and listened to my lectures and talks with great interest, admiration and regard, showing their great reverence for our ancient culture and astrology. The British astrologers were no exception. Toey were equally warm and kind in the welcome and consideration accorded to me.

20   America and India

The United States of America is a vast country made up of people of different nations. It is a land of rocky sea coasts, high mountain ranges, great forests, broad plains and fertile valleys, stretching 3000 miles from the Pacific to the Atlantic coasts and bound in the north by Canada and in the south by Mexico. It is a country of great diversity—vast cities and small villages, roaring factories and quiet fields and dazzling places of glamour and excitement and calm centres for meditation. New England in the East is noted for its attractive scenery while in the Pacific north-west you can see nature in her greatest extravagance—towering waterfalls and snowcapped mountains. In the California coastline vast beaches are gently touched by the blue waters of the Pacific. Sun-drenched beaches fringed with graceful palms are the peculiarity of the southern states.

The people of this land, though mostly draw from European countries, stem from different parts of the world. The Chinese, the Japanese, the Puertoricans, the Africans have all joined hands to fashion a nation that is United States. What is remarkable is that these multiracial people have fused themselves into a nation within the short span of 200 years and take pride in their being Americans.

Almost every known religion can be found in the United States, but most Americans belong to Protestant

churches. There are of course other groups—Roman
Catholic, Jewish, Russian orthodox, Greek orthodox,
etc. The United States constitution protects the freedom
of each American to practise his or her own faith and to
worship according to one's own conscience. The Government gives no funds to churches. Support of religious
institutions is voluntary. The separation of church and
state is a cardinal American principle. Americans and
Hindus have more in common in the matter of religious
tolerance. In India, people live and worship as they
please. Americans are also very tolerant. A keen
observer can notice the individuality of various relgious
groups in America and such group patterns—we have
them in India too—is perhaps a guarantee of demo-
cracy.

This vast country can be speedily and conveniently
spanned by airplanes, buses and trains. A network of
broad highways and fourlane super highways connect
city with city across the country. It is a pleasure to
travel in a car in these highways. The privately owned
automobile is the most widely used means of transportation. Motor trucks carry vast quantities of freight from
coast to coast. The trucking industry employs 6.5 million
workers using more than 10 million trucks. The rail
roads are owned by private companie ; and travelling by
traini s very comfortable. There are 7,000 civil airports
and "15 million landings and take-offs a year". For
instance, Washington alone handles over 2,000 such
arrivals and departures a year.

The living standard of Americans is very high,
perhaps 4 to 5 times higher than that of Indians.
According to their own statistics, in 1953 the average
person consumed "98 pounds of fruit, 24.8 pounds of
chicken, 145 pounds of meat, 148 pounds of fresh and

canned vegetables, 356 eggs and 18.3 pounds of ice-cream".

I was told that there is no illiteracy in America and that unemployment amongst the educated classes does not exist. It is estimated that there are 11,000 free public and 12,000 private elementary schools, 26,000 free public and 3,500 private high schools. Education is compulsory. America has 1,852 institutions of higher learning including "859 liberal arts colleges and universities, 311 professional and technological colleges, 193 teachers' colleges, and 513 junior colleges". About 3,80,000 academic degrees are awarded annually by colleges and universities. There is no glamour for government jobs.

What struck me forcibly was the existence of socialism in actual practice as different from theory. The Americans are wealthy but social distinctions have been reduced to the minimum. People rub their shoulders with each other without any trace of superiority. A worker in a factory in New York gets about 100 dollars (Rs.700/-) a week, a middle class farmer 5,000 dollars a year. The Americans have realised the dignity of labour. This aspect was brought home to me as soon as I got down in New York. In railway stations, airports, etc., passengers, young and old, carry their luggage, sometimes to 2 to 3 pieces, and they just do not wait for the porters. Here even in the India of 1976 many feel that it is below their dignity to carry their own luggage.

The first that thing impressed me was their uniform courtesy, warmth, friendliness, efficiency and helpful attitude. It looked as though the Americans are anxious to create a good impression about their country in the minds of the foreign visitors. Wherevr you go, whether it be a restaurant, museum, a private office, or a public concern, you will be greeted with a smile and the

receptionist will at once attend to you. While walking
in Chicago I once lost my way to the hotel and was
hesitating which way to take. An American, who saw
my dilemma, took me by the arm and led me to my hotel
talking a lot on the way.

The Americans are good hosts. They attend to the
smallest details in regard to the comforts of their guests
and they respect your sentiments. They found my food
habits queer but they showed great consideration to my
feelings. When weather permitted, I used to move about
at New York and other places in my usual *dhoti* and
uttariyam and I always found people appreciative of
what they called "sticking to national dress". Courtesy
and a helpful attitude characterise the conduct of transport drivers and conductors. Always smiling, they
appeared to be intent upon making the passengers comfortable. Aged persons and mothers with children are
helped to get into and out of buses. Passengers are not
hunddled into the buses like cattle, as we do here in
India, despite nationalisation of transport. I wish our
young men will take an example from their American
counterparts, when getting into and out of buses. Respect
to elders has been ingrained in our blood but apish
imitation of the West may be responsible to some extent
for the present degeneration of our youth.

The conduct of the American officials is also praiseworthy. Once I had to get some work done in a Government office. An official received me courteously and
attended to my work. All this took just 15 minutes. In
India though things are improving such a thing is still
not possible. False pride and an undue sense of importance are so common on the part of many officials. The
American officials seem to feel they are the servants of the

people and therefore they serve them efficiently. The people also seem to feel that the Government is really interested in their welfare.

Another feature I noticed in America was that many of the leading newspapers give as much importance to news of cultural, religious, scientific and public interest as they do to political news. They do not give exaggerated importance to the utterances of politicians. Scientists, philosophers, religious heads, etc., are considered equally important. The Americans seem to think that the primary responsibility of a newspaper is to the people and not merely to the Government of the country. The press seems to follow the public in giving the news it desires to have. Some of the leading papers in India give undue importance and publicity to the speeches of ministers and ministerial doings. Even where a function concerns a religious or cultural matter, the main emphasis is generally shifted, and the significance of the *occasion is obscured by the prominence given to the Minister—who is generally the inaugurator.

I was told that members of the cabinet rank and important Government officials would not waste their time in opening parks, churches, bridges, canals, etc., or indulge in similar acts of exhibitionism, as their counterparts do in India. It is a pity that tasks of inauguration, etc., which can be done by prominent citizens in other walks of life, are invariably entrusted to Ministers, many of whom convert the occasion to make propaganda for

---

* Most newspapers in India use astrology to boost their sales. As the editorial departments appear to be dominated by western educated Indians, they have queer and unscientific ideas about astrology. But the vast majority of the public are instinctively aware of the creative role of astrology in Indian social life.

their own party. Lakhs of rupees spent on these ceremonies can be utilised for better purposes.

Nor do political leaders in America go on airing their views publicly on matters which do not concern them.

Almost all cities I visited were neat and tidy. You cannot see any litter on the roads and pedestrians always walk on footpaths. I was told that city father vie with each other in providing amenities for the public. And you can see evidence of this in the fine parks, good roads and efficient municipal arrangements.

I think we have much to learn from Americans in the matter of punctuality, efficiency, courtesy, politeness, and sense of responsibility. American capitalists—Ford, Rockefeller, Carnegie, etc.—have invested millions of dollars not only in founding great industrial, cultural, historical and scientific museums which are of great educative value but also in creating huge trusts for charitable purposes.

Millions of dollars go to the different parts of the world for humanitarian purposes. The creators of these trusts have no personal motive to gain. They just want the money to be utilised for purposes of relieving the suffering humanity from disease and poverty. The Henry Ford Museum at Detroit is one such where American history comes to life. This 14–acre museum contains vast and varied collections which portray the major aspects in the growth and development of America from the pioneer days to present time. In the Greenfield village can be seen nearly 100 buildings representing every phase of national life as it was lived by their forefathers. The houses of famous Americans have been restored. The birth-place of the airplane, the shed where the first Ford car was built, the laboratory where Edison completed many of his famous inventions—these and many other historic structures stand as memorials to the departed owners as if their destines were as yet unfulfilled. Institutions run by private trusts take care of disabled while those able to work are provided with suitable employments. Though America is only 200 years old as a nation, American historians have been busy unearthing evidences to enable them to construct the past history of their country. Though India as a nation has existed for thousands of years, we are woefully behind hand in such matters. There is not a single satisfactory book on ancient Indian history written by an Indian. No attempt has been made so far to unearth the ancient astronomical treasures.

Americans do not seem to make much of their VIPs though as the world's nerve centre, there is no dearth for visiting dignitaries. An instance of this was witnessed by me while in New York. Once there was a traffic jam and the traffic was held up for 10 minutes. My driver drew my attention to a motorcade of VIPs held up on the other side of the road. In clearing the jam, the VIPs were not given priority. Nobody seemed to notice them and the traffic police were just concerned with clearing the traffic. I asked my host sitting next to me in the car why the VIPs were not given priority. He replied that public interest counted first and hence priority was always first given to the public.

Another thing that struck me was that American life appears to be dominated by the machine. In a sense life itself appears to be mechanical. Whether it is industry, agriculture, or even the home, there are gadgets which do everything—cooking, washing, sweeping and what not, so that not only human labour is reduced to the minimum but one can see the absence of the human touch. Despite this mechanisation of life and despite the fact that they are preoccupied with business problems consequent on their industrial civilisation, the Americans are intensely human and appear to evince keen interest in spiritual matters. Their interest is not superficial but real and genuine. They are intellectually inquisitive.

A number of American intellectuals seem to find that Hinduism is not only in harmony with the spirit of modern science, but it gives one a profound philosophic insight "into the relativity of knowledge and ideals". Each individual can try to understand the reality through methods which appeal to him. There is no question of a narrow and dogmatic assertion that only a particular prophet's 'revelation' can alone be true. The most distinctive trait of Western culture—individualism—is clearly brought out by Hinduism. Hence an increasing number of Americans have begun to appreciate the vigour and vitality of Vedanta which alone can make peace with modern science.

There is a growing body of opinion favouring a more serious understanding of not only astrology, Yoga and Vedanta, but also certain Indian values of life by adopting which they feel some of the social ills, peculiar to Western pattern of life, could be corrected. In all my lectures, the question time used to be lively. I encountered many questions but none inspired by malice. The questioners were genuinely eager to be enlightened. Many a psychologist and psychiatrist have become interested in the dynamism of Yoga being convinced that the psycho-analytical methods of the West with their neuerological preoccupations cannot deal with the problems of the 'psyche' as adequately as Yoga, There is also an awareness on the part of some of the leading psychologists in America that Indian psychology— Yoga though appears as ontological has always been insistent on the dynamic transformation of the human psyche.

A few words about the food habits of Americans. They are predominantly a meet-eating people. There are of course some partial vegetarians. They eat meat on occasions because they think it necessary as part of their diet. We must note that not all animals are flesh eaters. Why should man, who claims to be the pink of God's creation, have the equivalent of "tooth and claw"? Even the Bible says : "Thou shalt not kill". But Christian nations are the foremost meat eaters. At least one American who claimed he was a strict vegetarian said that today Western nations are gripped by the fear of destruction because the people prey on creatures less powerful than themselves. It is a pity that millions of animals are bred to be driven to slaughter houses solely to appease the appetite of man. The bad karma generated by these mass killings is bound to have its adverse repercussions. It is difficult to conceive how an otherwise kindly people, humanitarian and even loving petdogs and cats, allow themselves to be treated to animal food. Apart from the moral viewpoint, that much disease comes from meat-eating, especially meat tainted by fear when an animal is killed, is being increasingly noticed by Western dietecians. Stomach ulcers, cancer, and other forms of diseases are traced to meat-eating.

The majority of Indians have been strict vegetarians by tradition. But it is a pity that propaganda recently advocating non-vegetarian sources of protein "in the interests of health" is being carried on. To look "progressive" before the Western nations must we emulate their food habits ?

Enlightened opinion in the West is moving slowly towards the outlook on food which we in India have

12

advocated for thousands of years. Vegetarian food is materially the best type of food. The following remarks of the Secretary of the "London Vegetarian Society" are well worth serious attention by Indians. "It is now known, for instance, that the introduction of flesh food in the human diet causes changes in the intestinal flora. The ultimate effect of this is to upset the processes by which Vitamin B is produced in the intestines and made available within the organism for synthesising amino acids. Many people in the West appear to have lost this power and its recovery is most difficult. Until it has been restored it has been found that the purest form of Vegetarianism—free from dairy produce—is not possible without recourse to some external source of Vitamin B.

"No doubt peoples whose habits have included flesh-eating from generations past will continue to demand these foods until they become more enlightened, but for the millions of Indian vegetarians, who have inherited the purer vegetarian tradition, to be persuaded to such a perversion in the name of progress is sheer tragedy."

Some friends have asked me to say a few words about American home life. Home life is usually very informal. It is said that America is the most divorced country in the world and that there is one divorce for every three marriages, besides desertions and separations. The family I stayed with in the mid-West was similar to any Indian family, the youngsters behaving respectfully towards their parents and the elders showing all the affection for their kids. I was told that the majority of Americans are now anxious to restore the institution of family to its former sancity and importance and slow down the pace of divorce. America, being a new nation, with no tradition, burned for a time with a desire to originate something new —morgonism, marriages of convenience dissoluble at will and other freaks. They seem to have realised that these experiments have proved a thorough failure. Women in India, who want to become "progressive", can learn a lesson from the experiences of their unhappy sisters in the West. Some of the Women's organisations in India— their representative character of real Indian womanhood is doubtful because they are generally composed of divorcees, deserters, spinsters and widows many of whom appear to have never known the responsibilities and joys of either running a household or upbringing their children —are loud in their demand for the "emancipation of women".

The vast majority of Indian women however appear to be still inspired by the ideals of Sita and Savitri. Indians have always glorified womanhood. The Indian woman beginning from the Vedic times rightfully took her place by the side of her husband and occupied a position of superiority to be envied by her modern counterpart. She has always been the *mata* (mother) and *grihini* (the mistress of the household). Some of the misguided Indian women would like to descend to the level of rubbing shoulders with members of the opposite sex in the offices and factories and call themselves "emancipated". The social structure of life in India is quite different from that in the Western countries. The family has always been a stabilising social factor.

The image of an accomplished lady is one who is chaste, who loves her husband, who does not freely mix with men, who is simple in her dress and who knows how to train her children properly ; and not one who can simply play bridge, shake hands with gentlemen, drive a car, play tennis, paint her lips, have an independent income, drink, dance and smoke. She persists, despite increased contact with Western counterparts.

Today, when Western sociologists have begun to feel that even juvenile delinquency and sex crimes can be reduced if children are brought up in families which attach sanctity to marriage and which have not been exposed to divorce, separation, etc., it is a pity that some of our ill-informed social reformers want to pick up what is being rejected by the West.

Indian culture is built on such a strong edifice that traditional cultural and moral values are bound to assert themselves though obscured for the time being. Fortunately it is a negligible percentage of women that have caught the infection of 'modernisation' in the sense of westernisation. The love of the Indian woman towards her husband is proverbial. The heavier the adversity, the sweeter and the stronger becomes the Indian woman's love. This is an example which modern American women can emulate with great advantage. Americans now seem to feel that the family must be rehabilitated and to achieve this, I was told, both religious and social leaders have been sparing no pains.

We in India, inspired by some of our leaders, have been hugging to the illusion that science and technology are the only penacea for all our ills, despite the fact that in Western countries technological advances are becoming increasingly abused for the production of military power. I was told by some American friends that though they possess the highest standard of life and have every comfort that money and machines can give, many of them lack contentment. The average Indian not having even two square meals a day is more contented than his counterpart in America. In a sense the West has demonstrated that food and gadgets, even if plentiful, cannot make people really happy. Man does not live by bread alone. Some of the thoughtful Americans seem to feel that there is an awareness of the dangers to which their society is exposed as a result of too much of mechanisation, too much of insistence on material comforts and values and many of them feel that Indian values of life can wean them to some extent from their exaggerated belief in the right of man unaided by God.

Having seen a little bit of U.S., I must say that its type of life in many respects do not suit us. Our way of life is different, our values of life are more stable and we should stick to them. Many of our countrymen go to the West with the ostensible idea of learning. But most of them return with an air of superiority, copying their vices and abandoning our virtues. In a sense they return as denationalised Indians. It is therefore the responsibility of our Government to send to the West either on technical training or on diplomatic errands only such Indians, who are mature in their outlook and who have a traditional cultural background. Otherwise the cause of Indian culture is bound to suffer in the hands of men of immature outlook.

The Americans, I think, are a likeable people. They are very informal, extremely friendly, helpful, sincere, courteous, frank and tolerant. They have their dark spots too, just as we have ours. Let us ignore their vices and emulate their virtues. I immensely enjoyed my visit to America and I love to visit that country again.

I think, if Indians learned in their ancient lore, could go to America more frequently and thus maintain a continuous interchange of cultural ideas, not only the general cause of Indian culture could be promoted but an enduring edifice for international understanding laid.

21 Subsequent Visits to U.S.A., Europe and Japan

(A)

A cordial invitation extended by Mr. John Addey President, Astrologers' Association of England, that I should represent India at the Cambridge Astrological Conference to be held on 19th September 1970, and other long-standing invitations from different organisations in Europe and America to lecture under the auspices of various Universities, and cultural organisations made me decide to undertake again a tour of Europe and America.

Mrs. Rajeswari Raman had built up a certain reputation as a practical exponent of Yoga for the benefit of women and some of her foreign *chelas* who had been very much impressed by the benefits they derived from the practical courses in Yoga they had undergone at the hands of Mrs. Rajeswari were insistent that Mrs. Raman visit their countries and give demonstration-talks.

Our son B. Sureshwara who was then working for his doctorate in Engineering Science at Notre Dame University was insistent that his mother should take a holiday from the responsibilities of managing a big household and spend some days with him.

Thanks to the Passport authorities, the British High Commission and the U.S. Consul at Madras, passports and visas were easily obtained and the week before the date of departure (5-9-1970) was so packed with social engagements—dinners, tea parties, etc., arranged by friends, relatives and the staff-members of RAMAN PUBLICATIONS to wish us bon-flight that we had hardly any time left to spend with our children.

I cautioned Mrs. Raman about the difficulties she might have to face in matters of food, etc., but she just ignored my caution that none of these could daunt her from embarking on the trip as she was as anxious to carry in her own humble way, the message of our culture and ideals of Indian womanhood to her sisters in Western countries as was in our mission. In a sense, Mrs. Raman has more control over her palate, is more disciplined in her habits and stricter in her convictions than I am. Though not orthodox in its fanatical sense, she is a conservative Hindu, conservative in the sense that we should preserve the best in our traditions and way of life. Yet she is modern in her outlook as she is not averse to adopting the best in Western culture, such as personal integrity, sense of duty, etc.

There is not much difference in our fundamental outlook on life, the ancient values we should cherish and preserve and the extent to which we can adapt to modern conditions. Catholic in outlook, charming in disposition, unassuming and generally sympathetic towards the weaker sections in society she has a flair for befriending others and participating in their woes and weals. This quality is perhaps responsible for the scores of admirers and friends she has been able to earn for herself from amongst her pupils who come from different social, economic and educational strata.

In the Institute of Yoga for Women Mrs. Raman is conducting, no distinction is ever made between the rich and the poor, the educated and the uneducated, the elite and the rural, the Brahmin and the Harijan, the Hindu and the non-Hindu. In fact several Harijan ladies freely mix with the Brahmin and other Hindu, Christian and Muslim ladies and undergo training. As a mother, she is very much attached to all her children. She may show indulgence to their foibles and she is also intimate with them. But she is very particular that the children love and respect the parents and realise their duties towards the parents. Imitating cheap Western social codes is absolutely out of question.

I feel that the above digression, giving a brief picture of Mrs. Rajeswari's outlook, may be necessary to enable readers to understand what prompted her to make up her mind to accompany me. Finally the affectionate pressure of all the children that they would take care of the household and that she should have no second thoughts clinched the issue and we left Bangalore on 5th September 1970.

After a brief visit to Moscow *via* Delhi we arrived at Berlin on the 7th.

The sight-seeing in both East and West Berlin was interesting. Almost all the important monuments of historical interest including the place where Hitler is reported to have committed suicide are situated in East Berlin. The Berlin-wall between two parts of the city is not only made of stone and cement but also of political thinking.

Near the old Chancellory we accosted two policemen and made a friendly gesture introducing ourselves in English as tourists from India. The policemen were stiff robots. It was a relief to re-enter West Berlin and breathe the fresh air of freedom. A traffic policeman on duty near Tempelhof airport saw our predicament when we could not engage a taxi and helped us to get a conveyance. He said he was happy to meet two "Indian friends". His behaviour was exactly the opposite of his counterpart in East Berlin ruled by communists.

Berlin is a beautiful city. Unter den Linden is one of the finest and most spacious streets in Europe and is nearly a mile in length with a double avenue. Friedrich Strasse has chief shopping centres. It seems Hitler effected many improvements to make Berlin more beautiful. The river Spree with the Kurfursten bridge and the dome of the cathedral rising against the sky makes an imposing view. Berlin is a beautiful city worth seeing. We met the Austrian Consul in Germany and he showed interest in India's ancient cultural and scientific achievements.

Our visits to European cities coincided with the wave of hijackings that were just then taking place, In fact as we were flying from Moscow to Berlin three or four hijackings of planes were reported. On 5th September when we were in Frankfurt waiting to emplane for Vienna by Swiss Air, another hijacking of a Swiss Airplane was reported. This made us a bit anxious. In a sense Mrs. Raman is a psychic. She felt that nothing would happen to us and we should stick to our itinerary. The then current directional influences in our horoscopes were such that no such mishaps could befall us and we continued our flight reaching Vienna, the capital of Austria, the same evening.

Countess Wassilko, President of the Austrian Astrological Association, had arranged for a dinner meeting and I spoke on "Highlights of Hindu Astrology". In her Presidential remarks while complimenting me, Countess Wassilko felt that in her opinion the Western system was more suited to the Western culture and Western way of life ; while not under-rating the Hindu system she considered it "profound and difficult". She however conceded that the Hindu system could give more accurate results in the matter of timing events.

Mrs. Raman addressed the guests on the significance of Yoga and the audience showed keen interest.

Wien (Vienna), the capital of Austria, lies on the right bank of the Danube. Vienna had acquired a cultural leadership that placed it in pre-war days in the forefront of European cities. Impressive buildings and parks are numerous. Vienna is also richly endowed with museums, picture-galleries and other marks of cultural leadership. Kartnerstrasse is the centre of the city. The old Parliament building, the Opera House, the Museum of Natural History and Arts, etc., are all impressive buildings.

We went round the city in a car provided by an Austrian friend and visited many places of historical and cultural interest.

On the 10th September 1970 when we entered the restaurant of the hotel we had been lodged in, for morning coffee, myself in *dhoti* and shirt and Mrs. Raman in the typical Hindu dress, we were the centre of attraction for the vast number of Europeans and many ladies smiled at Mrs. Raman and introduced themselves as admirers of Indian Culture. We had to spurn the 'advice' of an Indian who met us in Vienna that appearance in public in *dhoti* would not be correct etiquette. We retorted that was the national dress of India and to look down upon it by Indians smacks of anti-nationalism. Learning that Mrs. Raman was a teacher of Yoga, several ladies met her privately and sought advice about their physical and mental problems.

On 11th September, we flew into Rome. A hostess who claimed to be a student of Yoga on "Air Italia" was all consideration in providing us with lunch suited to our sentiments and habits. She was about 24 but had lots of "emotional problems". She felt that Indian Culture could be a panacea for the "neurotic" Western world, "suffering from materialism and permissiveness" and "trampling on moral values and spiritual consideration".

Dr. Cragnolini, a scientist, accompanied by news reporters was at the Rome Air Port to great us. The same evening I delivered a lecture before a select gathering of psychologists, medical men, psychiatrists and astrologers. Several newspapers featured our visit. A cable from the Private Secretary to the Pope intimating that the Pope would receive us in a private audience reached us at Rome a day late when we were about to leave for Geneva.

Our sight-seeing covered not only the city of Rome but places associated with the names of Roman emperors, and the Vatican. Rome embraces more than 2000 years of history. It was once the capital of one of the most powerful empires of all time. The relics no doubt speak her mighty past and Rome's contribution to Western culture is indeed conciderable. But her perpetration of the Christian faith has its tragic aspects also because the Catholic faith arrogated to itself the wisdom of God and looked down upon the great Hindu and Chinese conceptions as 'pagan'.

The architectural splendour of the Colloseum built in the 1st century A.D. is to be marvelled at but it cannot stand comparison with the great Hindu temples in South India.

We visited the Vatican, St. Peter's Church, Olympic Stadium, Temple of Vesta, the Capital, the Pantheon and the Treyi Fountain. As we went round the place where Mussolini lived, our memory went back to the days when Mussolini at the pinnacle of glory and power, shook the European world and when we analysed his horoscope in the June 1989 issue of THE ASTROLOGICAL MAGAZINE and predicted his downfall and violent end. In this transient world, power like a soap bubble, can burst any moment. Wise rulers, knowing this will use power for helping the people and earning their goodwill, while arrogant rulers trying to become dictators are thrown out by popular hatred.

With its narrow roads and countless number of automobiles speeding up and down, Rome's traffic problem appears to be terrific.

Representatives of the Yoga Institute of Rome called on Mrs. Raman and urged her to pay a special visit to Rome and stay there for a few weeks.

From Rome, we flew into Geneva. The League of Nations building presents a desolate appearance. Geneva continues to be an attraction for visitors because of its climate. We met a number of Indian officials, Secretaries, etc., in the Central Government who were then in Geneva on "some official work".

Of all the hotels in which we stayed during our visits to Europe and America, Hotel Carnivara in Geneva was the last word in cleanliness. The maid-servant used to clean the bath room and make-up the bed twice a day. We had a small holiday in this beautiful lake-city and were quite refreshed by the time we reached Paris on the 14th September.

Paris is indeed the centre of French Culture, whatever one may mean by the term "culture". Mrs. Raman had her own interesting experiences which only strengthened her conviction of the soundness of the Indian way of life hedged in between rights and duties, moderation in pleasures and spiritual goals. Some well-meaning friends showed us round nocturnal Paris and some of the pleasure-haunts where men and women lose health, wealth and family life, for transient sense-pleasures and the so-called thrill.   At the Lido where in a sense we were guests of Monsieur Lenoisre we had the experience of being served *champagne* and dinner which we firmly declined with thanks.   We passed on the *champagne* to the two   Amarican guests who were with us and they grabbed the beverage with gusto.   We watched the entertainment till about midnight and were conducted back to our hotel by our hosts.   The night shows had their repulsive aspects and could not fit into our conception of innocent relaxation or healthy entertainment.   By no stretch of imagination could such cabaret shows be equated with clean entertainment and relaxation.   The contagion of aping the darker shades of western culture such as the cabaret, nude dance, disco etc., seems to have affected some upper class Indians in big cities to such an extent that many dancing women shamelessly expose in public their anatomy.   This is bound to adversely influence the youth, by instillting into their minds perverted ideas of art and culture quite alien to Hindu conception.   Vulgar and unrestrained display of the female anatomy in the name of art can only be obscenity : and Indian woman-hood should see that such exhibitions do not find a place in the Indian entertainment world either on the stage or even on the screen.

Paris has a lot of historical sights.   Place de la Concorde laid out under Louis XV is the scene of the execution of Louis XVI, Marie Antoinette and many victims of the French Revolution.   The Place de l'Etoila is the centre of 12 avenues radiating from it in all directions.   Champs Elysees is the Chief of these avenues.

As a student of Alison's *French Revolution*, I had developed an admiration for Napoleon Bonaparte.   I was much interested in visiting the historical places associated with the reign of this great man.   The *Arc de Triomphe*, which is said to be the largest triumphal arch in the world commemorates the military triumphs of Napoleon. Paris appears to be situated on both sides of the river Seine— South of the Seine are the Place St. Michel on the great centres of traffic in Paris. Palais de Justice is an attractive building having a fine facade in Greek style.

We were most interested in going round Hotel des Inavlids. Founded by Louis XIV as a retreat for infirm soldiers, it contained museums of military history and a gilded dome sheltering another Church. The central crypt of this church contains a fine sacrophagus of red parphyry, in which lie the remains of Napoleon Bonaparte, brought from St. Helene, where he died. Among other buildings we saw were the Palaise Royal, now occupied by the Council of State, the Palais Bourbon, the meeting place of the Chamber of Deputies and Palais de l' Elysee, residence of the President of third Republic. We went up the Eiffel Tower and from there had a breath taking view of Paris. Monsieur Bustros showed us round Paris.

As the Sun goes down and darkness begins to creep in, Paris becomes a fairy land, and the memory of Paris is bound to remain fresh.

On the 15th September, a number of ladies, some of them cabaret artistes in Paris night clubs in the age group between 18 and 20 years, met Mrs. Raman. Their main complaints were lack of peace of mind, restlessness and suicidal tendencies. That young blondes and brunnettes, earning fat salaries in the pleasure-haunts of Paris, lacked the simple happiness and contentment of middle class or even poor Indian ladies is a reflection on the type of society modern civilisation has evolved with its emphasis on materialism, mammon worship and sense pleasures to the exclusion of the real joy of a contented and regulated life based upon moral codes and certain social restrictions. Mrs. Raman listened to their woes patiently and within

the short period of our stay in Paris, initiated some of the
girls into certain Yoga-techniques, which, they are still
practising with benefit. A number of them have written
that they are no longer enamoured of the sinful night life
of Paris and are looking forward to getting married and
to leading decent lives of householders.

Our next halt was at Amsterdam in Holland where we
arrived on the 17th by KLM flight. We were received at
the airport by Mr. Mahajan, the First Secretary at our
Embassy in the Hague.

At the Hague we were guests of our Ambassador
Mr. Dhamija. He and his wife took special care of our
comforts. We were joined at the dinner by the industria-
list Mr. Bharat Ram who happened to be in Holland then,
and discussions ranged from astrology to international
affairs including of course India's role.

In the evening I delivered a lecture under the auspices
of the Indo-Dutch Friendship Society. Those present in
the lecture, in addition to the large Dutch audience,
included the Indian Ambassador, his wife, several officials
of the embassy and a few Indians.

Amsterdam is about 30 miles from the Hague where
the lecture was delivered. Part of the day was spent in
the Hague and the rest of the day at Amsterdam where
we camped at Howard Johnson Hotel.

The Hague is the real capital of Holland, the residence of the court and diplomatic bodies and the seat of
the Government. The Palace of Peace built to house the
international peace conferences is a fairly imposing
structure.

Amsterdam is a beautiful city. The countryside has
a fascinating appeal to lovers of nature.

The canalised river passes through the city and the
city is full of canals. We visited some important places

in the brief time we could snatch after fulfilling our engagements.

At Amsterdam we last our brief-case containing passports, air tickets, etc., and we were in a fix. Astrology helped us to expect the recovery of the brief-case. While the Indian embassy officials were getting ready to issue a duplicate passport, news came round that the brief-case had been delivered at the Air India Office by a passer-by who happned to find it near a bridge. This person wanted taxi-fare to be paid from the place where he noticed the bag to the Air India Office plus one pound sterling.

We landed at Heathrow Air Port, London, on the 18th September and the drive in the car from the airport to the hotel, where we stayed for nearly a week, took 75 minutes and we could see a part of Lodon during this long drive. We needed some rest badly and so spent the night quietly in our hotel as we had a crowded progromme the next few days.

The next morning we left by car to Cambridge to attend the Astrological Conference. Mr. John Addy and other organisers of the Conference were eagerly looking forward to our visit. I addressed the Conference at Fritz William College on "India's Astrological Heritage". I had an interesting discussion with Mr. Michel Gaquelin, a well-known statistician and psychologist of Sourbonne University, whose statistical studies have resulted in corroboration of many an astrological theory. There was a good gathering of well-known astrologers of Europe and America.

Our stay in London was availed of by a large number of Indian friends to visit us. Our sight-seeing included all the well-known places which have been detailed in the chapters on London. Only Mrs. Raman had not seen

them before. Mrs. Raman initiated a number of ladies
into Yoga. Two special lectures were delivered by me on
*"Nadi Astrology" (Appendix III) and "Hindu Predic-
tive Techniques" (Appendix IV) respectively at the
Astrological Lodge and the Astrological Association.
Our good old friends Mr. Cyrus D. F. Abayakoon and
Mr. M. K. Gandhi took special care of us. We had an
interesting discussion with our High Commissioner
Mr. Appa Pant who presented a copy of his book on
Yoga to Mrs. Raman. We meet several British astrologers
and had discussions with them.

We were living on fruits, milk and beaten rice and
naturally, we gladly responded to an invitation to lunch
with a Bangalore friend who had then been living in
London. He was to pick us up at our hotel and drive us to
his residence. When we arrived at his house, it was
already 3 p.m. though we had expected our kind friend
would give us the food by 1 p.m. The lady of the house
had just started cooking and one could imagine our
annoyance. Mrs. Raman helped the lady in preparing
the food and we had our meal at 5 p.m.

Life in London for the average Indian family does
not seem to be one of roses. There appears to be a certain lack of warmth and closeness generally evident in
most Indian families. A certain artificiality seems to
have made life mechanical. Wives not employed have
to spend most of their times attending to each and every
domestic work—unlike in India where domestic labour is
still available—living in a neighbourhood culturally and
emotionally cut off from the main stream : their children,
foreign to the customs, habits, beliefs and conventions of

---

* These lectures have been reproduced as Appendices III and IV.

13

their mother-country and culture and aping the Westerners—evoke our sympathy. Mrs. Raman's intimate talks with some of these ladies revealed how unhappy most of the ladies, especially if they are still "old-fashioned", are.

On arrival at New York on 24th September, we were met by our son Bangalore Sureshwara who was then doing his doctorate in Engineering Science at Notre Dame University. After a tight programme in Europe, we took the more needed rest at New York. Important places of sight-seeing described in the earlier chapters were covered as Mrs. Rajeswari Raman had not seen them. Our residence at New York was Hotel Taft, the same place where I resided in 1959. New York had changed. Atmospheric pollution, permissiveness and crime had all increased. Paradoxically there was increased interest on the part of the younger generation in matters extramundane. In the land of the almighty dollar where material civilisation and moral breakdown could provide everything needed for sense pleasures without hindrance, the people needed a spiritual and moral prop to give them the meaning of life, the aim of existence and real happiness. And Christianity with its dogma and church was no answer. They looked to India, to the Hindu way of life, with its emphasis on moral values, a spiritual goal and belief in the law of Karma and causation which could explain scientifically life's inconsistencies.

Mrs. Raman's help was sought by a number of women, young, old and middle aged, to initiate them into certain Yogic techniques, which would remove tension and give them confidence and peace of mind. She gave lessons in New York to a number of ladies.

A crowded programme awaited us at Washington. My lecture at Hotel Shilton arranged by the Washington Astrological Association dealt with "World Trends and Tensions" and Mrs. Raman spoke on "Yoga and Indian Culture". On the 26th morning, we addressed Press reporters at our Hotel and in the evening we were taken round Washington by Mr. and Mrs. Paul Grell and Mrs. Grant.

Since my visit 10 years before, Washington had not changed much except that the law and order problem had become very acute. Whites, it seems, generally lived in suburbs while the Blacks had monopolised the downtown. We were cautioned not to move without escort.

During our stay in Washington, we were guests at a dinner given by Mr. Parasuram, *Indian Express* representative and Mr. Thiagarajan of the Indian Embassy. We had also met Mr. Easwar Sagar, special representative of *The Hindu*, who drove us to the Air Port and saw us off to Chicago.

On 29th September I addressed a dinner meeting at the Lions Club, South Bend. The sophisticated audience showed keen interest in my exposition of the rationale of astrology.

My lecture at Chicago on the 30th September 1970 under the auspices of OASIS lasted for three hours. It was past midnight when we returned to South Bend accompanied by our son and his friend Dr. Rao. From 1st to 4th October, the programmes at New York were heavily sheduled—dinners, receptions, lectures, group meetings, discussions with prominent persons, etc., extending long after midnight. Lectures at the New York University, The Astrologers' Guild of America and the New York Astrology Centre drew large audiences. Purely technical lectures attracted the cream of the astrological fraternity.

Mrs. Raman gave a demonstration-talk at New York on 2nd October and the appreciations were spontaneous.

A busy programme awaited us at Boston, where we spoke to the New England Astrological Associaton, and Mrs. Raman gave a demonstration-talk on 'Pranayama'. We met quite a number of our old friends—Mr. Oscar Weber, Mrs. Clara Cotta, etc.

From October 5th to 8th, we had to participate in innumerable programmes arranged not only by astrological and cultural centres and Universities but also by our son Dr. B. Sureshwara. The engagements were so tight that it became necessary to cancel a few including our lecture at the Windsor University in Canada.

On the 6th our son drove us to Milwaukee in the State of Wisconsin which extended to us a warm welcome. "Yoga Incorporated" held a big reception in honour of Mrs. Raman's visit. There was a good gathering of Yoga teachers and pupils. Mrs. Raman was almost mobbed by the guests who attended the reception. Mrs. Hitchcock, the President of "Yoga Incorporated", was the spirit behind this function. Several Yoga teachers received initiation from Mrs. Raman. Mrs. Raman gave a demonstration-talk on "Certain Meditational Techniques".

The following is an extract from a report about Mrs. Rajeswari Raman, published in the *Milwaukee Sentinel* of Milwaukee, U.S.A., under the caption YOGINI FROM BANGALORE.

"A group of Yoga teachers—most of them housewives—gathered for coffee Tuesday afternoon to meet their counterpart from Bangalore, India, Mrs. Rajeswari Raman.

"And was she different? Yes and No.

"Mrs. John L. Hitchcock, W 140-N7905 Lilly Td., Menomones Falls, entertained members of Yoga United

(Yoga teachers) of which she is co-founder and vice-president, plus some of their pupils, in Mrs. Raman's honor.

"Mrs. Raman is a housewife. She also conducts Sri Surya Prakash Institute of Yoga for Women in Bangalore.

"The guest of honor was escorted by her husband, Dr. B. V. Raman, and their third son Dr. B. Sureshwara.

"Air pollution and women's equality being the questions of the day, the Ramans dutifully commented on these matters, although they do not share the prevalent concern with the topics.

"As for air pollution, they clean the air by the breathing process of Yoga and take in prana, they said, and every one benefits. Prana is a vital force assimilated into the body by disciplined breathing, according to Yoga belief.

"Mrs. Raman is the mother of eight children, the youngest 20. She is 5 feet 2 inches tall and weights 110 pounds. She does not look old enough to have a son in graduate school.

"She started studying Yoga after her marriage to Dr. Raman of whom she said, "He is my guru'.

"In her school, Mrs. Raman tailors a program to each pupil. She works up a veritable case history before starting. She sees each student once a week, and a course lasts three to four months. The sessions include *hatha* and *rajayoga* and *pranayama*.

"Serious Yoga followers are vegetarians and the Ramans are among the most strict.

"They do not eat anything from tins, no carbonated beverages, stimulants or alcohol. They believe meat has a pollution that cannot be washed away and which leads to ailments for those who eat it. "We don't want the body to be a tomb for dead animals," Mrs. Raman said.

"Likewise, Mrs. Raman said, "no cosmetics", although she wears the red circular mark on her forehead. However, she described bi-weekly oil baths, actually massage, with herbal oils subsequently removed with herbal nut-powder.

"A married woman's status is proclaimed in India by a nose ornament which varies in shape. Mrs. Raman's is a minute fan of diamond. It matches small clusters of diamonds in her ear-rings."

We were the guests of honour at a dinner meeting arranged by the Wisconsin Astrological Association, under whose auspices I spoke on "Hindu Astrological Techniques" at the Y.M.C.A. auditorium on 6th October.

A get-together party arranged by our son Dr. Sureshwara at South Bend gave us the opportunity of meeting the local elite. Quite a number of Indian friends were also present apart from local officials, University teachers, etc. It was an enjoyable evening.

My lecture at Notre Dame University on the 8th was on "Astrology and Its Relation to Psychology". The auditorium was packed and several Professors vied with each other in congratulating me on my "most scientific exposition". Mrs. Rajeswari Raman had a busy day. Under the auspices of Zellers' Yoga Institute she gave a demonstration-talk at the Y.M.C.A. The house was full. After the talk Mrs. Zeller complimented Mrs. Raman for what she called the "extraordinary performance of this Yogini from India". Late in the night we had to attend a tea party at the residence of Dr. Lee, an authority on Structural Engineering.

The 9th of October saw us back at New York. Our son and his friends gave us a warm send-off at South Bend. We were received at La Guardia Air Port by Mr. Weingarten and Miss Uma Barbara of Astrology

Centre and driven to our hotel at Times Square. **Mrs. Raman** spoke at New York Yoga Centre on "Some Important Aspects of Hata Yoga".

The same evening I spoke at the United Nations on the "Relevance of Astrology to Modern Times", a summary of which is given in Appendix v.

The Chef-de-Cabinets conducted us to the Dag Hammerschold Auditorium, where the lecture was delivered.

Before the lecture we had a meeting with *Mr. U. Thant, Secretary-General. He came out of an important meeting and greeted us with the remark "I have heard a lot about your wonderful work in the field of astrology and have watched with interest your activities for the past two decades".

On the same night we left New York by Air India *en route* to London and Bombay. As the plane was about to touch the soil of our motherland at Bombay, we remembered the words of the great Sage Valmiki put into the mouth of Sri Rama : *Janani janmabhoomischa swargadapi gareeyasi.*

Our visit to Europe and America in September–October 1970 was a great success. Though wielding no political or official position, we were extended V.I.P. treatment in all the places we visited. Our hosts spared no pains to make our stay in those foreign lands comfortable

---

* In 1968, Mr. U. Thant, due to some domestic problems had tendered his resignation from the Secretary Generalship of the United Nations. The Assistant Secretary General wrote to me : "Mr. U. Thant is very much interested in your assessment of his immediate future as he wishes to take certain decisions". I wrote back to Mr. U. Thant : "Even if you have made up your mind to resign Jupiterian influences in your chart are such that you will be obliged to continue for another term". And he had to withdraw his resignation and accept another term.

and enjoyable. We were enabled to stay in high class hotels. Our hosts who had arranged receptions and dinners respected our sentiments and provided us with our special menu. We made television appearances in U.S.A. and in the places we visited the Press prominently featured our visit.

Mrs. Rajeswari Raman in her graceful sari, prominent vermillion mark on her forehead, typically Indian bearing, and the easy manner with which she could demonstrate even difficult Yogic techniques attracted the attention of the public. At the various receptions many people "could not simply believe" that she was mother of a number of children. By her simplicity, friendliness and sweet manners and unassuming nature, Mrs. Raman created a very good impression about Yoga and Indian womanhood.

(B)

Within six months from the date of my previous visit to U.S., I was again prevailed upon to accept a cordial invitation from National Astrological Society to inaugurate the International Astrological Conference at New York.

Leaving Bangalore on 21st April 1971, I took off by Air India at Madras the same night for Rome. A warm send-off was given at Bangalore by Mrs. Rajeswari Raman and family members, friends, and press and office staff, and at Madras by my son Sri B. Suryanarayana Rao and a number of friends. The journey was not quite pleasant due to late departures from Madras and Bombay and somewhat rough flight. At Kuwait, the plane was grounded for nearly 4 hours for some repairs. I reached Rome four hours behind schedule.

Several friends were present at the Rome Air Port. At a meeting held in my room at Hotel Leonarda Da Vinci, discussions were held for starting an "Association for the Study of Hindu Astrology".

From Rome I flew into Zurich on 22nd April. Zurich is an attraction for visitors, what with its lake and beautiful mountain scenery. The helpful attitude of the local Air India Manager impressed me much. I did a lot of sight-seeing in Zurich, visited Mrs. Elizabeth's Yoga Institute and had a lively discussion with her. I also had the occasion to meet two of the pupils of Dr. Jung and discuss with them Dr. Jung's work in the field of practical astrology.

I arrived at Paris on 26th April and spent three days in this centre of 'French Culture'. I called on Mrs. Gaquelin and got acquainted with the work of her husband Dr. Michael Gaquelin— statistical analysis of thousands of horoscopes—with a view to proving or disproving certain assumptions of astrology. On 28th I addressed a big meeting under the auspices of 'Internationale D'Centre Astrologie'. Most of the leading French astrologers and astrological savants were present and the theme of my lecture was "Where Hindu Astrology scores over the Western Systems". The lecture was translated into French by Mr. Michael Bustros.

After my lecture, leading French astrologers prevailed on me to tell Gaquelin not to denigrate the predictive part of Western astrology under cover of his own studies and researches. In fact I was told that in France – and Gaquelin is a resident of Paris—he often ridiculed Western astrological principles, stating that they were not true.

Flight from Paris to Montreal in Canada was quite pleasant. While Air India jetted into the age of the Jumbo liner on 21st May 1971, I had my first experience of of Jumbo flight at least three weeks earlier, when I flew from Paris to Montreal by 747 Boeing. My first flight by air was in 1947—from Bangalore to Bombay. I have had the good fortune of flying in almost all types of carriers Dakotas, Constellations, Caravilles, Folker friendships H. S., Boeings, 707, 737, 727 and D.C. 9's, etc. But Jumbo 747 is a class by itself. It is something fantastic—more than 300 passengers spanning the Atlantic at 600 miles an hour at an altitude of over 30,000 feet! We were only a dozen passengers in the first class and the amount of attention paid to us by the stewards and hostesses of Air France was equally noteworthy. The pity, according to a hostess, who was all attention to me, was, I was so spartan that I could not enjoy the choice foods and drinks made available to first class passengers. Just before landing at Montreal, she presented me with a bottle of *champagne* which I passed on to an American passenger sitting behind me.

At Montreal Air Port, Mr. and Mrs. Pyarelal Khanna extended a warm welcome to me. I was lodged in a first class hotel—La Salle—and the Khannas spared no pains to make my stay enjoyable. Montreal is a beautiful city, the population being predominantly French. Canada seems to have its own language problem. It is bilingual.

I will have more to say on these matters in another book of impressions to be published shortly.

From Montreal I flew into New York on 30th April and was received at the J. F. Kennedy Air Port by my hosts and Dr. Rao, and lodged in a high class hotel—Grammarcy Park—in a quiet locality.

The Conference began on 1st May at the New York University auditorium and my address was on the "Relevance of Astrology in the Modern Times". The lecture was well received. In the evening, a party was given to me at the famous New York Hilton Hotel and there were nearly hundred guests—leading astrologers, medical men, scientists and others. There was a demonstration of E.S.P. by Mr. Jack London, which was quite enjoyable.

On 2nd May I again addressed the Conference on "The Spiritual Value of Astrology". The meeting was held at the spacious lecture hall of the New York Hilton. The other speakers were *Dr. Michael Gaquelin, Scientist Nelson and Dr. Razelli. It was Mr. Nelson that discovered the correlation between solar flares and certain "planetary arrangements". I had an interesting discussion with Mr. Nelson. My stay in New York till 8th May paid rich dividends. Classes were conducted on Hindu astrology and people of different walks of life called on me to discuss astrological and allied matters. On 5th May I spoke at Columbia University on "Astrology and Modern Science".

On 9th May, I left for Baltimore (Maryland) by Pennsylvania Express, accompanied by our hosts Mr. Weingarten and Miss Uma Barbara. The Aquarian University representatives met us at Baltimore Railway Station. In the evening I was taken to a community centre located in the beautiful countryside, and run by a group of young American men and women with the main object of "understanding the spiritual value of life". I was told the inmates lived the life of a Brahmachari—vegetarian

---

* In highlighting his researches in astrology, Mr. Gaquelin in a way underrated the existing Western astrological theories, as if they were of no consequence. I brought to Mr. Gaquelin's notice the apprehension of several French astrologers about the adverse effect of his denigration of the accepted Western astrological principles, on their profession ; but he just laughed : To me it appeared that Mr. Gaquelin lacked a clear conception and knowledge of Hindu astrology so that astrology still meant to him and men of his thinking what is only known to the Western world.

food, no alcohol, Yogic sadhana, etc. My address to the inmates was on "The Bhagavad Gita in Daily Life".

My lecture at the Aquarian University was on "Astrology, Yoga and Spiritual Life". There was a large and distinguished gathering.

Just before the lecture, I was interviewed by the well-known newspaper *Baltimore.Sun*.

On the 10th morning, I flew into South Bend where my son, B. Sureshwara, a staff-member at the Indiana University, received me at the Air Port. At his insistence, I had complete rest for three days, but a Press Conference could not be avoided. My son spared no pains to make my stay comfortable.

13th May saw me back at New York. On the same night, I left New York by Air India *en route* to London and Bombay and as the plane was about to touch the soil of our motherland, *a thrill* of joy ran through my veins.

(C)

On 10th September 1972 I left for Athens (Greece) *en route* to London and New York on a business trip. This was my fourth visit to foreign countries. Availing of this opportunity, I accepted invitations to speak on Hindu Astrology and different aspects of Indian Culture.

Thanks to my previous three visits to Europe and America, there was much demand for my publications and THE ASTROLOGICAL MAGAZINE in this part of the world. By my lectures, discussions, seminars, etc., on various platforms ranging from Rotary Clubs and Universities to the United Nations, I had been able to create some sort of a sustained interest not only in Hindu astrology but also in the Indian way and values of life, in the minds of a section of the cultured public in the Western hemisphere.

After a few hours of rest at Bombay International Hotel, I left by Air India Jumbo at 9-30 p.m. reaching Bejrut *via* Delhi by about 3-30 a.m. This was not my first flight by Jumbo. I had flown before from Paris to Montreal in April 1971—by Air France Jumbo—and therefore there was no thrill of any new experience.

In the first class we were about half-a-dozen passengers to be taken care of by 3 or 4 hostesses—a circumstance not quite in accord with our cherished objective of establishing a classless society. The Captain invited me to visit the cock-pit.

At Beirut, I was met at the Air Port by the Assistant Manager of Air India who drove me in his car to Hotel Phoenix a five-star hotel.

During my stay at Beirut of 6 or 7 hours, I could do some sight-seeing also. The drive on the shore of the Mediterranean Sea was exhilerating.

The City of *Beirut, capital of Lebanon, appeared to me to be a lovely place, situated as it is, on a triangular promontory, backed by the Lebanon Range. Beirut has some five squares but the bazaars are not very elegant. I was told that Beirut is a free trade centre—no restriction to bring in or take out anything. I could see many shops displaying luxury goods and the latest models of European-American and Japanese cars, available for immediate purchase. I felt somewhat envious of the Beirut citizen that for $. 2000 he could buy, without notice, the latest Japanese four-cylinder Toyota whereas to buy in India a new Fiat or an Ambassador, poorly constructed, and

---

* As we go press, Lebanon has been passing through a critical phase of her political existence. Civil war is going on unabated for months resulting in the deaths of hundreds of innocent people. It is hoped that a solution acceptable to all the political parties and Palestinians will be found soon.

unelegant, I should have to pay the huge amount of Rs. 23,000 ($. 4000). Now of course the price is more than a lakh.

Another factor I noticed in Beirut was that though the Muslims constituted nearly 45% of the population, there was no *purdah* observed by the Muslim-women. Only three women were found in burqua at the Air Port and on enquiry I learnt that the three ladies belonged to the retinue of a Shaik. But even in my home town in Secular India, Indian Muslim women barely appear in public without covering their faces.

The headquarters of the Palestinian guerillas, I was told, was about 50 miles from Beirut and just then there was much tension as the Israelis were attacking the Guerillas in their bases.

At 3 p.m. I left for Athens by Swiss Air. The security at the Beirut Air Port was tight and the luggage of all the passengers was carefully searched. Probably because I was an Indian, I was asked merely to identify my baggage and emplane.

My stay at Athens for three days was quite fruitful. A lecture delivered at the Athens Rotary Club attracted the attention of the elite of the city. The lecture hall was jam-packed. I spoke in English on the scientific and cultural indebtedness of Greece to ancient India and my lecture seems to have made a good impact on the audience. Among those who attended the meeting were the Japanese Ambassador and his wife and the Belgian Ambassador. I explained the similarity in the teachings between the masters of ancient Greece such as Socrates, Aristotle, Plato on the one hand and Indian masters like Vyasa, Parasara and Sankara and upheld my thesis that Greek astrologers and philosophers were indebted to India for their knowledge.

Mr. D. Tripodakis, President of the Club, was in the chair.

I was the chief guest at this dinner meeting and my Greek-hosts were particular to respect my sentiments and provide me with fruits, milk and corn-flakes.

Except my lecture, the rest of the proceedings were conducted in Greek language and a summary was given in English for my information. The Greeks appear to be highly conscious about their language and ancient culture. Though every member who attended the lecture knew English, they employed their own language. But in our country, while as things stand, there could be no objection to use English as link language between people hailing from different states, I fail to see the *raison d'etre* for using English in Rotary and Lions Club meetings. Kannada is the language which should receive the pride of place in Bangalore. Obviously our elite still seem to be averse to switch on to the language of the region. Such an attitude could be a reflection even on our nationalism. When Indians are not proud of their languages, their cultural values, their philosophical attainments, their scientific achievements and the high moral integrity practised by their forbears, it amounts to a certain degeneration to which we have wittingly or unwittingly fallen. The thinking of many of our educated people appears to be generally Western-oriented. The goals and values of life, propounded by the sages, are of perennial interest and universally applicable. Let us not therefore allow ourselves to be looked down upon by the future generations that because of our indifference, they were deprived of the benefits of our glorious heritage.

The object of my visit to London was to seek a suitable representative for my books and magazine. A number of well-known publishers were contacted and it was a pleasure to find the increasing interest evinced by the publishers to sell standard books on Hindu astrology, Vedanta, etc.

On my previous four or five trips to London, my visits were confined to libraries, museums and other historical and cultural places. I was interested in visiting the slum areas to acquaint myself with the conditions there. The impression of many people in India that all is well in Western countries and that the slums are the monopoly of only Indian cities is wrong.

My London residence was at Strand Palace Hotel. A Miss Lynette Turner, a post-graduate student of Oxford University, with whom I had got acquainted in a book shop, called on me to discuss about 'Indian Culture'. When I expressed my desire to visit parts of London City inhabited by the poor, she suggested that the next morning she would take me round East London in her car. She drove me through several slum areas. East London seems to have a large Indian population. I was surprised to find some large Indian families living in two room flats in unhygienic conditions. Many of these Indians seem to feel that it is far better to live in a slum area in London and work in a British factory rather than live in India. These Indians, unwanted in Britain, exhibit a false sense of prestige. Miss Turner had a strange notion of Indian history, largely gathered from British sources and I corrected many of her misconceptions.

I visited the residence of Dr. Johnson and the beer cell where a cup of beer offered to me was politely declined.

Another feature I noticed this time in London was the presence in the hotel I stayed of a certain racial feeling. More attention was paid by the management to cater to European visitors and it looked as though they wanted to make the Indian visitors feel inferior. Paradoxically in India in some of the so-called five-star hotels run on Western lines and having nothing Indian to show except the colour of the bearers, a cringing attitude is employed towards foreign guests while Indian guests receive a somewhat indifferent treatment.

So long as we continue to imitate Westerners in dress, in habits, in food, in entertainments, etc., and lack the nationalistic outlook needed to present in our Western type hotels intended for foreign tourists, Indian styles of dancing, music, etc., such a state of affairs is bound to continue.

The pity is, most of the middle class foreign tourists, especially West Europeans and Americans, want to see something really Indian—Indian food, Indian music, Indian dancing, etc. But they are provided with a cheap imitation of Western type of entertainment, cabaret dances, etc. I wish our hotels would imitate Western hotels in the matter of efficient service, cleanliness and hygienic preparation and distribution of food.

On arrival at Kennedy Air Port, New York, on the 18th, I was met by my fourth son B. A. Kumar Babu and his friends. Kumar Babu had been doing his M.S. in Engineering Science at the famous Brooklyn Polytechnic Institute. The flight from London to New York by T.W.A. was smooth and enjoyable. The T.W.A. have their own customs lounge and an official of the T.W.A. facilitated clearance without any hitch. A hostess, Spanish by nationality, who meticulously attended to my comforts while on flight, had a surprise for me. She was herself a keen student of astrology and extra-sensory perception. She spent most of the flight time discussing Hindu astrology.

14

At Jacksonville where I arrived from New York on the 20th I was met by Dr. and Mrs. Monckevisz who drove me from there to Gainesville, a distance of 60 miles. The countryside through which we passed reminded me of Kerala.

On the same evening I lectured under the auspices of the Santa Fe College on "Astrology and Spiritual Progress". There was a large gathering of professors and students. The next day I addressed a group of students of the college on "Hindu Ideals of Life and Evils of Permissive Society".

Late in the night a get-together had been arranged at the countryside residence of Mrs. Monckevisz. About 100 students had gathered there with a few Professors to receive "initiation" of a mantra which would give them peace of mind and which would help them in spiritual progress.

Some interesting sidelight could be thrown on this meeting. Most of the students (girls and boys) belonged to the age group of 20 to 25 and were scantily dressed in clothing patched up here and there. When I asked why they were so dressed, the reply was that it symbolised their "revolt" against what they called "the materialism" of their parents. Among other things, they said : American society is degenerating : ninety per cent of the boys and girls assembled there had pre-marital sex ; they hated materialism ; they were convinced that Indian Culture could help them recover their lost soul and that given a chance they would all like to come away to India.

Two professors of the Florida University, one of Sociology and the other of Psychology, who had a private meeting with me, were sore over their shattered family life and sought comfort in "the Indian way of life". When I asked the Sociology Professor what exactly she was expected to teach, she said "groupbehaviour". I suggested that in the ultimate analysis the nature of group-behaviour towards each other depended upon the nature of behaviour of an individual towards family members, towards the public, etc. Of course she had no answer. Why family ties were breaking down and group-behaviour descended to the level of group hatred, in spite of all their "advancement" in Sociology, Psychology, etc.? The woman in her asserted. She confessed that she had four children of 6 to 14 years age, that she had asked for divorce from her husband and that she was now living with another Professor (father of three children) whom his wife (who had three children from the Professor) wanted to divorce and whom the lady Professor wanted to marry. All this looked rather very complicated and brought to prominence the type of family and social relations now obtaining in the most powerful and the most materially advanced country in the world.

The lady Professor of Psychology had her own tale to tell. She did not like her husband, a noted medical doctor, leading a normal family life and spending the evening with his children at home. She was for extra-marital relations and sophisticated social life. Hence she was suing him for divorce !

When I explained to them how even today, family ties are quite strong and mutual loyalty of the husband and wife are a normal phenomenon in India, she could only marvel that things should still be so good in India.

After being seen off at Gainseville Air Port by Dr. and Mrs. Monckevisz, on the 22nd, I flew into Chicago. My son Dr. B. Sureshwara and daughter-in-law Srimathi Sumati drove me to Desplaines where Dr. Sureshwara had been working as an Engineer.

On 24th September I lectured at 'Oxford House', Chicago, on "Political Astrology" under the auspices of NASO. The audience showed keen awareness of the technicalities of such a difficult subject.

After 3 days stay at Desplaines where my son and daughter-in-law took affectionate care of me, they drove me to Detroit. Prof. Mehta was there to receive me and to take me to Windsor University in Canada which is on the opposite bank of river Detroit. Prof. Spellman, Head of the Department of Asian Studies, introduced me to several other Professors. My lecture at the University was on "Astrology—the Space Age Science".

On return from Windsor to Detroit the same night, I was scheduled to speak at the Kannada Koota. The meeting had been arranged at the residence of the Chairman Mr. M. Krishnappa. Several Kannadigas, scattered within an area of 200 square miles, had come to the meeting to greet me. Mr. Krishnapppa said that he learnt about my visit to U.S. from Press reports of my lectures, etc. One Mr. Gurunath of Bangalore working in the Ford automobile factory at Detroit who phoned to me the previous day to Desplaines was very particular that I met the Kannadigas when I visited Windsor. I readily agreed. It is always a pleasure to be in the midst of your own countrymen. An address of welcome was presented to me by the Chairman and I spoke in Kannada on "The Duty of Indians Living in Foreign Countries".

The Kannada Koota is an association of all "lovers of Kannada living in America and Canada". The 'Koota' was started on 3rd April 1971. Within the short period of 18 months, it seems to have made considerable progress in the membership-drive and in starting branches in different U.S. Cities. The main object of the Sangha is the "cultivation of Kannada culture".

Kannadigas in Karnataka should extend full co-operation to this Koota. It was distressing to be told by the
President that it was very difficult for them to get free of
any expense even a good Kannada film from India, by
Air, and that some of the distributors wanted air freight,
etc., to be paid.

When Kannadigas, scattered in different parts of
America, want to get together for cultural meets and for
preserving, subject to the conditions obtaining in
America, appropriate aspects of their culture, it is the
duty of all patriotic Kannadigas — or for that matter all
Indians—to extend the best of help and co-operation.

I was much delighted to spend a couple of hours with
Kannadigas and this meeting is bound to remain indelible
for a long time.

Baltimore was the place of my next halt. Holiday Inn,
where I stayed for 2 days, attracted many visitors who
wanted to meet me. I had a busy schedule and delivered
two special lectures, one at the Aquarian University on
"Yoga Psychology" and the other at the Theosophical
Society on "The Spiritual Value of Astrology".

Baltimore, the chief city of Maryland, lies at the
head of tide-water upon the river Petopso. Blacks out-
number whites. The Mayor was also said to be a black.
John Hopkin's University is a major institution of higher
learning. There are two major arts galleries and also a
museum of local history. Baltimore is a city of large-scale
industry and is considered "the northernmost southern
city, the southernmost northern city, the westernmost
eastern city, and the easternmost western city". I visited
a number of historical places also.

On 29th September Mrs. Belle Carter and her fiance,
both Attorneys, drove me to New York, a distance of

about 140 miles. A crowded programme was passed through during my stay of over a week in New York.

A suite consisting of a bed room, drawing room and a kitchenette had been reserved for my use at Hotel Gramnarcy Park, where I stayed with my son Sri B. A. Kumar Babu, who was doing M. S. at Brooklyn Politechnic.

This time there was no food problem as Kumar Babu did the cooking and attended to all my personal comforts.

As chief guest at the luncheon meeting of the Rotary Club of Philadelphia I spoke on "Astrology and the Modern World". The Conference Hall where I spoke was jam-packed and after the lecture several Rotarians were heard commenting that "astrology could no more be considered a superstition". Mr. Russell Urqachart presided. The lecture was at 1–30 p.m. I reached Philadelphia at 1 p.m. by rail accompanied by Miss Uma Somerfield, who acted as my Private Secretary throughout my stay in New York and adjacent places.

Philadelphia the third city in population and fourth in manufactures in the United States has several celebrated structures and libraries. The Philadelphia Museum of Art provides a panoramic history of art. This is also the place of the American Philosophical Society, which has published recently some ancient books on astrology and an Ephemeris giving planetary positions for 5000 years.

After returning to New York, the same evening I spoke at the New York University on "Astrology and Spiritual Life". My another lecture at the same venue on the next day was on "Planetary Afflictions and Remedial Measures". The question hour was very lively and interesting.

In response to an invitation from Mr. Rao of the New York State University I drove to Albany on the 6th accompanied by my son A. K. Babu, my Secretary Uma Somerfield and Mr. Henry Weingarten of NASA. The subject of my lecture was on "Astrology and Atmospheric Sciences". Those present at the lecture included the Professors of astronomy and atmospheric sciences, a new name for meteorology.

"Pure Andhra food" offered by my hosts at Albany turned out to be a flop. The atmosphere was more American than Indian and I excused myself from taking the food. While the majority of Indian boys and girls in U.S. seem to be keeping up our food and social habits, there is also a small minority who slavishly ape the Westerners in all matters—food, social behaviour, entertainment and the mode of life. One of the Andhra gentleman I met hailing from Rajahmundry from an orthodox Brahmin family, seemed to me to be ultra-western, preserving nothing that is Hindu and Indian, except for his brown complexion.

Some of the Professors I met at New York State University expressed appreciation of ancient India's unique contribution to culture, science and civilization. They also felt there was much in the ancient lore of astrology which merited the attention of meteorologists. It seems some of their researches have revealed an incidence of correlation between Jupiterian movements and years rich in rainfall.

By the time we returned to New York it was 1 a.m. In the morning's New York papers, the weather forecast had predicted rainfall in the afternoon. But unfortunately we had a beautiful sun and there was no trace of rain until we left Albany. In the course of my lecture when I referred to the strange phenomenon of meteorologists' forecast of heavy rain but the skies being free from even thick clouds, the audience burst into laughter.

I met a few Mysoreans at Albany working as Engineers. Though fully qualified they could not get suitable jobs in India and they had to leave their motherland.

For two days, advanced courses in Hindu Astrology were held at new York Astrology Center. The teaching was restricted to about a dozen persons who were all well-versed in astrology and some of whom were practitioners with local and all-American reputation. The pupils were able to pick up some of the abstruse principles of Hindu astrology without much strain. One of the pupils was black, aged about 26 or 27. He was a bartender serving liquor and eatables in a way–side bar. But his interest in Karma theory and Hindu astrology was very pronounced. He never missed my lectures, always used to take careful notes and also tape-record the proceedings. He met me privately to have a discussion about his horoscope. Hailing from an obscure Negro family of Harlem he passed through bitter experiences of poverty, strife and persecution. His interest in astrology was roused, he said, when by chance a local astrologer he met a decade ago, read his past correctly. He said that his Jupiter was well placed in the meridian and this made him study astrology. Subsequently, he attended my lectures in 1970 and 1971 and decided to learn Hindu astrology. No astrologer among the blacks, he confessed, had a scientific grasp of the subject. He wished to become a leading astrologer from amongst the Blacks and a specialist in Hindu astrology. I assured him that most of his aspirations would be fulfilled. He believed in the theory of Karma. He hated the ignorance, the squalor and the crime which still persisted amongst the Negroes of New York.

I took leave of my son Kumar Babu on 9th October and arrived at Minneapolis in the State of Minnesota.

The City of Minneapolis is situated midway between the equator and the north-pole and adjacent to the City of St. Paul. The city lies on both sides of river Mississippi. The city is clean with wide streets and many fine public and business buildings. The main campus of the University of Minnesota lies on the east bank of the river and the Department of Sanskrit is headed by an Indian, who could not find time to attend my lecture though specially invited by my hosts. The leading papers are in English, I was told, but weeklies in Swedish and German are also published. I was interviewed by the Press about astrology, Indian Culture, Indian social life and the coming American elections and the interview was prominently published in the papers. My lecture at the auditorium of the Gnostic Society was on "The Social Function of Astrology". Mr. Carl Wascheck, Proprietor of Llewellyn Publications, took a leading part in arranging my visit to this beautiful city. The same night I was given a dinner by Mr. Wascheck. A number of Indians holding good positions are settled here.

The version of a Punjabi gentleman who was present at my lecture, as to the extenuating conditions which compel many a qualified Indian to wish good bye to their mother country merits the serious thinking of our rulers. He is a Ph.D. in Physics, was a scientific officer at I.I.T., Delhi. Sheer favouritism, casteism and political ideology and not academical distinction or merit, he said, weighed with the authorities in dealing with the staff-members. Disgusted with this, he resigned his job came to U.S. and at Minneapolis, he lectured at the University, has a textile shop and practises Palmistry. In his own words : "The people here are good and helpful. There is no restiction to pursue any avocation you like so long as you pay your taxes correctly. No licence, no permit, no harrassment of businessmen to curb initiative. Nobody in his senses would like to lead a miserable life in India !'' I tried to persuade him that his primary duty, no matter whatever be the economic and political conditions, was to India. Personal interest may have to be sacrificed a little for the sake of the country. I am sure, the gentleman would not have agreed with me.

My next halt was at Denver in the State of Colorado. Mrs. Eleanore Kimmel, President of the Cosmobiology Centre, was at the Air Port to receive me. A dinner in the evening, followed by a lecture at the Y.M.C.A. auditorium on "Hindu Astrological Techniques", discussions with several astrological groups and a Press Conference rounded off my visit to this place.

Denver is a pleasant place to visit. Its altitude is exactly one mile above the sea lying at the edge of the great Plains, in the river vally with rocks, mountains as a snow-capped background. The climate is said to be favourable throughout the year. The city has broad streets and a system of boulevards and parkways.

The Colorado State Capital situated in the center of the city is a massive structure of granite topped by a dome overlaid with gold. The civic centre is beautiful.

At Denver I met two Indian doctors, one a Gujarati and the other a Tamilian, working in the General Hospital. A middle-aged American nurse, mother of 3 children, showed me round the city in her car. Her main problem, as were the problems of the majority of women I met, was separation from her husband. She was herself an astrologer and some of the hospitals in Colarado, said this nurse, were using astrological diagnosis also, a statement I could not personally check up with the doctors.

12th, 13th and 14th October were packed with engagements in the city of San Francisco where I arrived on the 12th morning. Three lectures were delivered here, at Metaphysical Centre on "Hindu Astrology.", at Metaphysical Association on *"Political Astrology" and at the California Institute of Asian Studies on "Astrology and Spirtual Awakening" respectively. Groups of people, many of them University lectures, lawyers and doctors, interviewed me at my residence "Hotel Oxford". Among those that attend my lecture, quite a few had come from Los Angeles and other places. At my lecture at the California Institute I met Dr. Rama Murti Misra, M.D., who is now in U.S. propagating Hindu Philosophy and Yoga. Dr. Misra is a highly talented person. Disgusted with modern medicine—he has several foreign medical degrees—Dr. Misra said he was now back to the Indian way of tackling the human body and mind by the grand Hindu system of Yoga. His "Fundamentals of Yoga", a copy of which he presented me, is a masterpiece within its restricted scope.

After my lecture at the Metaphysical Foundation Centre, my hosts took me to an election meeting addressed

---

* In my lecture I dealt specially with the horoscopes of Nixon and Mc Govern and said that Nixon would be elected with a thumping majority but that he would not be able to complete his term because when Saturn transited he would be getting into a situation which he could not anticipated and which would result in his fall from power. Subsequent events have justified these forecasts. I was told that my prediction about Nixon secured wide press publicity in U.S.A. both when I made the prediction and when Nixon resigned.

A summary of the lecture was published as Leader article in the December 1972 issue of *The Astrological Magazine.*

by Democratic candidate McGovern who was then in San Francisco.

I must record my special thanks to Mr. Paul Grell, Secretary, American Federation of Astrologers, for over a decade and now engaged in astrological activities in San Francisco, and his wife for making my stay in their city enjoyable. Mr Grell drove me to almost all the important places of interest in and around San Francisco, the premier financial center of the Pacific Coast. San Francisco bay is said to be one of the finest harbours in the world. It looks as though the city itself is built on hills. Most streets are at right angles. Among the scenic boulevards are the Marina, Twin Peaks, Market Sreet Extension Lincoln, and Great Highway paralleling the Pacific Ocean. The Oakland Bay bridge and the Golden Gate bridge are great attractions. The former is said to be longest bridge in the world over navigable water. The city has several attractions for a visitor. After the immense havoc caused by the earthquake which occurred in this city on 18-4-1906, new structures were planned and a beautiful San Francisco arose from the debris.

My original plan was to spend a quiet day at Honolulu in the Pacific Island of Hawaii and do some sight-seeing. But one Mr. William Lindsay Spight telephoned the day before I was to leave San Francisco that I must consent to address a dinner meeting of the local astrological group as they wished to know something of Hindu astrology and astronomy.

I spent 40 hours in Hawaii. The first impression of Honolulu was that it could be a part of South India. Coconut trees line several roads and the Hawaians looked ethnologically closer to us, though, after Hawaii became one of the U.S. States, Americanism could be seen in all walks of life.

The dinner in the evening consisted of a variety of fruits, nuts and raw vegetables. The menu was prepared after ascertaining my taboos and habits. There were about 20 men and women guests, some claiming to be well-versed in Yoga and some in Hinduism and some in astrology. The Yogi teacher, a woman of about 30, demonstrated *asanas* satisfactorily and the party closed at midnight after which I was taken round Honolulu to have a glimpse of how the city looked during night. The city extends to about 12 miles along the shore and about 5 miles inland across a plain and up ridges and valleys to a mountain range 2 to 3 thousand feet high. There are many drives and parks, the largest being Kapivlani Park. Numerous palms, variegated croton shrubs, bouganville, Jacaranda trees, etc., varieties of hibiscus seem to render the whole city a botanical garden. There is an excellent art museum having extensive Polynesian collections. I paid a visit to the famous Pearl Harbour, which was attacked on 7th December 1941, involving America and Japan in mutual hostilities in the 2nd world war.

At a small party the next day, I was treated to a performance of Hawaii dancing. The Honolulu beach is held to be famous what with hundreds of tourists mostly from U.S. and Europe taking sunbaths and lying on the sands in nude and semi-nude states without any qualms of what Indians would call "decency", sipping tender cocoanuts.

Leaving Honolulu at 3 p.m. I flew into Tokyo by JAL 747 Jet at 6-20 p.m.

Pretty Japanese air hostesses, some dressed in kimano, were all attentive to first-class passengers. I was the only Indian travelling by first class. Strangly, though I had been assured by JAL Office at San Francisco that I would be provided with a fruit meal, the air hostess regretted no arrangement had been made for me and that she would serve whatever vegetarian food could be sorted out from the Japanese menu. I had to rest content with a cup of milk till reaching Tokyo.

Two special features attracted my attention, *viz.*, Japanese passengers talked only in their language and they were served only Japanese food, to be eaten with chop-sticks. Some of the Indian passengers, occupying the second class, were served, perhaps with European food and forks and spoons.

A Chinese businessman who was sitting next to me, was eating with chop-sticks and when I asked him what type of food the Japanese consumed. his answer was, apart from rice and vegetables, all sorts of sea-worms!

When we crossed the international line, the date changed. 15th October became 16th October so that one day in my longevity was lost! If I had flown from Tokyo to Honolulu 15th would have become 14th and I would have gained one day extra for my longevity! A certificate was issued to all passengers who were in the career just as the Jet was crossing the International date line.

Mr. *P. J. Rao, First Secretary of the Indian Embassy, met me at Tokyo Air Port and drove me to the Prince Hotel. Later in the night I had dinner. "pure vegetarian food," at the residence of Mr. Rao. Thanks to Mr. P. J. Rao, an Andhra Brahmin gentleman, my stay in Tokyo was enjoyable and fruitful.

The next morning I could do a lot of sight-seeing, thanks to the Indian Embassy, who provided me with a conveyance and an interpreter Mr. Waichiro Kawai. I visited the famous Buddha temple in Asakusa and was

---

*Mr. Rao is now the First Secretary, Permanent Mission, of India to United Nations, at New York

introduced to the chief priest. The temple is frequented by thousands of Japanese and tourists. The Hindu practice of removing footwear and washing hands and feet before entering the temple is continued. Incense is burnt as in Hindu temples and flowers offered at the altar. A Hindu feels quite at home in such an environment, unlike in a church where the environment looks alien. Mr. Kawai gave me a ride in the Tokyo Tube which, compared to the Tubes (underground trains) in London and New York, are more efficiently and punctually run. My guide explained that the Japanese, though westernised in drees and appearance, retained their age-old customs and values of life—respect for parents and elders, chastity and love of family life.

Tokyo is perhaps the largest city in the world and I propose to write my impressions of this visit as a separate book.

The Japanese have advanced economically and industrially to such an extent that they could compete successfully with the Americans in their own country. I visited some car and radio manufacturing concerns and was impressed by the stupendous advancemeut made in technology. It is remarkable how a country devastated by war just 25 years ago, could have recovered economically and financially to such an extent as to be at par with any technologically advanced country in Western Europe or America.

My lecture on *"Hindu Attainments in Positive Sciences" delivered under the auspices of the Japan-India Society evoked considerable interest amongst the educated Japanese. Dr. Yasamaki Nara, who presided on

---

* Published as Appendix IV

the occasion, expressed surprise that ancient India had
developed physical sciences (astrology included) to a
degree unmatched by any other nation of that time. The
same night the office-bearers of the Society hosted a
dinner in my honour at Hotel Fairmount. It was attended by a number of leading Japanese. Dr. Nara and the
other professors expressed the view that India's national
prestige could go up if the ancient national language,
viz., Sanskrit replaced English. For a people who have
never been ruled by any Western power—save for a brief
period of Americrn occupation after the second world
war and who have developed their own language in a
way capable of expressing the most advanced scientific
terminology, it seemed odd that an ancient nation like
India whose spiritul conquest of the whole of Asisa is an
acknowledged fact, should still be using an alien tongue.
Japanese are proud of their language and their attainments. Their economic policies are based on pragmatic
and not on ideological considerations.

Leaving Tokyo by Air India on 19th October, I was
back at my hometown Bangalore the next day. But for
the grace of Almighty, my fourth trip in Europe, America and Japan from the point of view of propagating
Hindu astrology and certain aspects of Indian Culture
could not have been as successful as it turned out to be.

Before concluding this chapter, I think I should revise
my earlier views (expressed in Chapter 15) after the 1970,
1971 and 1972 trips, about the customs inspection in
India. Both while leaving India and on returning to
India, the Customs official were more courteous and the
procedure adopted was also simple. I do not think I
would like to change my opinion as regards the usefulness of Indian Embassy officials towords visiting Indians,
though there were exceptions as in Amsterdam and Tokyo.

In 1970, the Public Relations Officer of our embassy at Washington had written that he "could get together a couple of reporters from Washington newspapers" to meet me "along with correspondents of the Indian newspapers". But when we arrived in Washington and when one of the correspondents of a leading Indian newspaper tried to contact the official, he was conspicuously absent from Washington ! Of course a press Conference was held at Hotel Roger Smith in spite of the official's bungling. Similarly in important cities like London, Paris and Rome the embassy attitude was generally cold.

During 1971 and 1972 visits, Air India was quite helpful in catering to my requirements. But still I should like to make a few remarks about our well-known national Airline.

Except perhaps for the dress of the hostesses and some window decorations, there does not appear to be anything Indian. The reputation Air India has earned for its excellent airworthiness should be matched by a certain degree of efficiency and Indianness. When I checked in a New York Air Port (in 1971) for our return journey as a first class passenger, I was ushered into the "Maharaja lounge". I had a few American and Indian friends with me who had come to see me off. When alcoholic drinks were offered, I preferred to have milk or coffee.. The mini-skirted girl in charge of the 'bar'—she was either American or English but not Indian—asked my friends, "Do not people Drink in India?" Air India should correctly brief its employees regarding the social customs, food habits, etc., of Indians, the vast majority of whom still do not drink.

The atmosphere is thoroughly Western whether inside the carrier or in any of the Air India Offices at London, New York or Paris. As you enter the plane, you are

15

treated to Western music and not to Indian music. A conservative Hindu—and there are thousands of such Hindus who visit foreign countries—is made to feel embarrassed when vegetarian and non-vegetarian dishes are brought on the same trolley and served to passengers. A Hindu passenger, who was sitting behind, remarked that he was being served only with western food. Another feature we noticed was that the stewards and air hostesses bestowed more attention on foreign nationals. This inferiority complex must go. When an American passenger was greeted with *namaste* by the Air Hostess, he asked the steward : "Namaste is very graceful. What does it mean?" The steward said it was a religious symbol! I corrected him and said it was a dignified and graceful way of greeting.

The Managers of Air India at New York, London and Paris do not seem to bestow much attention on the requirements of Indian passengers. They could be more courteous instead of being self-centered. On the contrary the Managers at Rome, Zurich, Geneva and Frankfurt were very co-operative and helpful.

There appears to be no co-ordination between Air India and Indian Air Lines in the matter of providing accommodation to International passengers whose destination is not Bombay. It would be worthwhile investigating if there is any racket behind the denials of immediate connections from Bombay.

It is hoped the authorities of Air India will spare no pains not only to make the atmosphere within the carriers and their counters in cities like New York and Paris more Indian and also cater more satisfactorily to the requirements of Indian passengers. They will also do well to brief their overseas employees about the culture, manners, social life and food and drink habits of the majority of Indians as different from the minority of westernised ladies and gentlemen.

22 Fifth Visit to U.S.A.

Accompanied by Rajeswari Raman, I arrived at Paris on 9th May 1981 at 6–30 a.m. by Air France, leaving Bombay on the 8th at 12–30 a.m. The flight was quite smooth. Amongst the 4 or 5 Indian passengers travelling with us in the 1st class, were the film magnate Raj Kapoor and his son. We exchanged a few thoughts with Mr. Raj Kapoor.

As usual the first class passengers were busy helping themselves with champaign and other varieties of liquors, some of them had already become inebriated.

Inspite of the assurances given to us by the Bangalore and Bombay representatives of Air France, our food requirements—good milk and raw vegetables and fruits—were not properly attended to. It is a pity that while Air India and Indian Airlines sometimes even go out of the way to satisfy the food requirements of European passengers, the European air lines, inspite of loud publicity given by them in the press about the availability of Indian food show themselves helpless in meeting even the sparion requirements of passengers like me.

Accommodation for our stay had been reserved at Hotel Meridien, 81 Blvd.Couryia St., Cyrtela,Paris. But still we had some problems. We were dropped at a place two furlongs away from the Hotel and language was the main hurdle in our way of locating the hotel. A French professor who happened to know English helped us. This casual acquaintance resulted in the professor arranging on the 10th May a group meeting of some local astrological savants and intellectuals at the Hotel lounge.

The theme of my talk was "Astrology and Determinism".

I said that if astrology was completely deterministic, as some of its opponents wrongly supposed it to be, this argument might carry some weight. But according to Hindu sages, astrology depended upon the tendency of earthly events to run parallel with certain configurations in the heavens. There is analogy without determinism.

After explaining the philosophical basis of astrology, I set forth the cosmological background of the Hindu Yoga theory which placed men in true perspective in relation to the universe, showing how ill-founded were the objections which had been brought forward to controvert the astrological point of view. I said that it was lamentable that in certain scientific and religious circles in the West, astrology was still regarded as a pernicious error. This was mainly due to the ignorance of the ecclesiastics and the scientists who took a purely materialistic view of the universe.

Dealing with modern psychology, I explained briefly the many psychological schools which differed and wrangled and which, when compared to the profundity of yogic attainments in probing the mysteries of the mind and emotions, was still in an elementary stage. Quoting Dr. Jung, I said that while Indian sages trained their minds in introspective psychology for thousands of years, the Europeans began their psychology, as Dr. Jung said, "not even yesterday but only this morning".

Illustrating on the basis of the horoscopes of Hitler, Mussolini, etc., I pointed out the peculiar structure of their psyche and how certain planetary groupings were responsible in making them resort to aggressive wars and how, if their mental dispositions had been known earlier, their aggressive designs could have been given less play.

Dealing with the theory of Karma *vis-a-vis* astrology, I pointed out that the horoscope indicated the trend of future events to happen—some sort of a blue print—and that with suitable effort, the evils could be minimised to some extent or the good augmented.

Concluding my talk, I commended the profound discipline of Yoga and astrology to the attention of the French thinkers.

Mrs. Rajeswari Raman, in her brief exposition of Yoga, pointed out how with the aid of certain yogic techniques, she was able to give relief to a number of ladies in regard to their physical and emotional troubles.

Mrs. Elizabeth Teisser, a well-known astrologer in Paris called on us to seek some clarifications on Hindu astrology. She took us round Paris and we spent an hour at her residence. She had a computer for casting horoscopes and within a couple of minutes she was able to cast my and Mrs. Raman's horoscopes.

I explained to her that computers could enable one only to save time but prediction was an art which only a trained and experienced human being could handle.

Another friend Elechuri Venkatakrishna Rao, an Andhra settled in Paris, and married to an Argentine lady was much helpful to us. He and his wife took us to the famous Versailles and other places of interest.

Versailles is 12 miles west of Paris. It is famous for the grand palace built by Louis the XIV. We spent nearly three hours in this grand structure. The church of Notre Dame is also nearby. In the great court of the palace stands the statues of Riche Lieu, Conde and other famous Frenchmen. The palace contain galleries and halls of historical pictures and sculptures and other apartments, the most famous of which is theatre built under Louis XV. The banquet to the Gardes du Corps, the toasts at which provoked riots that drove Louis XVI from Versailles, is the most famous historically. It was again here that the National Assembly met from 10th March 1871 till the proclamation of the constitution in 1875 and the Senate from 8th March to 1876 till the return of the two Chambers to Paris in 1879.

The queen's apartments and the rooms of Louis XIV are on the first floor. The ante-room where the courtiers waited till the King rose is quite attractive. It leads to the bed room in which Louis XIV died and which Louis XV occupied from 1722 to 1738.

The Gallery of the Republic and the First Empire is in the south wing on the ground floor. There is also the room where the Chamber of Deputies met from 1876 to 1879.

Then there are the beautiful gardens, the ground falling away on either side from a terrace adorned with ornamental basins, statues and bronze groups. The marble statues are remarkable for their fine sculptures. It is said there are 1200 croya trees in the garden. The alleys of the park are ornamented with statues, voes and regularly cut yews and bordered by hedges surrounding the shrubberies.

Versailles is also famous for the "treaty of peace" that was signed at the close of World War I by the representatives of the Allied and Associated powers and of Germany on 28th June 1917.

The palace is a magnificent marble structure, comparable perhaps to the palaces of Jaipur and Udaipur.

We went round the town of Versailles and also visited the church of Notre Dame.

Leaving Paris on 11th May 1981 at 13 hours by Air France we arrived at New York at 3-30 p.m. A number of friends and admirers received us at the Kennedy Air Port, and were taken to Park Meridien Hotel for our stay. Miss Uma Somerfield and Henry Weigarten attended to our comforts and were of much help to us.

On the 12th May 1981 I addressed a luncheon meeting of the New York Lions Club on the "Role of Astrology in Modern Times". After dealing with the evolution of astrological and astronomical thought in India I explained the significance of astrology in relation to day-to-day matters and how in regard to judging compatability in marriage, partnership in business etc., horoscopes could play a vital role in enabling one to select a right partner. After the lectures several Lions were heard remarking that astrology was something more than sun-sign readings doled out in the popular media and that Hindu astrology could be of much popular value.

In the evening we visited the New York Astrology Center and Saw a demonstration of casting horoscopes by computer. I was informed that most of the astrology—computers in U.S.A. were designed to cast sidereal horoscope also on the basis of what they called "Raman Ayanamsa".

The next morning in response to an invitation by Swami Muktananda of 'Ganeshpuri, Bombay, we were driven to his Ashram at South Falsburg by Mr. Henry Madden, an ex-movie actor and presently famous in the New York theatre world. During our two hour discussion I felt that Mr. Madden was deeply interested in Hindu philosophy and Yoga. Mr. Madden told us that whatever money conferred on him—comforts, name, fame, influence—did not satisfy his soul and he had felt that he was lacking something which could give him happiness. The way was shown by Swami Muktananda and he now felt, Mr. Madden said that real joy consisted in making others happy, sharing our happiness with others and seeking solace in spiritual values.

I and Mrs. Raman had a private meeting with Swami Muktananda. I felt that the Swamijee was an evolved soul and that he was indeed doing remarkable work in carrying the message of India to the West. The Ashram was spacious. In the big compound, statues of Lord Siva, Adi Sankara etc., had been prominently installed. The atmosphere was thoroughly Hindu. Scores of American desciples of the Swamiji we met said that the Swamiji enabled them to secure peace of mind and that they were all now after transcendental truths. A vegetarian kitchen run by American disciples provides healthy food. Much credit goes to Mr. Chakrapani Ullal for arranging our meeting with the Swamiji. His health was not good and he had some problem. In a general discussion of his horoscope I had hinted that *1982–83 might be critical for him.

Immediately after returning from South-Falseburg another important engagement awaited us, a meeting at the Ganapati Temple in New York arranged by the local *Kannada Koota*. The temple precincts had been jam packed with *Kannadigas* and non-*Kannadigas* and some American friends also drawn from various walks of life were present. As the meeting was convened by the *Kannada Koota*, I preferred to speak in Kannada. But the audience consisted of a large number of non-Kannadigas. It was decided that I should speak in English and Mrs. Raman in Kannada.

Speaking on "Hindu doctrines and modern thinking", I dealt with the evolution of Indian thoughts, philo-

---

* Swami Muktananda passed away at Bombay in 1983.

sophical and scientific from the beginning of Kaliyuga. I said : "the flowering of ancient Indian genius produced an array of disciplines that the West could only think of in later days of renaissance and some of them had not yet had any parallel in the whole gamut of European thought, ancient or modern".

. I said the theory of Aryan immigration into India made by a section of modern historians was "arrant nonsesnse", and that it had played a great deal of havoc in encouraging disintegration of political forces. The so-called Aryans and Dravidians were all original inhabitants of India and were natives of no other foreign country.

. Dealing with the scientific advancements made in ancient India, I detailed their attainments in astronomy, medicine etc.

I said "an image has been created not only by a section of Western scholars but also by an influential section of their Indian counterparts that all that ancient India could boast of in matters of science was a reflection of early Greek civilisation and that the Indians were only hair-splitting philosophers, not conversant with the so-called positive sciences, and that ancient India had neither scientific talent nor a scientific outlook".

I observed that even 22 years after the dawn of political independence, our educated people, particularly our youth, continued to be nurtured on the fantastic theories of a superstition-ridden ancient India. The distorted notions of history entertained by a section of our influential leadership–political, social and even educational– stood as a formidable barrier to an impartial and scholarly appreciation of her well-founded claims in scientific superiority at an age when the rest of the world, including

Europe which today boasted of a high material civilisation, was steeped in ignorance.

I gave plenty of textual detail in support of my
thesis, both from Indian and foreign sources. From
Paninian linguistics to mathematical theories, the whole
fascinating field of Indian thought and scientific endeavour
was replete with originality and achievement.   From
astronomical speculations to the concept of illness as an
expression of the personality of the patient, there was
hardly an area where Indians of yore did not strike an
original and surprisingly modern note. In fact it had
taken all the advance in space and nuclear sciences to
appreciate the daring concepts of ancient Indians. They
were not content to remain idle speculators, I observed,
but had attained heights of glory which shed lustre all
over Asia and beyond and gave meaning and content to
millions of people.

Making a passing reference to the importance and
uniqueness of astrological achievement of ancient Indians
I pleaded for restoring Indology to its rightful place in any
scheme of educational reform.

Mrs. Raman spoke on the need for Yoga and the
duty of Indian womanhood based in western countries.
She cautioned her sisters that they should all consider
themselves as ambassadors of Indian womanhood, which
stood tolerance, motherhood, patience, and a happy
sharing pursuits with her husband. She said that even
today in India it was the mother that was really the pivot
of family life, and the mother always occupied a superior
place. She wanted Indian women settled in the west to
preserve the best in our culture and imbibe the best in
western culture. She however emphasised that life values
as understood and practised by our fore-fathers should
never be bothered away in the name of modernism,

progressivism etc.—words coined by those who lacked roots in their own culture.

Dr. Chandrasekhar, President of the Koota presided.

On the 14th we flew into Chicago and were warmly received at O'Hera Airport by our son and daughter-in-law Dr. and Mrs. Sureshwara and driven to their home at Lake Zurich.

On the 16th at a get-together arranged by Dr. and Mrs. Sureshwara attended by a cross section of the Indian community consisting of medical men, engineers, professors and business magnetes, Mrs. Raman gave a demonstration talk on the need for Yoga in daily life.

Explaining the importance of yoga Mrs. Raman said: "Yoga is typical of Indian civilisation in the concern for the whole personality of man and his upliftment. Whatever be the immediate focus, no Indian discipline or endeavour ever divorces itself from the main stream of life. Yoga is an example for *excellence*. The discipline of Yoga has its rigors, particularly because it helps man to become a better individual in all his human splendour. It provides no happy escapist outlets. To make a person truly human has always been the most difficult task in this world. Yoga attempts to achieve this with a unique flair of its own".

Mrs. Raman observed that man was an instruement and Yoga realising this sought to perfect this instrument for the betterment of the individual. Man had always been more than a mere structure of bones, muscles, nerves, etc., with a brain atop. He had been more than an individual and mere than a social being. Yoga was aware of this trend and tug of forces beneath the surface of human existence and had oriented itself in that general direction. All the while it never lost sight of its immediate objective of making man a true measure of things, things outside and things inside, she said.

Even as a physical exercise, Mrs. Raman said, Yoga was incomparably great and far beyond the reach of any known system. Many a person in the rough and tumble of modern life might not have the time or inclination to reach out for the spiritual horizons that Yoga unfolded but *asanas* or it coupled with a little of *dhyana* or meditation was of utmost relevance particularly today. It put man at peace with himself and at ease with his environment. Asanas toned up muscles and nerves and by regulating the internal secretions so vital to life but so difficult to reach, made man a better image of himself. By tapping the vast reservoirs of vitality that lay hidden deep inside, it supplied his deficiencies, and catered to his vital needs. With the help of Asanas, a practitioner was able to give a better account of himself circumscribed though he might be by birth and heredity. It gave him self-confidence and human dignity, she pointed out.

In conclusion, Mrs. Rajeswari Raman said that Yoga was a package deal for man's physical betterment, social well-being and spiritual uplift. What more could one bargain for, she asked.

After her talk, she gave a demonstration of some important techniques including the different methods of *Pranayama*. She exhorted the ladies (and the gentlemen too) to practice Yoga regularly so that the health of the body and the mind was assured.

In the course of my lecture on the Relevance of Astrology, I explained the high level of ancient Hindu astronomical and philosophical attainments and how the common factor between philosophy and astrology was the theory of Karma.

I said that the entire fabric of Hindu astrology rested on the broad principle of evolution in time. The Hindu astrologer believed that man's actions in this world had a long tie with his moral principles. To him this cult seemed to conform with perfect logic. Being guided by a series of observations and intuition he had discovered that certain mathematical coordinates gave satisfactory answers to his queries regarding the divining of future events. According to Indian tradition the horoscope–indicated the results of past karma.

Regarding the present-day thinking, I pointed out that the trend of modern scientific thought seemed to have failed to take note of a unique branch of knowledge that linked man with the celestial order. It was only astrology that tried to tackle the problems of life in its various aspects. Where the basic issue of free will versus determinism was involved, astrology went to the root of the matter.

I further continued: Despite astronomy being an "exact" but costly science, the greatest of astronomers differed as to the fundamental question whether the universe was finite or infinite but were agreed on there being billions of universes which certainly was no improvement on the ancient Indian concept that regarded God as the lord of billions of universes—*akhilanda koti brahmanda nayaka.*

Speaking about the great antiquity of Indian civilisation and culture and its theory of *maha yugas* or cosmic cycles which was evidence of the highly developed scientific thought amongst ancient Indians, I said that it was not safe to assume as correct the western habit of tracing the origin of Hindu astrology or Hindu astronomy to Greecian or Chaldean sources. There was hardly a modern science or discipline that the ancient Hindus did not tackle.

Comparing the western approach to the ancient Indian approach, I said that the knowledge of the ancient Hindus was far more deeply based on and intimately correlated to the realities of life than dreamt of in modern times. Particularly Yoga, Vedanta (philosophy) and Jyotisha (astrology) were fully systematised and completely developed. Long before the time of Egyptian, Babylonian and Grecian civilisations, the Hindu studied astrology in a scientific manner and had invented algebra and trigonometry to suit their studies.

According to tradition, I said, Astrology was propounded by the sages but sage Parasara's work formed the basis of Hindu astrology. At least 5000 years ago, Jyotisha was planned and developed entirely by Indian genius. Derived from the Vedas, astrology was rooted in Hindu philosophy and tried to determine the relationship which the present individual life bore to the whole. The theory of karma was based on cause and effect relationship on the physical, mental and moral planes.

Karma operated through a series of births till moksha was attained. There were three categories of Karma— *sanchita* the accumulative, *prarabdha* the operative and *aagami* the prospective—and the horoscope indicated the *prarabdha*. Therefore the astrological predictions were tendencies on their way to fulfilment.

Instancing proofs of the correlations between luni-solar movements and human psychological phenomena, I observed that the ancient Hindus considered the eighth lunar day as best for commencing medical treatment, which corroborated with the modern observation that on that day the Sun and the Moon, the two big pulls on the earth, being 90 degrees apart diminished each other's attractions on fluids and the blood in the human beings remained comparatively undisturbed.

The 14th lunar day with the two luminaries about 170 degrees apart marked a critical phase for skin diseases, insanity, epilepsy etc. So was the 29th lunar day.

Birth could only occur when certain cosmic radiations could materialise within the fertilised egg and deaths preponderated near and about the full Moon and new Moon days. Great significance was attached to birth in specific constellations and Hindus classified human beings corresponding to 30 lunar days and 27 constellations, which enabled one to construct a fairly accurate picture of an individual, his temperament, his likes and dislikes, his weaknesses and his abilities.

Delting with the remedial or curative aspect of Hindu astrology which regarded disease, mental worries or spiritual affliction as resultant of past karma and prescribed specific remedial measures such as medicines, *mantras* and yogic practices, I said that even when viewed from a purely scientific angle the horoscope could be considered as the mathematical interpretation of the energy—quanta with which the human system—biological and psychological, was endowed.

Concluding my lecture, I said : "Hindu astrology in its original form is being most successfully used all over India. In view of the differing social and cultural traditions in the West, some of the principles required re-formulation to suit the changed conditions—political, social and economic—in the modern times.

Dr. Sureshwara introduced me and his mother to the audience in choice words breathing respect and regard for his parents.

On 17th May we were driven to Cedar Rapids by our fourth son B. A. Kumar Babu, who is working in U.S.A. as a computer scientist. We spent a few days with Kumar Babu and his wife who took care of our comforts and returned to Lake Zurich on the 22nd. During our stay at Cedar Rapids, Kumar Babu took us to the computer-centre and explained the working of different types of computers.

On the 23rd, Dr. Sureshwara drove us to Cleveland. After a night's halt there, we arrived at Pittsburg, Pennsylvania and had the Darshan of Lord Venkateswara. The temple built on a small hill can compare favourably with the Thirupati temple. I found the *archakas*, who hailed from Hyderabad, well versed in the performance of various types of *sevas*. Every Hindu must feel proud that a Venkateswra temple has been built in U.S.A., thanks to the devotion, interest and munificence of the Hindus settled there. We were informed that the Hundi collections in the temple every week were to the tune of about four thousand dollars or so. Sri Venkateswara Temple at Pittsburg, Ganesha Temple at New York, the Meenakshi Temple at Houston have already become nucleii of Hindu spiritual activities, affording Hindus living in U.S.A. opportunities to satisfy their spiritual and cultural quest. America is indeed secular in the sense that freedom of worship has been guaranteed. We learnt that some fundamentalist Christian priests and institutions were subtly working against the establishment of Hindu institutions. But the American public in general appear to be free from any religious fanaticism. In fact an increasing number of American people are becoming conscious of the fact that Hindu philosophy and Hindu religious practices are not dogmas but represent a unique approach to God-head which could be attained by any one, irrespective of what his own religion may be. The Karma theory and the doctrine of reincarnation offer the most rational explanation of the incongruitics and inconsistent genacies found in our lives and how, in the final analysis, we alone are the authors of our weels and woes in this life. I found that most Indians who were generally indifferent towards their cultural and religious practices while in India had changed their outlook in America and had become staunch temple-goers.

But in India itself some of our educated persons in the name of psuedo-rationalism, pseudo-scientific outlook and pseudo-progressivism, and clutching to theories, fashionable in the west 25 years ago, are putting up an air of superiority looking down upon the vast majority of people believing in traditional values. Nearly 40 years have elapsed since the dawn of political independence. But paradoxically, many educated persons are still not free from intellectual slavery.

One need not be surprised if in the near future the Hindu way of life and Hindu beliefs come back to us via the West, especially U.S.A.

A number of engagements in Illinois, Texas, Florida, Virginia and California had to be cancelled as we were prevailed upon to rest for a few days by our sons and daughters-in-law who spared no pains to make our visit pleasant and enjoyable.

On 28th May 1984 we were seen off at the Chicago Air Port by our sons and daughters-in-law. Reaching Paris on the 29th morning and halting there for a couple of hours we left for Bombay and returned to Bangalore on 30th afternoon.

16

APPENDIX I
Astrology in India

Address delivered at the Special Conference organised by
the Astrologers' Guild of America, at Hotel Astor,
New York, on 11–10–1959

Ladies and Gentlemen,

It is indeed a great pleasure to meet you all. I feel it
a privilege to have been considered worthy enough by my
esteemed friend Mr. Charles Jayne Jr. to address this
special Conference of astrologers. I ventured to accept
his kind invitation because of the conviction that it gave
me one more opportunity to place before American astrologers, a picture, however inadequate, of an important
aspect of Indian Culture, *viz.*, Astrology, which even
today has been playing a vital role in the lives of millions
of Indians. When Mr. Jayne left the subject of the
address to my discretion, I felt a bit embarrassed for a
time, but after a little reflection it occurred to me that a
general lecture on 'Astrology in India' would be instructive to my esteemed audience.

Before taking up the subject matter of the address, I
feel I must tell you something about the general cultural
and astronomical background of the ancient Hindus.
India is the house of an ancient but still vital civilisation
which differs to some extent from the civilisation of the
West. The civilisation of India is the greatest factor in

the lives of people who today number one-fifth of the human race and perhaps it would be no exaggeration to say that this civilisation is India, because it provides the common basis which gives the whole country a fundamental unity. Tens of centuries before the Christian era, India had attained proficiency in almost all branches of knowledge secular and spiritual. Whether in positive sciences or philosophical speculations. Hindu ideas and methodology have deeply influenced the current of thought both in Asia and Europe. No other country, except perhaps China, can trace back its language and literature, its sciences and arts, its religious beliefs and rites, its domestic and social customs through an uninterrupted development of more than five thousand years.

In the recent times, however, the political subjugation of India stood as a barrier to an impartial appreciation of her well-founded claims to her high cultural attainments in ancient times. Any dispassionate student of history, after making a thorough study of the indigenous sources, can easily come to the conclusion that the Hindus have evolved an independent civilisation and a culture of remarkable continuity which have been preserved even unto this day with superficial and surface changes due to the impact of modern industrial and technological onslaughts.

In surveying the history of astronomy from the earliest times to the present day, modern astronomers sign to have completely ignored the contribution of Hindu astronomers, and the vast strides made by them in astronomy for nearly five thousand years, have been dispensed with the epithet that the "Hindus received their astronomical knowledge from the Greeks". I do not think that except for a few oriental scholars like Bailey and .Mon. Williams, any serious attempts have at all been made to

probe into the antiquity and nature of Hindu astronomical conceptions, which can be done only by getting into
the original sources. In modern India, as in ancient
India, the same term *Jyotisha* is used both for astrology
and astronomy.

Ancient Hindu Achievements

It has been suggested that the age of Copernicus saw
the transition from the astronomy of the ancients to the
astronomy of the moderners. We are told that before
Copernicus it was believed by most people, including the
popes and emperors, that the earth stood still, that the
Sun and the stars revolved round it and that the Universe
was controlled by some external power. And of course
whoever denied this theory was a heretic. Such conceptions might have existed in the Europe of middle ages. But
the case was different in India. Copernicus lived in the
15th century. At least a thousand years before Copernicus, the Hindu astronomer Aryabhatta, was upholding
what he called the ancient theory that the rising and
setting of the planets and stars were due to the movements
of the earth while the still more ancient astronomers had
already propounded a conception of an inherent natural
order. Of course, this conception was nobler than Newton's mechanical view of the Universe. They were fully
conversant not only with the astronomical laws regulating
the movements of the celestial bodies but had also formu-
lated spiritual and moral laws corresponding to these
physical laws. Hindu astrological, astronomical and
philosophical thought will be found to be remarkably
consistent with science. This claim may seem strange to
those whose knowledge of Indian Culture has been derived
from books written by certain oriental scholars whose
sole aim was to trace Indian Culture to Roman or
Grecian sources. The Hindus believed that the Universe

or *Brahmanda* is non-mechanical and that it is the result of a gradual unfolding of the creative power inherent in the primordial substance. As you all know, the intelligently ordered and the non-mechanical nature of the Universe is being increasingly endorsed by modern science. Ancient astronomical literature reveals that the Hindus were not only well versed in observational astronomy but had also entered the borders of abstract conception. One of the most important features of Hindu learning is that important truths of astronomy, astrology, yoga and medicine, are always kept veiled. The Vedic hymns and other astronomical and astrological works are composed in a formula of speech which could be understood only by the initiated and which taken in an outward sense carefully covered their true meaning and secret. Indian astronomical thought has its firm roots in the *Vedas*—the most ancient literature of the world. The theory of Yugas which has as its basis the general conjunction of planets is not without its cosmological significance. And the *Suryasiddhanta*, the most important work on Hindu astronomy which even to this day is held in great esteem, which is supposed to be at least 3 to 4 thousand years old and which, as is evident from the very first chapter, is said to reveal only the 'secret' knowledge contained in the *Vedas*, gives what is called the circumference of the celestial ellipse which more or less corresponds to galactic universe of today, as 18,712,080,864, 000,000 Yojanas or roughly 16000 light years and the age of the solar system as (195,58,85,060) about 1956 million years. Even amongst contemporary cosmologists— Eddington, Jeans, Einstein, de Sitter, there is no unanimity on any vital aspects. That as early as five thousand years ago, the Hindus could have imagined the earth to be about 2000 million years old and the galactic universe to be 16,000 light years, speaks volumes in favour of their gigantic intellectual achievements. E. M. Plunkett in his book *Ancient Calendars and Constellations* writes : "The opinion of the Greek writers at the beginning of the Christian era may be quoted as showing the high estimate in which Indian astronomy was held. In the life of *Appolonius of Tyana* the Greek astrologer and philosopher, written by Philostratus about 200 A.D. the wisdom and learning of Appolonius are set high above his contemporaries because he had studied astronomy and astrology with the sages of India".

And all these astronomical achievements of the Hindus were only a means to an end, the end being the development of astrology. Hindu astrology has been founded upon the fact that human life is intimately connected and interwoven with the motions of the cosmos. Another feature of ancient India was that religion, science, philosophy, and art proceeded on a common ground and formed a harmonious unity.

Philosophical Basis of Astrology

I do not know, what astrologers here say by way of philosophic basis for this science but I would like to tell you something about what Indian astrology has to say in this regard, for, without understanding the philosophical basis of astrology, one cannot understand the significance of astrological prediction.

According to Hindu astrological and philosophical works, the basis of human existence is an intricate network or inter-relation of events and actions on all planes — physical, mental and moral. The law by which the individual progresses towards *Moksha* or spiritual liberation is the *Karma* or action in the sense of cause-effect and their intimate relationships. The *Karma* doctrine in a way is akin to Newton's third law of motion that action and reaction are equal and opposite; but applied to moral and mental realms of life. Whatsoever we are reaping today, we have sown in the past, may be in this life or in the life or lives previous. The man who suffers the effects is the man who generates the effects. If I think ill of others, I generate evil *Karma* and I have to suffer the consequences of this evil *Karma*. Therefore by controlling my thoughts I can regulate my *Karma* also. *Karma* is thus antithesis of Fatalism. There is a blue print of my future life in this birth, as a consequence of my action— good, bad, and indifferent—done in the past lives and my horoscope just reveals what these consequences would be.

While the horoscope indicates past *Karma*—the *Prarabdha* or the operative portion of the *Karma* being our destiny in this life, the expression of these indications as events would follow certain sequence in accordance with the movements of planets. Thus if as a result of past Karma one is to lose one's child in his 45th year, in the horoscope of such a person, there would be a certain grouping of planets indicating the event. It is not the view of the Hindu sages that the Sun, the planets and stars are just dead matter rushing about under the pull of blind forces. On the physical plane, we do find planets influencing terrestrial affairs. But as ancient works on Hindu electional astrology make it clear, every moment has a certain special quality, and you may call it occult, if you like, which is akin to the ego that enters the terrestrial life as a separate being on that moment.

Fate and Free Will

Hindu astrology does not suggest man's subordination to something that is absolutely predestined. The planets by themselves do not bring about human destiny. They give an indication. Man has got a certain circumscribed scope in life but within that scope it is upto him to work out his best by recourse to remedial measures, which have also been suggested in ancient books. A man s destiny is forged by his *Karma*, the effect of his actions in the past. There is a perpetual tug-of-war between free-will and destiny and our actions at any moment are a resultant of these two forces. In the ordinary man, free-will is not very strong. His actions in life will, therefore, correspond, to a very large extent, to the forecast given by his horoscope. But, in the case of persons of great spiritual development, there will be some variation, even though the general pattern will remain the same as indicated by the horoscope. In this world of relativity, neither fate nor free-will could be supreme. It is some sort of a conditional liberty which man enjoys.

Astroloy and Modern Science

Some people go so far as to say that astrology is not a science because some of the scientists still regard as fantastically improbable the fact that the relative positions of celestial bodies could have anything to do with the intricate drama of human lives played on the earth. If by the term science is meant an organised body of knowledge, then astrology is certainly a science. It cannot be an exact science in the sense of Physics or Chemistry because the latter deals with only matter whereas astrology is concerned with life and its activities and therefore it is much more than a science. In Sanskrit astrology is called by the term *Hora Sastra* or the Science of Time as it unravels what is contained in Time. Astrologers can certainly produce demonstrable proof in support of their claims that correlations exist between certain planetary groupings in a horoscope and the nature of results likely to happen in the life of person concerned But he may not be able to present proof in terms of known laws of science. But that is no reason why astrology should be treated lightly.

Sidereal Basis of Hindu Astrology

The Hindus use a Zodiac which remains fixed in position with reference to the stars, while western astrologers use a zodiac that remains fixed with reference to the equinoxes. The Hindu seers knew that the precession of the equinoxes produced an ever-changing relationship between the constellations and the degrees of the movable zodiac and consequently founded their system of predictions upon the fixed or sidereal zodiac. The Sanskrit terms *Sayana* or with precession and *Nirayana* or without precession, used in the most ancient books are self-explanatory. According to the advocates of the movable zodiac, not only the planets move in their orbits from day to day but also the ecliptic in its circuit amid the stars and constellations so much so that if the degrees of the movable zodiac have anything to do with influencing the destiny of man, they derive from the vernal equinox to which they stand at a constant relation but not from the stars and constellations which constitute only an ever-varying environment for them. It will thus be seen that the Hindu fixed Zodiac is sidereal in its basis and conception while the western zodiac is solar if not equinoctial in its origin and construction. It is a matter for investigation whether the western conception of the astrological zodiac has any sanction in the writings of Ptolemy who is usually regarded as the father of European astrology and who was so much indebted to India for the astrological canon that he has handed down to posterity. The sidereal basis of the Hindu Zodiac brings into relief the relative importance which the ancient Indian sages have assigned to the remote stars and hence to other Suns than ours, in shaping human destiny inspite of their lively consciousness of circumstance that our immediate overlord is our own magnificent Sun. These adepts were better aware than the

modern astronomers, of the shifting character of the
equinoctial point and the facility it afforded as a landmark
for noting the position of celestial objects and the further
calculations that were deducible therefrom. But, as I have
already said, the means of astronomy were by no means
the ends nor even the methods of astrology and hence the
help which the shifting vernal equinox afforded in fixing
readily the celestial latitude and longitude of the planets
did not induce the Hindu astrologers to mistake its vocation and dignify it to the position of the vital centre of
astrological zodiac. To the Hindu, the fixed zodiac is a
perennial sidereal sphere with definite constellations and
star points to indicate the range and limits of its various
mansions. The twelve signs of the sidereal zodiac, the 27
asterisms and the 9 planets which exclude the trans-
saturnine bodies but include the Moon's Nodes–form the
basis of all Hindu predictive art.

Main Features

There are three schools of predictive astrology, *viz*.,
Parasara, Jaimini and the Nadi. Parasara is perhaps the
most widely used system and it has its own distinct
methodology of interpretation, which varies to some
extent from the other two.

I shall touch on a few important features pertain
ing to Hindu astrology as a whole. In the Nadi works,
which I shall elaborate shortly, and which contain the
applied or experimented aspect of the astrological literature of India, it is clearly suggested that of the three
moments—the moment of conception (*adhana*), the moment
of the appearance of the head (*sirodaya*), and the moment
of complete birth when the baby is dropped to the ground
(*bhupatana*), the last one alone should be considered for
erecting horoscopes, as the other two cannot be known
correctly. On practical grounds, the so-called conception

horoscope is not favoured. The actual moment of birth
—and the Nadis fix the time correct to an *amsa* or 24
seconds—should be discovered by an astrologer on the
basis of his experience and predictive skill. Such factors,
as the situation of place of birth, whether it is a village,
small town or big city, whether one is born in the house
of a parent or a relative or in a hospital, whether the
delivery was easy or difficult, the number of brothers and
sisters, etc., should all be considered. Thus when the
Ascendant is Taurus, the thrimsamsa or the 1/30th part is
that of Venus and the sensitive-point is the 1st part
Komalamsa one will be the eldest issue, the mother will
have suffered much at the time of delivery, birth will have
occurred in the residence of the maternal grandfather, the
house facing south on a road running east-west, the place
of birth being ordinary town situated on the banks of a
river. If the sensitive point is the latter half of the
Komalamsa, the Ascendant, etc., being the same, then
the subject will be the eldest issue, by the circumstance of
the other elder-born having been dead, the residence will
be facing east on a road running north-west and the place
of birth would be an important city. In other words, it
is on the basis of life events that the exact moment is to be
ascertained. For each such *amsa* or minute division,
details of place, number of brothers, sisters, etc., whether
parents are alive or dead and similar other details are
given in the Nadi works to enable an astrologer to ascertain the moment of birth.

In the evaluation of a horoscope, there are two
factors to consider. One is the analytical and the other
the synthetic. The Hindu astrologer evaluates the strength
or vitality of each planet under different asterisms and
based on certain point-rating system. He finds out the
various *yogas* or special planetary groupings in respect of

each house and then tries to synthesize, when and under what conditions, the various events will take place. Apart from the signs and the sub-divisions occupied by the planets, the constellations and certain sub-divisions within the constellation are also equally important.

The Moon's Importance

The Moon has a very vital role to play in the Hindu system. She is said to rule the mind. The Indian system of psychology going under the name *yoga* attaches tremendous importance to the mind. It is through its agency or instrumentality that effective functional contact is established with external reality. The self or soul ruled by the Sun, is taken for granted to exist. That is the sheet-anchor of Indian thought. The self or *atman* – comes in contact with the mind or *manas*. The mind in its turn comes into contact with specific sense organs or *Indriyas*. And the sense organs in their turn come into contact with the object or this or that fraction of external reality. As a result of contact continum, knowledge or external reality is secured. Hence it is the position of the Moon in the horoscope with reference to the Sun and certain asterism points, that gives a clue to the behaviour pattern of an individual. It invariably happens that the Moon and the Sun in certain mutual geometrical positions occupying the constellations of the Nodes or Mars, direct the mental energy into certain destructive channels conferring on the native certain abnormal traits. For instance the Sun and Moon having the same parallel of declination and this is known in Hindu astrology as *Vyathipatha*, is not at all favoured as this constitutes an adverse combination denoting mental imbalance. Apart from the Moon's intimate connection with the mind, the Moon is the pivot of a large number of yogas or specific combinations going under the name of *Chandra Yogas*, which indicate different grades of status, rank and destiny. These gradations and the nature of their manifestation again revolve on the beneficial or malefic character of the various soli-lunar constants such as *tithi* or the lunar day, *nakshatra* or the asterism, the *yoga* or the period during which the joint motion in longitude of the Sun and the Moon amounts to 13° 20′, and the *Karana*, or half-lunar day. Whether in natal astrology or electional astrology, the Moon plays a very important role. Many of these astrological rules, tested for thousands of years, have been given in the shape of formulae, universally applicable, with adaptations consistent with modern social, religious and cultural conditions The importance attached to the Moon becomes equally evident if we remember that each asterism has been assigned certain distinctive astrological qualities which will be experienced by one born under its influence. To give you a sample: Let us take the constellation of Mrigasira or Orion corresponding to the arc 53° 20′ to 66′ 40′ in the Sidereal Zodiac. Birth in this asterism makes one hopeful, god-fearing, respectful towards parents and elders, intelligent, timid, shrewd and learned in the occult lore. If the birth is in the 1st quarter (the Moon's longitude being 53° 20′ to 56° 40′) : one will not look healthy, he rises in life by sheer effort. If the birth is in the 2nd quarter, one will be shy, devoted to mother, but clever in speech. Mars rules this constellation. Persons born under this star will be susceptible to danger from weapons, reptiles, poisons or poisonad gases etc., in the 3rd year; danger from convulsions in the 3rd week of birth; disgrace or misfortune in the 25th year; and loss of wife in the 50th year. The periods of happening of these events differ, according to the different parts of the asterism.

Mercury who is symbolically considered the son of Moon is also associated with the mind. Moon and Mercury in mutual quadrants, unassociated and unaspected and occupying the constellations or constellational parts of the Nodes are said to cause what is called *Paisacha Yoga* denoting insanity. When these two planets occupy the constellations of Saturn, the personal life of the individual will be filled with periods of stress, struggle, boredom, mental depression and a rebellious attitude. The disposition of the Sun, the Moon and Mercury are very important and ancient Hindu astrologers have evolved a number of formulae involving these three bodies, which give us a clue to ascertain very important details affecting the mind, character and destiny.

Aspects

As regards aspects, vital differences exist between the Hindu and Western systems. The western belief that nothing but good can emanate, say from a trine—a harmonious aspect and evil from discordant aspects—square or opposition—does not find acceptance in Hindu astrology. The nature of the aspect—trine, square or opposition—depends upon the nature of the planets involved and their situation in the horoscope. I do not think that merely on the basis of harmonious or discordant aspects, the merits of a nativity can be judged. The aspects between planets, during a day, except perhaps for the Moon, remain practically the same. I have seen horoscopes of persons born on the same day with almost similar aspects but poles apart in their mental outlook. The strong man of Italy (Liug : Borras *alias*) Milo and a very saintly Indian scholar Dr. Bhagawan Das were born on the same date. In these two horoscopes while the aspects are more or less similar, the *Yogas* as per Hindu

astrology are quite different. Sepharial gives the horoscopes of a mentally defective girl and Pope Pius XI as
born on the same day. The Pope was a master of 22
languages and possesses a powerful combination called
Soubhagya Yoga where as mentally defective girl has an
unfortunate combination called Paisacha Yoga. Such
considerations must make us to look to factors other
than mere planetary aspects and here Hindu astrology
can supply the deficiency. The Sun and Jupiter in trine
is described as a beneficial aspect. My esteemed friend
Mr. Carter says that this aspect "confers mental powers
above the ordinary, quiet benevolent disposition, success
by means of intellectual achievements and so on". But
in Hindu astrology, aspects as such are not mutual, except
when the planets are in mutual opposition. When the
Sun and Jupiter are in trine, it means, it is actually
Jupiter that casts his aspect on the Sun and not vice-versa.
The results of this aspect depend upon the rulership which
the Sun and Jupiter hold in the concerned chart. Thus
for example, if Taurus is the Ascendant with Jupiter in it
and the Sun is in Capricorn, it is not a good disposition
for, as lord of the 8th and 11th, Jupiter becomes a malefic
and his aspect on the Sun, lord of the 4th is not condu-
ctive to the prosperity of the 4th house indications.
Firstly the Sun's position in Capricorn especially in the
asterism of Mars makes one quarrelsome, pessimistic and
devoid of happiness. Secondly, Jupiter having become a
temporary malefic by virtue of ownership of the 8th and
11th augments the evil results due to the Sun's position
so far as general happiness is concerned, but as lord of
the 11th or house of gains, aspecting the lord of the 4th
(real estates, immovable properties, etc.) the house invol-
evd being the 9th or house of fortune, Jupiter favours

acquisition of properties, houses, etc. One of the major dictums of sage Parasara, propounded thousands of years ago, is that any planets in Kendras or angles—1st, 4th, 7th and 10th houses—form an exceptionally strong disposition denoting prominence. Next in vitality are those disposed in *Panaparas* or succeedent houses suggesting some sort of a slow action and the least significant are those posited in *Apoklimas* or cadent houses giving rise to insignificent results. If the planets are *Yogakarakas*, *i.e.*, (conferors of fame, positions etc.) the merits of the nativity become clearly established.

In all such cases, Hindu astrology employs certain methods of assessing the functions of the various planets and the extent to which such functions manifest, etc., so that a correct estimate of the future can be had. It is this dictum of Parasara that some of our friends in the West are using in the names of *foreground*, *middle ground* and *background*. But unfortunately how and when the planets in the various *grounds* produce effects, they have not yet been able to appreciate.

The next point I would wish to consider is the directional system. As far as my humble acquaintance with Western astrology goes, I think not much emphasis is laid on the possible effects of the signs of the zodiac except in so far as they use these for the delineation of character and psychology. I must confess that, in this regard, western astrologers have definitely made for themselves a mark. But so far as predicting specific events or the determination of the rank, status and position are concerned, Hindu astrology provides more satisfactory methods.

With the aid of Yogas or certain specific combinations, it is possible to assess fairly accurately, what rank or position one would attain and whether one would become a political high-up or a business magnate or a church leader. These specific combinations are all based on experience of thousands of years. To ascertain as to when the indications in the radical horoscope would manifest, we have the Dasas or directional systems, the most important and the most reliable one being Vimshottari Dasa based on a 120–year cycle. You have of course the primary directions, the secondary directions, the tertiary directions and also certain symbolic directions. Their importance need not be under-rated. While with a flair for mathematics, you may discover a dozen arcs of directions concerning all the planets, which may measure closely to the date of an event, in actual practice, with the aid of the same train of directions, a future event such as birth of a child or the death of a person cannot be anticipated with certainty. But the Hindu Dasa system plus the transits can enable an astrologer to anticipate with a fair degree of accuracy, important landmarks in the life of a person.

The ruling period or Dasa at birth is determined by the asterism the Moon is in. The distance yet to be traversed by the Moon in the asterism occupied by him is equated to the corresponding planetary period to be undergone at the time of birth.

The extent of an asterism being 13° 20' of arc, the full life cycle allotted to this Dasa system, viz., 120 years covering 9 asterisms corresponds to 120°. In a way, the progressing of the Moon by a degree has been equated to a year of life. This may be symbolical, or it may have a rational explanation. We do not yet know. But it is in the peculiar scheme of arrangement of the 9 asterisms corresponding to 120 years and the disposition of the

17

Dasa rulers, in a certain specific manner, that the future events can be predicted. It is in the manner of interpretation that the skill of the astrologer lies. Planets owning the 3rd, the 6th and the 11th houses become evil-lords. Suppose there is a yoga or typical combination for high political power and the period of the planet causing the said Yoga is operating. If the plane concerned is in association with the lord of the 6th, the constellation involved being say that of fire like Krittika (the 3rd) or that of destruction like Bharani (the 2nd), there may no doubt be high political success but during the sub-period of the 6th lord and corresponding to the time coinciding with the transit of the same asterism point, or one of its trines by the 6th lord, the person will be pulled down.

Let alone ancient masters. The correct manner in which the results are portrayed in our Nadi Granthas or collections of ready made horoscopes is the despair of modern astrologers. Nadi Granthas are manuscripts written on palm leaves, we do not know when, and they contain thousands of horoscopes which may belong to those dead and gone, those living and those yet to be born. If you locate your horoscope—to trace one's horoscope it sometime requires several days as horoscopes are cast for intervals of 24 seconds of time each—there is an intimate description of your life, your character, your past history and even affairs which can be publicised only at considerable risk. Not only details pertaining to this life—past and future—are given but also those concerning one's previous incarnation are also revealed. How is it possible to think that astrology is false when your own horoscope is to be found in an ancient book, and when events in your life—and you may not have been even born when this horoscope was written—are so intimately narrated. Even assuming that these manuscripts are only one hundred years old, it is amazing to find references to atom bombs aerial flights, telephones, radios, and the Railways and Newspapers. This Nadi literature I think should reinforce the faith of any sceptic in the validity of astrology. There are dozens of Nadis available in different parts of India and we have been able to find in some of them horoscopes of quite a number of non-Indians also.

In the famous Sukra Nadi of Satyacharya, the English translation of which I intend to bring out in due time, a unique approach is made to the art of prediction. The real predictive clues are hidden in the Nadi literature and it is only recently that these treasures are being unearthed. Each sign of the zodiac is divided into 150 parts so that each *amsa* or minute part becomes equal to 48 seconds of time or 12' of arc, each such minute part being again subdivided into 2 parts. If you could lay your hands on the exact *amsa* or point of your Ascendant, a broad outline of your future could be obtained by applying the suggested combinations. The details can then be completed. Thus a person born in *Komalamsa* of Scorpio and has what is called Gaja Kesari Yoga, *i.e.*, the Moon and Jupiter being disposed in mutual quandrangular signs, will have his marriage in the main and sub-period of the planet ruling the 2nd asterism from birth. For one having Saturn in Aquarius, and the Ascendant in Aries—the point being *Komalamsa*—there will be ferquent breaks in career and he will have two marriages. Similar results and combinations causing them with reference to each of these minute parts are all sketched so elaborately that an entire picture of the future can be had. The transits or Gochara are only secondary in importance and are controlled or dominated to a large extent by the radical horoscope. In predicting an event, some sort of a blending of the influences of the directions and transits are to be made. According to this particular branch of Hindu astrology, patterns of destiny rise at the horizon every 24 seconds of time, so that in a day there are 3,600 basic patterns. These basic patterns can be fitted into any horoscope and the influences exercised by the planets should be studied only in the light of these basic patterns.

Prominent features of Hindu astrology which may be profitably studied by Western astrologers are the doctrine of Yogas or specific combinations enabling us to judge the rank, status, etc., of a person; the Dasas or planetary periods; and the methods of evaluating the planetary potencies so that the functions of the different planets in the horoscope may be clearly ear-marked. All this ancient knowledge experimented and highly developed is preserved even unto this day by the Hindu astrologers. In India, we have not botherd ourselves about philological or etymological researches. Words like cosmo-biology, cosmo-psychology, astro-dynamics. celestial dynamics, etc., are not used by us. The Sanskrit word *Hora Sastara* which means Science of Time or the English word Astrology seems quite adequate and no serious student of astrology in India feels inclined to apologise for the use of the word Astrology. I find that some of our friends in Europe seem to be somewhat touchy about the name. But we do not find it necessary to dispense with the time-honored name.

It occurs to me that many a gap in the astrological doctrines of the West can be bridged over by a proper use of the Hindu astrological priniciples. I am aware that there are quite a number of astrologers in the West who are favouring the adoption of the Fixed Zodiac. Mere adoption of the Fixed Zodiac without making use of the Hindu methods of prediction will not be of much use.

Nor would I suggest to my Western friends to reject the Movable Zodiac. They have evolved in their own way, certain systems of predictions and progressions which they should further develop. My appeal to you is to give Hindu astrology the attention it merits. Side by side with your own systems, Hindu methods can be used especially in regard to prediction of events. A hotchpotch of the Hindu and Western methods, instead of helping astrology will further confuse the issue. At this stage, attempts at synthesis of the eastern and western systems are premature. The Indian system of astrology has not ceased to be progressive as some astrologers think. It is a magnificent edifice with a strong foundation, and any accretions that may be attaching to it are being cleared. What is needed is a certain orientation to suit modern conditions of life. If the aim of the astrologer is to attain precise prognostication, he must not feel shy to make use of the real knowledge from weatever source it may come. There is a store of amassed knowledge on the subject of astrology in India and there is no use running the risk of wasting one's efforts in research aspects of astrology that have already been covered.

In India, astrology has always occupied a unique place and found illustrious supporters. Many an enlightened ruler not only made use of astrology for the benefit of the country and the people but also encouraged its study. It is only after the advent of British rule that there was some sort of an indifferent attitude shown by a section of so-called educated Indians. Today however astrology is not only being revived on an unprecedented scale but efforts are being made to unearth valuable ancient treatises such as the Nadies which are the repositories of great astrological truths. Astrology in India is a national science and in the not distant future it is bound to occupy

the same important position in the comity of other sciences
as it did in the past.

Ever since my coming to your great country and my
meeting with several American astrologers, I have noticed
that astrological activity in America has been organised
in a commendable manner. The United States is the
home of modern progressive scientific thinking. I do
hope that she will also be the home of progressive astrological thinking, assimilating what is best in the eastern
systems and thus forging ahead in the further development of astrology.

Ladies and gentlemen, I have taken much of your
time and I thank you all for patiently hearing my address.
But before I close I must pay my humble tribute to my
esteemed friend Mr. Charles Jayne and his associates for
organising this special Conference in honour of my visit
and for enabling me to tell you all something about astrology in India. Mr. Jayne is a serious and sincere worker
in the field of astrology. He is a man of scientific outlook
and I am glad to see that in understanding astrology and
in expounding astrology, he is adopting the method of
science which strives for objectivity and an impersonally
critical attitude.

United States of America and India have many things
in common—a representative form of Government, freedom of expression and freedom of thought, a regard for
moral and spiritual values, and above all a regard for the
dignity of man. It is my firm hope that if American and
Indian astrologers co-operate by pooling their findings
and by maintaining a continuous interchange of astrological ideas, not only the general cause of astrology
could be promoted but an enduring edifice for international understanding and goodwill can also be laid.

APPENDIX II

Prof. B. V. Raman's Visit to Cambridge

*Report by *Dr. Kedarnath Prasad, M.A., Ph.D.*

India's great exponent of Astrology Prof. B. V. Raman, Editor, THE ASTROLOGICAL MAGAZINE, Banga lore, paid a visit to Cambridge (England) on the 7th November 1959. This was the Annual Poppy Day. The students, boys and girls, of the University of Cambridge were out in the open in all funny costumes (resembling Holi festival in Northern India) to raise funds for the disabled men of the two Great Wars. Prof. Raman arrived at Cambridge in the afternoon. At the station he was received by me—a *shishya* of his. I had arranged for a large Tea Party in honour of his visit at 52 St. Barnabas Road. Those who attended the party represented various professions—teachers, research scholars, doctors, etc.

Prof. Raman was introduced to each guest. All the guests were longing to meet Prof. Raman. He talked to them on a number of subjects concerning India—her culture, her contributions to art and literature, her current problems, the interest of the American people in Indian affairs, and so on. His remarks were greatly appreciated by the guests.

------

*Dr. Prasad is now the Head of the Department of Economics, Patna University.

After tea, I introduced Prof. Raman formally to my guests. I said: "It is my proud privilege to introduce Prof. Raman to you this afternoon. I have known him for quite some years. I regard him as my Guru (teacher). He is one of India's greatest living astrological savants. As the Editor of THE ASTROLOGICAL MAGAZINE for over twenty years, he has made many startling forecasts about world affairs such as the second World War, death of Hitler, upheavals in Soviet Russia, etc., which has turned out to be true. As man, he is the perfect embodiment of the Indian saying 'plain living and high thinking'. He is one of the finest and kindest persons I have ever met. I place him with the Sages of India. He is a true Yogi. He has been travelling such a great distance in the West at a time of the year when it sometimes get well below freezing point so very lightly dressed and remaining a strict vegetarian. He is the grandson of Prof. Surya narain Rao, said to be the reincarnation of Varahamihira and he fulfils the triple qualities of a true astrologer as laid down by Varahamihira— he is so learned, he is so experienced and he is so self-less. I know you are all anxious to hear him speak on such a fascinating subject as Hindu Culture and Hindu Astrology, and I therefore request Prof. Raman to give us his talk."

Thereupon Prof. Raman got up and spoke for about an hour. He explained the fundamentals of Indian Culture. He traced the origins of Hindu Astrology. He cited several instances from his own experience of how correct predictions could be. He referred to some of the old astrological scripts such as *Bhrigu Samhita, Nadi Samhita,* etc. He stated how recent studies have confirmed the propositions of the ancient astrologers of India. He discussed the influence which the phases of the Moon have an human physiology in matters like diseases, menstruation, conception, etc. He pointed out how the practice of tallying the horoscopes of the boys and girls at the time of marriage constituted an important factor in the stability of Hindu marriages. But he warned that astrology in India was meant for serious and good purposes. There has not been a fetish of it. Only when man's commonsense failed him that astrology was sought. He regarded himself as a 'keen student of astrology'. And he wanted to pursue his astrological studies in that spirit. In a word, to him Astrology 'was an engine for the discovery of truth'. He said that much research was going on in the field of astrology throughout the world and yet much was needed. It is only by such means that astrology could be made to serve humanity fruitfully.

I circulated among guests old volumes of THE ASTROLOGICAL MAGAZINE. Prof. Raman then answered many queries put by members of the audience. The Tea Party ended with a vote of thanks proposed by me and seconded by Dr. Curtis. I presented each of my lady guests with a garland of flowers and Prof. Raman with a Cambridge University Pocket Diary as a token of remembrance. Later on may guests wrote to tell me that they had never attended such a wonderful party to meet such a wonderful scholar.

In the evening, Prof. Raman was taken by the members of the *Majlis* (a society of the students from India, Pakistan, Ceylon and Burma at the University of Cambridge) and shown round the University. Later on he was entertained to an Indian Dinner at Kohinoor (an Indian Restaurant at Cambridge). At 8-30 p.m. he met a number of students in one of the halls of King's College where he talked to them about various interesting points in Astrology

Prof. Raman returned to London the same night.

APPENDIX III
Nadi Astrology

Mr. President, Ladies and Gentlmen,

When I received a letter of invitation from my esteemed friend and your worthy President Mr. Ronaled
C. Davison to address the well-known Astrological Lodge
of London I was not only gratified but a bit embarassed
also because Britain and India having had a close historical relationship for nearly two centuries and having parted
as good friends, it would in a sense mean renewing old
ties of friendship and understanding ; and embarrassed
because Mr. Davison left the subject of the talk to my
choosing. However, it was not difficult for me to overcome this initial embarrassment because I could easily
decide that the subject to be dealt with should be the one
that should not only be movel but also instructive to the
members and I could not think of a more appropriate
theme than Nadi Astrology, a subject in which I have
been making investigations for over twenty years. I must
also seek your indulgence in advance for having to use a
number of Sanskrit terms, for which no suitable English
word capable of conveying the spirit of the original could
be thought of, even though I shall try my best to give the
nearest corresponding words in English.

Before I take up the subject matter proper, I think I
must tell you—and I am sure most of you already know—
certain distinctive features of Hindu Astrology and its

philosophy. Hindu astrology does not endorse the theory
of absolute fatalism. Astrology and the doctrine of
Karma are intimately connected. According to Hindu
philosophical works, man is a combination of a physical
body, the mind and the selfconscious self or *atman* which
is spiritually present. It is the individual's Karma or
actions done in past or previous lives that determine his
present life. There· are two main categories of Karma,
viz., *Sanchita* (accumulative) and *Prarabdha* (operative).
The present course of life is indicated by the Prarabdha
or operative Karma, i.e., deeds or actions whose seed
has already sprung up and whose machinery has been set
in motion towards their fruition in the present life. The
Sanchita or accumulative Karma pertains to actions that
are still lying latent "like seeds stocked up in a granary for
fruition in future lives". The horoscope indicates our past
Karma, the Prarbdha or operative portion of our Karma
being our destiny in this life and that astrological predictions are tendencies of nature on their way towards
fulfilment or manifestation and that to some extent we
can either strengthen or weaken their momentum in the
direction desired by suitable remedial measures. The
celebrated ancient astrologer Varahamihira whose works
are still considered authoritative points out that astrology
reveals the lines along which the destiny of Individuals
would be unfolded.

The first and the most important of the distinctive
features of Hindu astrology is that it is based on the so-
called fixed or sidereal zodiac. This is divided into 12
parts called the signs of the zodiac or 27 equal parts or
asterisms or Nakshatras of 13° 20′ each. The fixing of
the first point of the zodiac—the end of the constellation
Revathi which some identify with the modern Zeta Piscium
—so as to make it the same for all time is an important

feature of Hindu astrology and this shows a fundamental difference from the European system of reckoning in which all longitudes are measured by arcs of the ecliptic, the origin being the equinoctial point at the time of observation. This does not mean that precession was not know to the Hindus. The very Sanskrit terms *Sayana* and *Nirayana* — to distinguish between the two Zodiacs— mean, with precession and without precession. In fact the precession of the equinoxes was discovered by our Sages long before anything about it was known to any other nation. In actual practice, it is the arcs of 13° 20′ measured from the 1st point of stellar Aries that are really important for astrological purposes. They of course bear the names of the brightest stars—or Yogataras of the star-clusters that lie on or near about the arcs concerned.

In India astrology continues to occupy a very important place socially and culturally, in the lives majority of Indians whose requirements of astrological consultations are generally dealt with by astrologers well versed in the traditional systems, which are preserved even unto this day in the same form, as they perhaps existed three or four thousand years ago. The stars and constellations have been associated with Hindu astrology from times immemorial and their significance in prediction is considerable. Nor does Hindu astrology take into account the extr-saturnine planets, *viz.*, Uranus, Neptune and Pluto. The Moon's ascending Node, *viz* ., Rahu and the Moon's descending Node, *viz.*, Kethu are given great prominence. Even though the Hindus were aware that the Sun is a star ; the Moon, a satellite of the earth ; and the Nodes, points of inter-section between the orbits of the Sun and the Moon— all these were termed planets for astrological purposes. The term 'planet' for the Sun, the Moon and the Nodes in modern astronomical parlance is no doubt a misnomer, but the Hindus had their own reasons to call them Grahas, which for want of a better term, in English, we call as planets. Graha in Sanskrit means a "centre of energy" capable of the properties of attraction and repulsion. You will thus see that in Hindu astrology when the term planet is used it may be the Sun, the Moon, Mars, Mercury, Jupiter, Venus, Saturn or the Moon's ascending or descending node. It is mainly on the nine planets, 12 signs and 27 constellations that the entire predictive art of the Hindus has been developed.

Some of the general principles such as rulerships, exaltations etc., are common to both the Hindu and Western systems. But regarding aspects, there is divergence. For example, Western astrology considers, a square or an opposition as always bad and a trine or a sextile as always good. According to the Hindu system, however, no aspect by itself can be good or bad. It is the nature of the planets involved in the aspect and the type of ownership they hold with reference to the Ascendant, that determines the nature of the aspect. An aspect like Moon-Jupiter square or opposition, in the words of late Mr. Carter, denotes in addition to the "same good humour that we find with the good aspects, a more restless and sometimes even combative disposition." But I think on the whole you consider a square aspect as bad. But according to Hindu astralogy, such a disposition causes what is called Gaja-Kesari Yoga—indicating respect, name, fame and position. Even here, the nature and extent of fame or position rests upon the type of lordship, the two planets hold with reference to the Ascendant, the nature of the constellations held by them and the vitality the two planets have secured and so many oth   factors such as their dispositions in the various sub-divisions, etc. Where for example the Ascendant is Sagittarius with Jupiter in the constellation of Moola (*i.e.*, the 19th) and the Moon is in Pisces—in the constellation of Purvabhadra (25th), the fame and name will be on the plane of philosophy, but of a non-traditional type because Jupiter would be in the constellation of the Moon's descending Node, while the Moon is powerfully placed as he occupies both the sign and constellation of Jupiter ; or again if we take Virgo as Ascendant and Jupiter in Libra in the constellation of the Node (Swati–15th) and the Moon in Aries in the constellation of Venus (Bharani–the 2nd) it is indeed a splendid combination for success and fame in occult matters which in a sense includes astrology, theosophy, and possibly psychology. In such a yoga, Jupiter aspects the 6th house giving opposition, antagonism and also sucess over the opponents, while his aspect on the 10th is generally favoured as it gives the person certain settled convictions, and also the faculty of prevision.

The other distinctive features of Hindu astrology are Yogas or typical combinations of planets which enable us to ascertain clearly the rank and status of a person, and the Dasas or methods of progression enabling one to time events :

The Nadis or Nadigranthas are compilations by the masters of the science of astrology—the Maharishis or the Sages—the very same masterminds who have written treatises on every aspect of Indian Culture and whose forte was observation and meditation. They contain not only hundreds and thousands of ready-made horoscopes and horoscope-patterns but also valuable astrological formulae.

The Nadi literature should be regarded as absolutely speial and original to Indian Culture and genius : While the West has been able to achieve remarkable control over the forces of nature, in the development of star-lore the achievements of India are indeed noteworthy. Until perhaps 1930's, Nadi astrology was a sealed book to many of the Hindu astrologers themselves as they could not procure the texts. They were available, as palm-leaf records in various Indian languages—Sanskrit, Tamil and Telugu—and deposited in temples or their trustees, and somehow came into the hands of uncultured people who played a lucrative trade with them. It is about 25 years ago that a Nadigrantha, that is, a work on the Nadi system came into my possession. I am working on an English translation of this work and God willing I expect to publish it in 1972. This work, I am sure will make a definite contribution to predictive astrology by placing in the hands of astrologers reliable methods of prediction.

I have heard it said by some of my learned astrologer-friends in Europe that the "key to astrology was lost with the burnning of the library at Alexandria or it perished with the Atlantis people" and so on. But in India at least the key appears to be quite in tact, perhaps because of a certain continuity of culture for thousands of years and because of the fact that astrological knowledge is still being taught orally in the shape of aphorisms or certain code-language.

Hundreds and thousands of people make use of the recorded horoscopes contained in the Nadis for knowing not only their future in this life but also about their past lives. There are different types of these Nadis. Some of them give entire life histories of persons in each case substantiating their deductions by astrological reasoning while others merely give predictions of both the past and the future without much astrological discussion. There are yet others, which merely give the horoscope on the

basis of certain palm lines, the delineation being left to be
looked into in other works. But the bulk of them are
based on radical or birth horoscopes. The horoscope
when correctly traced indicates the entire life-history of
an individual from cradle to the grave. Easy or difficult
child-birth, description of the lying-in chamber, birth-place
in reference to village, town, city etc., caste, details about
the parents, number of brothers and sisters alive and dead
education, future attainments, number of marriages,
private life, diseases, friends and enemies and a lot of
other details pertaining to an individual are stated.

The various charts given should be taken as typical
and representative or symbolic and they can be fitted into
person's horoscope, which has almost a similar pattern.
Thus for a given horoscope, many judgments are given,
which agree with one another to a period and then differ.
I think even Sepharial refers to the Nadis in one of his
works. My revered grandfather, the late Prof. B. Suryanarain Rao used to tell me that when Sepharial met him
about 60 years ago and his reading was read from the
Sukra Nadi, he was almost dumbfounded at the uncanny
way in which his life had been revealed. There are a
number of Nadis scattered in different parts of India. In
North India, they are known by the name of 'Samhitas'.
The Nadis which I have seen are *Guru Nadi, Sukra Nadi,
Markandeya Nadi, Nandi Nadi, Kowmara Nadi, Suka
Nadi, Budha Nadi, Saraswathi Nadi, Dhruva Nadi* and
Satya Nadi. Each Nadi sets before it a certain number
of particular questions relating to life incidents that
appealed to the authors to be of real value to the people.
Some of these Nadis are also available in Oriental Libraries in India but in most cases, the keys are lost so that
it is rather difficult to trace the pattern of the horoscope
required. Chandra Nadi, for instance, is available in a

mutilated condition in the Oriental Manuscripts Library at Madras. Generally each Nadi work is classified into 12 parts, each part dealing with one house of the horoscope. Each of these twelve parts is again divided into nine sub-parts corresponding to the nine Navamsas or 1/9th divisions of a sign or into 12 sub-parts corresponding to the 12 Dwadasamsas or 1/12th division. Then there are the Dasas and Bhukthis or progressions. These palm leaves contain predictions of events on the basis of the main periods and sub-periods, the reading starting from the time of birth and covering the important landmarks till the time of consultation and further on till the time of death. Three more parts deal with what are called Yogakhanda, Karmakhanda and Shanti Khanda. The *Yogakhanda* gives with great precision one's spiritual, political, scientific and social attainments. the degree of status and wealth, sudden elevations and falls and significant fortunes and misfortunes with appropriate planetary combinations. In *Karmakhanda* are enumerated the sins one is supposed to have committed in one's past life and in what manner the effects of such sins have manifested upto the time of consultation, and will manifest in the remaining part of this life. And in the *Shantikhanda* are prescribed remedial measures which consist of medicines, yogic practices and mantras or certain regulated forms of sound vibrations, to ward off or minimise the evil.

Some of the Nadis are voluminous. For instance, Saraswathi Nadi has about 1000 bundles of palm leaves, each bundle having about 200 leaves—each leaf measuring about $8'' \times 2''$. One bundle contains at least not less than 50 horoscopes, so that the work as a whole has nearly 50,000 horoscopes.

18

There is one work called Satyasamhita in which, as early as 1935, the horoscope of Mahatma Gandhi and King George V could be traced. This Satyasamhita is a stupendous work consisting of 125 volumes. Each volume in its turn has 300 palm leaves. Its author is supposed to be Satyacharya, a very honored name in classical Hindu astrology, who is said to have lived about 2000 years ago gracing the illustrious court of Emperor Vikramaditya, the last and the most colorful of Hindu monarchs. The amazing part of this work is that terms *Nyayavadi* and *Nayadarsi* are used to denote modern distinctions between an Advocate and a Solicitor. The Satyasamhita has the following to say about Mahatma Gandhi's horoscope. "The native will be born in a holy city on the Coast of the Ocean. His father will be a Dewan or Prime Minister. At the age of 20 he will go to a foreign country. His mother will die at the age of 22 in his absence. His father will die when he is 16. He will have four sons of whom three will be engaged. He will marry at 13. At 32, he will be a lawyer. He will consider the whole world as his family; will always speak truth and will be pure hearted. Pride and arrogance will not touch him. There will be no distinction between his thoughts, words and deeds. While living as a *Grihastha* or house-holder he will live as a hermit at heart. At 62, he will be very unhappy when running through the period of Rahu. At age of 66, he will fare well and achieve some success in his mission. Before 65, he will profitably meet the Emperor of the White People. His father will have more than one wife and he will be born of the second wife. He will resort to fast for the good of the world and will live above 70". This is the test reading of Gandhi. When the test reading is correct, then one can get the detailed reading by referring to the appropriate key number and page.

But it is Dhruva Nadi and Sukra Nadi that are really superb. They not only give horoscopic patterns but also horoscopic discussions. I would like to give you a summary of a horoscope, picked at random from Sukra Nadi. It reads as follows :—"The person who has *Komalamsa* point (Taurus) rising at birth is born in a small town near a temple of the God Shiva, in the house of his relative. If the 2nd part of this amsa ar sensitive point (Taurus) is rising, then the birth would be within the preincts of a temple itself. Jupiter in exaltation occupying the Navamsa (1/9th division) of Scorpio, and Saturn in Leo occupying the Navamsa (1/9th division) of Aries, and the Sun in Sagittarius, birth will be on a Thursday, in the dark half of the lunar month, in the 1st quarter of asterism of Pushya (8th star). The appearance of the head will be in Taurus itself. The birth will be in the hora (half division) of the Moon and Drekkana (decanate) of Virgo, Navamsa (1/9) of Taurus, and Thrimsamsa (1/30th division) of Jupiter. As the Ascendant is aspected by Mercury the mother will have suffered only ordinary labour pains at the time of his birth. If the birth is in the 2nd half of the sensitive point, the labour will be difficult. As the lord of the 9th is in inimical house (it is Leo here) he will not have much happiness from father. Having been born in the Komalamsa of Taurus Ascedant and the Thrimsamsa (1/30th part) being that of Jupiter he will have a golden-coloured complexion. He will be highly intelligent with a well-proportioned body. Not avaricious, he will possess a bilious constitution. As the lord of the 2nd house is aspected by Mars and as the 2nd house is aspected by the Sun, he will be sensual in his thoughts and capable of knowing others' mind. Highly learned, he will not only be an expert in three languages, but a capable writer also·

The 10th lord being in the sign of the Sun, his occupation would be that of serving others. As the lord of the fourth house Sun is in the 8th and the Moon is in the 3rd in her own sign with exalted Jupiter, he will have happiness from mother who will be a good-natured lady highly devoted to her husband.   In the main and sub-periods or lord of the 2nd asterism from that of birth, when Jupiter transits the end of Pisces, mother's death takes place.   Lord of the 11th Jupiter exalted and in the sensitive part of *Kinna-ramsa*, and the Ascending Node occupying the 11th, the elder brother will be a famous author. He will marry in the main period of 2nd asterism-lord, in his 21st year when Jupiter transits Aries". The length of life given in 68 years, death taking place when the Sun transits his debilitation sign, on a Wednesday. This is what is called a test reading to be followed by a detailed reading in which the vitality or otherwise of the various lords have been discussed and the main-periods, sub-periods and the transit positions in which different events take place, are all given.

A careful investigation of these various Nadi Granthas has revealed certain very interesting factors, which may be of great practical importance to astrologers—Hindu or Western—and which when properly used may enable us to make predictions with a degree of accuracy that is conspicuous by its impossibility today. It is also clear that the Nadi writers, in formulating their methods of predictions have made use of the exhaustive literature on astrology attributed to Sage Parasara. Most of the great mass of this literature has been reduced into the form of *sutras* or apothegms for securing brevity and concentration and also as memory aids. Each sign of the zodiac has been divided into 150 parts called *amsams*. Each division thus comprises an arc of 12' or about 48 seconds of time. Each of these 150 divisions of a sign is given a certain proper name, such as *Vasudha, Vaishnavi, Brahmee*, etc., and in a certain order, which holds good in all movable signs. The order is reversed in the case of fixed signs. Thus, while the first amsa (minute) of Aries, Cancer, Libra, Aquarius is Vasudha, the same unit will be the last in Taurus, Leo, Scorpio and Aquarius. In the case of dual or common signs—Gemini, Virgo, Sagittarius and Pisces —the count commences from the 76th amsa. The name assigned to the first unit of a movable, the last unit of a fiixed and the 76th unit of common sign is the same.

This minute unit or amsa of 12' of arc is again sub-divided into the first and the second parts so that actually, the time of birth should be determined with very great precision (24 seconds). The results are bound to vary with each such minute. While birth in the 1st part of this unit in Aries (*i.e.*, Aries 0° 6') Ascendant makes one an educationist, birth in the 2nd part (Aries 6' to 12') makes one a politician. In Taurus for instance, the 5th unit refers to the horoscope of a hawker ; the 7th to that of a dancing girl, the next one to that of a magician, the next one to an engineer. One born in the next unit—of course with certain definite types of planetary grouping— will make one a great King who lives for 110 years but who by his yogic power will. increase it ten fold. It is also hinted that no such human being would be born in the Kaliyuga or the present iron age—in this particular unit and particular grouping. Nadi astrology makes it obligatory that predictions should be given only after a careful scrutiny of not only this specific amsa or unit from amidst the 150, but also the other 9 sub-divisions into which a sign is divided. The other 9 divisions are Shastyamsa (1/60th) Thrimsamsa (1/30th), Shodasamsa

(1/16th), Dwadasamsa (1/12th), Navamsa (1/9th), Saptamsa (1/7th), Drekkana (decanate) and Hora (1/2). The lords of the sub-divisions occupied by the nine planets and the Ascendant should be determined.

The minute unit (that is 1/150th part of a sign) that is exactly on the eastern horizon at the time of a birth is the principal indicator of the course of life and the fortunes and misfortunes a person faces. It looks as though a certain pattern of events is shown within this small compass of 12' of arc. Since in the whole zodiac there are 3600 such divisions, there are obviously 3600 basic-patterns of destiny. Each of these patterns turns up once each day, due to the apparent revolution of the zodiac. It is these 'patterns' that really form the basis of all secondary analysis, furnished by the asterisms in which the planets are found. The actual Ascendant is the very zodiacal point which is coming up over the horizon at the moment of birth. In strict fact, this zodiacal point should be located upto six minutes of space. A difference of six-minutes of space marks a world of difference. It places a birth in an entirely different pattern of destiny. But during a whole series of minutes at twilight. if Sagittarius or Capricorn be seen on the horizon, birth will be followed by instant death. Twilight is the period of 48 minutes before sunrise and after sunset. It therefore follows that from December 15th to February 14th birth in the early dawn or from May 15th to July 15th immediately after night-fall is generally invested with fatal possibilities. A statistical vindication of this finding of the Sages is a contribution which an earnest researcher owes to astrology.

According to the Nadi astrology, the moment of birth has to be determined by reference to three phenomena. One is *Adhana* or the moment of conception; the second is *Sirodaya* or the first appearance of the head of the child; and the third is *Bhupatana* or the actual moment of the contact of the child with the earth. Of these three which is to be preferred? Satyacharya is emphatic that the first and the second, *viz.*, conception and the appearance of the head, cannot be correctly determined, so that the third, *i.e.*, actual birth is alone to be taken. Questions such as what constitute the moment of contact with the earth may be asked. The nurse or the obstetrician may receive the child first. Can this be taken as the moment of birth because the nurse or the obstetrician stands on the earth? The original Sanskrit word, BHU-PATANA is clear and specific, *i.e.*, the moment of being dropped on the earth. It is this moment that should be related to the basic unit or amsa. There are so many practical difficulties to note down such a moment. Perhaps anticipating such difficulties, Satyacharya says that as it is improbable that the exact moment of birth would be recorded, the astrologer should determine it on the basis of his experience and skill and then gives a number of details, such as the nature of place of birth, the caste, the surroundings, number of brothers etc., which would be the case in respect of each amsa.

I just give two or three examples. If the Ascendant is Taurus and the sensitive point is *Kumaramsa* 1st part the person will be third issue to his parents; he will be born in a big town on the bank of a river, in the house of his own father, situated in a street running north-south and the house facing the east. The delivery will be easy. If the birth is in the 2nd part of this sensitive point the place of birth will be a small one, birth having taken place in a relative's house, situated in a street running east-west and the house facing the south. He will be the 4th issue, the

eldest brother having died. The delivery will be difficult.
In either case, the Thrimsamsa (or 1/30th division) will be
that of Venus. If the ascending Node is also in the
Thrimsamsa of Venus, as a result of his past sins, he is
liable to suffer from epileptic fits. In the sub-period of
Jupiter and the major period of the 2nd asterism lord,
when Saturn transits the end point of Taurus or the
beginning of Gemini, mother's death takes place. Again
in the Ascendant being Taurus, if the sensitive point is
Komalamsa 1st part the person's birth takes place in a
relative's house, situated in a street north-west-south-east,
the house facing north-east. The delivery will be easy.
In the 2nd half, the birth takes place in a hospital situated
near a temple in the person's mother's house situated in a
street running north-south and delivery takes place after
much suffering for the mother. The person will be the
3rd issue to his parents, the first two brothers having died.
The Thrimsamsa or 1/30th division being that of Jupiter,
denotes a body inclined to corpulence. If the sensitive
point is *Mangalamsa* 1st part the birth will be in a small
township near a big river. He will have a number of
brothers but only one sister. He will suffer from lot
of infantile troubles. His complexion will be blood-
red. If the birth is in the 2nd part the birth will be in
an industrial town. The delivery will be difficult. He
will be fair-complexioned and he will have, alive, two
brothers and two sisters. The father will be a petty
official.

In this manner are given particulars in respect of each
sensitive point. The amsas or the 1/150th parts cannot
be ordinarily used by an astrologer unless one is able to
pick-up the exact *amsa* by the verificational methods I
have just now mentioned.

The Nadi Granthas provide some interesting facts which can be of great value to predictive practitioners. The Dwadasamsa or the 1/12th division indicates a certain general pattern of future, the Thrimsamsa or the 1/30th division, a more specific pattern and the Nadi amsa, the exact pattern. When one is not able to locate the exact basic point, he can study the horoscope on the basis of the Dwadasamsa pattern which takes into account influences for every $2\frac{1}{2}°$. This will be useful in predicting important events, even though, the event cannot be narrowed down to days or months. The Ascendant, the asterism and the Dwadasamsa are all linked. The number of asterisms being 27, and the number of Dwadasamsas being 12, the number of combinations for each sign will be 324. I shall just give a few random combinations from the *Nandi Nadi*. Details have to be filled in by planetary influences.

Ascendant Aries ($22\frac{1}{2}°$ to 25°): Dwadasamsa 10th ; Moon in Rohini (4th star). Belongs to higher middle class ; proud, war-like and arrogant ; very independent in views. Generally a strange career. Hasty, passionate, audacious and desirous of prominence. Aggressive and rash. Marriage unfortunate. Marriage takes place in the third main-period and the sub-period of Venus, when Jupiter transits a trine from Venus. At the end of the main period, the husband or wife will fall seriously ill or die. At the age coinciding with the commencement of the fifth main period, he will meet with enmity and misunderstanding and in Rahu's sub-period, coinciding with his transit of the (1st, 3rd, 5th or 7th star) he will have a sudden fall from position. If the horoscope warrants birth of issues, he will have the first issue in the sub-period of Jupiter in the third main period. He will

die in the 5th main period and the sub-period of the 7th
lord.

Ascendant Taurus ($12\frac{1}{2}°$ to 15°): 6th Dwadasamsa:
Moon in Rohini (4th star). Excellent future, high rank,
diplomatic. secretive, obstinate, self-willed. If Venus is
involved in a Raja Yoga (combination for fame) gives
high education and fruitful imagination. Lord of the 9th,
in a destructive constellation, father's death in the 3rd
main period and Sun's sub-period when Saturn transits
the birth asterism. Mercury in Vargottama (same position in the Rasi and Navamsa charts) in the 2nd house,
eminence is attained by writing. Marriage in the main
period of the 4th asterism lord and the sub-period of
Venus when Jupiter transits a trine from Jupiter. Great
honour in the main period of the 5th asterism lord and the
sub-period of the Node. Death takes place at the end of
the main period of the 7th asterism from birth-star.

Same Ascendant ($12\frac{1}{2}°$ to 15°) and Dwadasamsa but
Moon in Bharani (2nd star). Obstinate, sensitive, sensual,
self-willed, short-tempered : a master of fore-knowledge,
recorder of events. Marriage in the 2nd main period
when Jupiter transits the 6th asterism. Great prosperity
and eminence during the main period of the 6th asterism
lord. Not much happiness on account of children ;
great ability in writing; highly learned; devoted to religion
and God. Livelihood by trading. World famous, if
Mangalamsa rises. Father's death in the 4th main period
and the sub-period of the Moon when Saturn transits an
angle from the Sun. Mother's death in the 3rd main
period and the sub-period of the Moon (1870) when
Saturn transits the 8th from the Moon. His own death
in main period of Saturn and the sub-period of the
Moon.

Ascendant Virgo (25° to 27½°) : 10th Dwadasmsa and Moon in Bharani (2nd star) ; An unostentatious person, ordinary rank ; has a good brain with power of intuition and reasoning ; fortune unsettled ; gain through women ; Family life not happy. Religious fervour, philosophical inclinations ; moral character good ; retiring nature, critical, thoughtful and vacillating. Lacking in drive and ambition, success only in the 2nd part of life beginning from the main period of the lord of the 5th asterism from birth; Marriage takes place at the end of the 3rd main period, when Jupiter transits a trine place from the Moon. Death in the major period of the 7th asterism, when Saturn transits the 12th from the Moon.

Libra Ascendant (5° to 7½°) ; Dwadasmsa 3rd ; Moon in Purvashada (20th asterism). Strange and quixotic views; ill-temper; Marriage not likely. Born in a humble middle class family. Slow but sudden rise in life. Parents die at the end of the 1st main period or the beginning of the 2nd main period, coinciding with Saturn's transit of Scorpio (1902 or 3). Incarceration in the 4th main period and the sub-period of Saturn. Eminence in the 5th main period and fall when Saturn transits the constellation occupied by the Node.

From what I have said hitherto, you will notice that Nadi astrology gives an important place to the basic pattern of the horoscope revealed by the Dwadasamsa for a general outline and the Nadi amsa for a comprehensive survey. The details such as attainment of rank, position and status, success, occupation etc., are filled in by the planets and the various Yogas or typical combinations formed by them. In actual practice, these principles can be easily demonstrated by applying them to well-known horoscopes. But that will only be a *post-mortem* study. After an event has happened, we can justify it in some way or other but it is in the prior application of these principles and prediction of events to happen in future that the real value of astrology lies. Just for the sake of curiosity, one may note that Hitler's Ascendant—as determined by me—falls *Sankaryamsa* of Libra. For this basic pattern the description is : Not educated but well-informed, likes music, a virulent orator, knows three languages, deceitful nature, suffers greatly in the first and second Dasas. Becomes famous and rich in the 5th period, strange connections with women and tragic end in the 7th period ; But for a Kokilamsa (21° 50′) all events will be same but the person will be a religious head.

What is astonishing is the discovery of certain patterns of destiny capable of application to thousands of individuals born in different parts of the world. In the Nandi Nadi, it is mentioned that subject to a small error, the types of human birth recur on a certain cyclic basis, so that these horoscopes can be considered as more or less valid for any number of years. This aspect of the question, we have yet to investigate. The Nadi writers have demonstrated in unmistakable terms the validity of the principles of traditional astrology, for apart from the destiny—patterns which they have discovered, predictions are given only on the basis of the traditional principles. The existence of palm leaf manuscripts containing some kind of ready-made horoscopes, universally valid is no fiction. It is a reality and a fact of experience. Anybody who visits India can have an experience of Nadi reading. India is still conservative and is a country of traditions. And since most astrologers who possess these nadi-works are tradition-bound, they hold these manuscripts in great reverence especially that their authorship is traced to sages of yore ; they cannot be moved from place to place and least of all taken outside India.

Investigations into the Nadi system of astrology have brought out several important matters of astrological and philosophical interest. *First :* the existence of certain basic patterns of destiny ; We do not know whether these 'basic patterns' were obtained by observation and study or by intuitional methods or by a combination of both the processes. But there they are. The method does not matter. In the evaluation of results, some of the Nadis go a step further and suggest that planetary influences also vary with regard to each minute unit used for determining the basic patterns of destiny ; I think the nearest in approach to the Nadi amsas, to be found in Western astrology, are the degree-influences, most of them being symbolical. *Second :* Nadi aslrology demonstrates clearly that Hindu astrology gives great importance to the fixed-stars, for the author of *Sukra Nadi* lays emphasis on the 27 asterisms and the 108 quarters. He says that the stellar zodiac is something like a cosmic ocean in which the celestial bodies swim like fish in water. *Thirdly :* There are certain conditional predictions given in respect of some bad events in certain horoscopes, such as for instance, serious sickness or death of a wife, etc., suggesting that the evils can be overcome by suitable remedial measures implying thereby scope for exercise of man's volition.

Fourth : In regard to prediction of events, the Dasas or the directions or progressions are of primary importance. What is not shown in the birth horoscope cannot happen, whatever be the strength of the transit influences. Transits are only secondary in importance. They probably act as cataclytic agents. But there should always be a blending of the directional and transit influences for the happening of an event.

Fifth : The subject of house-division which appears to puzzle many an astrologer in the West does not bother Hindu astrologers. The controversy in house division seems to me to be some sort of a profitless amusement. You have for instance, the systems of Regiomantanus, Campanus, Porphyry, and so on. Most astrologers in India employ either the method of *Sripathi* which corresponds to the Porphyry in the West, or the equal house division. The Nadi system is based upon equal house division, that is to say the Ascendant is first determined with reference to the place and time of birth and each house extends for just 15° an either side of the Ascendant point. Obviously the cusp is taken as the centre unlike in the West where the cusp is the beginning. Nadi Granthas and for that matter, all the systems of Hindu astrology base their technique of predictive astrology in terms of the planets in the angles (Kendras), succeedent houses (Panaparas) and Cadent houses (Apoklimas)-the maximum power being exercised by the planets in the angles. Of course, the nature of the influence, the events affected by the influences depend upon the nature of the planets, the type of ownerships they hold as from the Ascendant and the nature of the asterisms involved. It is this principle of Parasara that some of our American friends have been expounding as 'foreground', 'middle ground' and 'background'. But they have yet to grasp the real technique of their application. The proof of the pudding is in the eating thereof. If a system gives accurate results, the mathematical principles upon which it is based are quite immaterial except as a matter of purely academic interest Hindu astrology furnishes us with facts.

In the matter of delineation of character, Western astrology has really done a wonderful job. If only some of the techniques of prediction employed in Hindu astrology could be adapted by the Western astrologers, of course in the light of the social, cultural and religious conditions peculiar to their lives, I am sure, astrology can be restored to a place of honour and dignity.

I thank you, ladies and gentlemen, for the patience with which you have heard my lecture.

APPENDIX IV

Hindu Predictive Techniques

Lecture delivered at Cambridge, England on 21-9-1970

Friends,

I am glad to have had this opportunity to meet you all and to tell you something about Hindu predictive techniques. As suggested by Mr. Addy, the President, I propose to address you this evening on an important aspect of Hindu Astrology, *viz.*, the significance of the sixteen-fold divisions or Shodasavargas.

Before dealing with the subject proper, I feel I should explain some of the fundamental concepts of Hindu astrology.

There are three schools of horoscopic interpretation, *viz.*, *Parasari*, *Jaimini* and the *Tajak*. Horoscopes can be tackled successfully according to any of these systems, provided the astrologer is fully conversant with the concerned system. But in regard to determination of longevity, the Jaimini system has certain special virtues.

Hindu astrology does not much concern itself with the description of general character even though behaviour-patterns and mental abnormalities are pointed out on the basis of soli-lunar relations. It concerns itself more with the delineation of future and predicting events.

The precision in forecasts is due not merely to knowledge and experience but also to what is called intuition.

There is a saying in India that all astrologers cannot be successful predictors and all medical men cannot be successful doctors. But those who are not born astrologers can yet deal with horoscopes with a fair degree of accuracy if one knows the clues correctly.

As in Western astrology, there are twelve houses in the Hindu system signifying all the important events in a man's life. Just as a house signifies an event, each planet also signifies an event. Kendras or squares and trikonas or trines are common to both the Hindu and Western systems but the interpretations are different. According to the western system the square aspect is always evil perhaps denoting conflict and obstacles while the trine is constructive often bringing good luck. But Hindu astrology interprete the aspects taking into account the nature of the planets involved. For example, a square or opposition between the Moon and Jupiter is a highly beneficial aspect going under the distinction of Gaja Kesari Yoga and capable of lifting a person to High power and influence. In the horoscope of the late Indian President Dr. Rajendra Prasad, the Moon and Jupiter are in square aspect involving the Ascendant and the 9th indicating a high status, a firm will and idealised outlook.

Hindu astrology has devised an exact system of numerically determining the strength of planets and houses called the Shad-balas or six-fold strength. A high rate of strength for Sun and Mars denotes a great intensity of striving for recognition. A low value will give rise to frustrated life. Highly ambitious, he will be a disappointed man. A high lunar value indicates that he will be liberal and capable of enduring hardships, a man of power running high as a wave, firm in friendship and happy in the middle and concluding portions of life. A low lunar

19

value denotes a weak-minded and an unscrupulous not
caring for prestige or fame. Saturn's high value denotes
one becoming a mass leader. Venus and Mercury having
high values give rise to persons whose lives are generally
easy-going. Intellectual eminence, integrity, a noble
disposition and high attainments are the requisites of
Jupiter. In all these cases, the exact type of eminence or
attainment depends upon whether or not the concerned
planet has acquired certain other requisites such as special
ownerships etc.

To predict an event, the lord, the house and the
karaka or indicator are carefully examined. If the house
is strong, existence, i.e., the effects are there. If the lord
and the indicator are in good position, the effects will be
enjoyed. If the lord and the indicator are in a bad position, the effects cannot be enjoyed. If the house is weak,
the effects are not there; but if the lord and the indicator
are good, the effects however feeble will be experienced.

Then each house of the horoscope has its gross and
subtle aspects. If you take the 5th house for instance,
the subtle aspect is *Pratibha* or intelligence while the
gross aspect is *Putra* or children. Here again, whether
the gross and/or the subtle aspect manifests and when
and in what manner such manifestation takes place has
to be judged. There are clues for isolating the exact
function of a planet in respect of a house. In the matter
of health for example, the allocation of the 5th house to
mental illness and the 6th house to physical illness is a
feature of Hindu astrology. If the affliction is between
the 5th and 8th lords, then the origion of disease is in the
mind-anger, fear, desire, sorrow, etc. If the 6th and 8th
lords are inter-connected, then the trouble will be in the
body.

The two most distinctive features of Hindu astrology are Yogas and the Dasas. When a horoscope is presented to a Hindu astrologer, he scans through the whole of the chart to track down the Yogas, after examining the longevity.

Yogas in Sanskrit astrological nomenclature mean special planetary combinations for the production of high political and social power and influence, great wealth philanthropy, asceticism, misery, debts, demoralisation and corruption. In all horoscopes, these yogas must be properly scrutinised along with the application of the usual astrological rules. Important yogas make or mar a man for, if special *aristas* or unfortunate combinations are found in a horoscope, the person will be always miserable, even though, according to ordinary astrological rules, such a horoscope is a promising one. The word Yoga is quite indigenous and such a system cannot be found in the astrological principles of other nations. A clear comprehension of the technique and application of these yogas is necessary to make them applicable to western social, religious and cultural conditions.

The yogas may be Raja Yogas–producing high political power; Dhana Yogas or combinations for great wealth; Gnana Yogas or combinations for higher spiritual knowledge and renunciation of the world; and Arista Yogas–series of misfortunes of the most baneful nature. If Sanyasa Yoga in the horoscope of a Hindu makes him to take to yellow robes with a view to giving relief to the suffering humanity by ministering to their moral and spiritual needs and by upholding the transitory nature of human existence; in the horoscope of an American millionaire, it may indicate social service, philanthropy, helping humanitarian causes or founding endowments for the study of philosophical subjects. There are thousands of such tested yogas given in the original Sanskrit works in the shape of Sutras or aphorisms. It is the proper application and interpretation of these yogas that are still kept secret. The results ascribed to each yoga will completely manifest themselves if the *Yogakarakas*, *i.e.*, planets producing such yogas, are not afflicted. Again in regard to the yogas, the strength of the planets causing the yoga, their aspects etc., should be taken into account. Of the innumerable yogas with which the Indian astrologer is generally familiar, pride of place is given to what is called *Pancha Mahapurusha Yogas*—or five great combinations which arise by virtue of Mars, Mercury, Jupiter, Venus or Saturn occupying an angle identical with the planet's exaltation or own house. Thus if Libra is the Ascendant and Mars is in Capricorn or Aries—in either case a quadrant, Ruchaka Yoga is caused, involving the 4th house or the 7th house according as Mars is in Capricorn or Aries. The results ascribed to this yoga are that one would become famous, ruler or an equal to him, and leader of an army. It is not by accident that this yoga could be present in the horoscope of Hitler. Mars is very strong here. Therefore this yoga made Hitler, daring, aggressive, a great leader and perhaps a tyrant ; though born in humble circumstances, he became ruler of a great country. Mars is of course afflicted by the association of Rahu or the Moon's ascending Node and hence there is a strong element of destructiveness in the horoscope. You will see that a similar combination—*i.e.*, RUCHAKA YOGA is present in the horoscope of Stalin also. When this special combination affects the 7th, there is not only an instinctive sense of dominion but an aggressive nature. Humbler people with a similar yoga may become little Hitlers in their own spheres of activity.

If Jupiter is in an angle identical in his own or exaltation sign, then another great Yoga—Hamsa is caused. Hamsa is the swan and it is symbolical of purity. You have this yoga in the horoscope of the former British King George VI involving the 10th house. Hamsa Yoga is very strongly disposed with the result George VI found himself in possession of an Empire under circumstances rarely witnessed before in the annals of English history. There are then what are called Neecha Yogas—combinations which bring down the most powerful dictator to an abysmal fall. Such combinations can be recognised without much difficulty and the anticipation made as to the stature in life one would attain. To give an illustration : In Mr. Roosevelt's horoscope, Leo is the Ascendant. Jupiter, lord of the 5th a trinal house, and Saturn, lord of the 7th a quadrangular house are in association in Aries, the 9th from the Ascendant. This is supposed to be a Raja Yoga. The special combination is further intensified by Saturn's debilitation being cancelled, so that Roosevelt's political career was of a very high order. Saturn also happens to be the lord of the 6th or house of disease, occupying the constellation of destruction while the other lord who has contributed to the political eminence of Mr. Roosevelt, is also lord of the 8th, another malefic place and he is also in the constellation of destruction. It was at the end of Saturn's major period that Roosevelt had an attack of paralysis. A planet capable of lifting a man up in life can also affect his health adversely.

Similarly horoscopes with a bias for spiritual enlightenment can be sorted out by studying carefully the presence of Gnana Yogas, such as in the case of the Budha or Sankaracharya or Jesus Christ. It is this unique feature of yogas that makes Hindu astrology unique. There are innumerable formulae in Sanskrit giving out these yogas covering every aspect of human life, so that by carefully distinguishing them and studying their strength a Hindu astrologer will be able to declare without much ambiguity the general future of an individual without reference to the period when it will come to pass.

I think that according to Western astrology the magnitude and importance of one's employment is generally determined by the power, elevation and aspects of the ruling planet, their being angular or oriental of the Sun, etc. In actual practice, it may not be quite easy to distinguish between a secular head and a spiritual head. But according to Hindu astrology, it is possible, by the employment of the yoga theory to sort out such charts.

As regards the timing of the events, you will find the Hindu system much more handy and reliable. I do not think that any satisfactory and reliable methods of predicting events has so far been developed in the West inspite of the fact there are available a number of astronomical and symbolical systems. Whether it be primary directions, secondary directions or the one based on Franklad's measures, one can demonstrate their efficacy only after the event has occurred. Same directions between any two planets may recur more than once in the course of a normal span of life. The delineation of events correctly is rather difficult according to these directional systems. But with regard to Hindu astrology, the case is different. One can give a survey of the whole life and all important events.

The position of the Moon at the time of birth marks the initial main period and the other periods succeed in the order of the Sun, the Moon, Mars, Ascending Node, Jupiter, Saturn, Mercury, descending Node and Venus. In the case of Hitler for instance, the ruling period at the time of birth was that of Venus remaining for about 16 years. Venus as the lord of the Ascendant is in association with Mercury lord of the 9th ruling father. Venus in his own constellation is in the subdivision of the descending Node in association with Mars and aspected by Saturn. Venus was qualified in causing the death of his father before the end of his period.

That a contact between the lords of the 1st, the 7th and the 6th, or the 1st, the 7th and the 8th lands one in prison, is an astrological maxim. Here Venus is lord of the Ascendant and the 8th, Mars is not only with such a lord but is also aspected by Jupiter owning the 3rd house. It was therefore during the period of Mars that Hitler found himself in prison. His most eventful period was from 1933 to 1945 covered by the major period of Rahu. Rahu is in the 9th or house of fortune exalted. This lifted Hitler up, during his period, but Rahu occupies the constellation of Jupiter lord of the 3rd and 6th and the sensitive point of the Sun, causing his downfall. It is also a cardinal principle of Hindu astrology that Saturn's disposition in the 10th aspected by Mars or a Node would result in downfall. Hitler's character and his achievements, and his sudden rise to power and collapse are clearly explainable on the basis of Hindu astrological principles.

It does not mean that in predicting events transists are ignored. They have their own important role to play but their importance is only secondary. Thus in the case of Hitler, death could occur only when Saturn transits the sign or constellation held by the major lord Rahu, viz., Gemini or Aridra and the sub-divisions of Venus within the constellation of Aridra.

When the Dasas or the main periods and the Bhukthies or sub-periods have been marked, general prognostication covering intervals of from 4 months to 3 years can be given with a fair degree of accuracy.

Suppose one is having the major period of a planet owning the 3rd and 6th houses and the sub-period of a planet owning the 8th house. During such a period, he will meet with great suffering, reversals, disappointments and a generally uneasy time.

There are combinations indicating more than one marriage. Under the directional influences of planets causing the combination, the event happens as a matter of course. Where greater details are needed and more accuracy is desired there are special rules and aphorisms of interpretation which involve the consideration of the Ascendant and the *sensitive point*. I shall just give a sample maxim for your information.

If Taurus is the Ascendant and the sensitive point is Kumaramsa (29° 48' to 30°) and Venus is in Taurus, the birth constellation being Poorvashada (*i.e.*, the Moon's position will be 253° 20' to 266° 40') and the lunar day is the 8th of the dark half and the week day is a Monday, the native will lose his mother when Saturn transits the end of Taurus. Father's death takes place in the sub-period of the 2nd main period, when Saturn transits the end of Sagittarius. In the sub-period of Mars, he will be successful in political or official life. In the third main period, Sun's sub-period, there will be acquisition of a house. In Rahu's sub-period, when Jupiter transits a trine, there will be birth of a daughter. In this way, for different sensitive points, the likely periods and sub-periods in which different events will happen, have been elaborately sketched. With some experience it is possible to predict and time events correctly. These are called sutras or some definite principles of facts and are not merely speculations.

With this general background of Hindu astrology, we can understand the significance of the Shodasavargas or sixteen forms of division.

Here I must emphasize the fact that Hindu astrology is neither fragmented nor lacking in sound principles. All the schools of Hindu astrology have a common meeting place. Hindu traditional astrology is an integrated system comprehensive, unalloyed and self-sufficient. It has preserved its diverse traditions in a magnificent and orderly form.

Though the Varga divisions are sixteen in number, the actual number of divisions adopted differs according to how they are used. For determining the positional strength of a planet, 7 Vargas (Saptavargas) are considered. For a rough and ready estimate of the strength of planets, 6 or Shadvargas are used. But for studying important aspects of the chart, ten to sixteen vargas are used. The divisions are the sign itself (Rasi), half-sign (Hora), one-third (drekkana), one-fourth (Chaturthamsa), one-seventh (Saptamsa), one-ninth (Navamsa), one-tenth (Dasamsa), one-twelfth (Dwadasamsa), one-sixteenth (Shodasamsa), one-twentieth (Vimsamsa), 1/24th (Siddamsa), 1/27th (Bhamsa), 1/30th (Thrimsamsa), 1/40th (Khavedamsa), 1/45th (Akshavedamsa) and 1/60th (Shastiamsa). This reckoning is according to the great sage Parasara.

After these sixteen charts are cast, the placement of planets in their own, friendly or inimical divisions are considered. A planet occupying his own division in more than one divisional chart secure a certain distinction. If, for instance, the Sun is situated in his own division in all the 16 charts, he attains Vallabhamsa, the most eminent distinction. If the owner of the chart is a political leader, he can hope for securing the highest political position, provided he is capable of conferring Raja Yoga. If Mars is in his own Varga or division say 11 times, he gets the distinction of Dhanwantari Amsa. Dhanvantari is great name in Hindu medical tradition. One having Mars so disposed can reach the highest position in the medical line, provided Mars is free from afflictions. The larger the number of own divisions occupied by a planet the greater the potentiality it derives either for good or bad.

I should like to be somewhat prolix in my treatment of the Navamsa chart.

Its first and most important use, as I have already said, is in balancing for good or bad, the main chart so that the horoscope as a whole is assessed correctly. The most powerful Raja Yogas or combinations for royalty get tempered or even neutralised if the planets causing such Yogas are afflicted in the Navamsa. Conversely, even if the main chart is somewhat weak and the planets causing affliction are well placed in the Navamsa, the main chart secures strength. The Sanskrit saying is *Amsakam Balamuttamam i.e.*, the strength of the Navamsa chart is the most significant.

There is a special system of reckoning longevity called Amsayu on the basis of the Navamsa. According to this system, planets contribute as many years as are representrd by the number of the sign occupied in the Navamsa chart.

In the ecliptic there are nine cycles each of 12 navamsas. Therefore a planet in Aries in the Navamsa chart gives one year. A planet in Pisces gives 12 years. These are the gross values. These values derived in the Amsa chart are increased or decreased by virtue of the positions of the planets in the main chart. Planets occupying invisible half of the ecliptic lose a part of their gross contribution, a malefic planet in the 12th for instance negatives all its contribution while a benefic in the 12th loses 1/2 of its contribution. In the 11th, the 10th, the 9th, the 8th and the 7th houses, a malefic loses 1/2,

1/3, 1/4, 1/5, 1/6 of its contribution and a benefic, half of what a malefic does. This is called Chakra Pata Harana. The grossterms of longevity are increased or decreased by certain multipliers, in consonance with the situation of the planets in own, exaltation, friendly or inimical places.

According to Jaimini system, the planet whose longitude is the highest in a sign becomes the Atmakaraka or the prime Controller of the horoscope. The Navamsa sign in which such a Prime-Controller is placed goes under the name of Karakamsa and this plays no mean role in predisposing one to certain physical dangers and diseases. For instance if the Atmakaraka is in Gemini Navamsa, one will suffer from skin troubles; in Sagittarius, accidents from weapons ; Capricorn—drowing ; Pisces—watery diseases etc. Here is a vast field for research. Afflictions to the 6th from Karakamsa give rise to serious health troubles while affliction to the 8th house generally indicates death by suicide, accidents, etc. The Node in the 8th house from Karakamsa produces strange psychical experiences and shows danger of death through poisoning, suicide or violence. May a mental patient has Mercury in the 8th from Karakamsa. The Navamsa Chart is extremely important.

When the birth time is fairly accurately known, say within a couple of minutes difference, then the exact moment is clinched by what is called Navamsa—Dwadasamsa chart, according to which male births can always be in male signs and female births always in famale signs. In the Navamsa-Dwadasamsa chart, each Navamsa is divided into twelve parts, so that each part gets 16′ 40″ of arc equivalent 0° 1′ 6″ of time. If for instance, Aries 4° is the Ascendant, the Navamsa-Dwadasamsa will be Leo, which is a male sign and hence the given time can be treated as correct.

I shall now deal briefly with the other sub-divisional charts.

The life-chart or the Rasi Kundali is indeed the basic chart upon which rests all the other charts. In it is hidden all the various factors which will come to fruitition in the course of the present life of an individual. But it must be dissected into other charts so that a clear history of each one of the factors of life is obtained. Quite often the evidence which seems important in the Rasi or the main chart is modified by the evidence furnished by the subsidiary chart. Sometimes events of a startling nature occur and these are not traceable in the life-chart but in the subsidiary or division chart there will be potential indication. The general strength of the horoscope, the psyche of an individual, etc., should always be looked into in the basic chart.

The Hora chart is the second in the order of rockoning. We can study the wealth factor and personal emotional ties from this chart. In a way the Hora chart furnishes details about one's character. It indicates the person's sitality, temperament, intensity of nature, the complexion of his skin, etc. It can indicate whether an individual under certain degrees of pressure and emotional conflicts will and obstacles shown in the birth chart will break down or stand the strains and stresses.

The third subsidiary chart is the Drekkana or decanate. It describes the brothers and sisters and family ties and indicates the limitations which these ties impose on the native's hopes and aspirations. In a sense this chart exposes all family skeletons. Family ties conflict many a time with one's desire and career and the manner in which these opposing forces can be resolved, can be discerned in the Drekkana chart.

The next in importance is the Drekkana or the Decanate. This is employed for predicting the nature of death apart from its use for predicting brothers and sisters. All the 36 decanates typify certain effects and the nature of death will be according to the nature of decanate falling in the 8th house. Decanates denoting Ayudha (weapon), Nigala (noose) and Sarpa (serpent) cause death by poisoning, accidents, shooting, assassination or suicide.

The allocation of special meanings to the decanates has a long history. The problem of interpreting them is difficult and calls forth on the part of the astrologer great intuitive capacity.

The 4th divisional chart—Chaturthamsa—can be used for assessing the immovable property, whether or not it will be mortgaged and whether the native suffers any troubles due to property affairs.

Spiritual inclinations should be read from the fifth divisional chart or Panchamsa. It can also reveal one's spiritual evolution and whether one has a leaning for religion, philosophy or even atheism. The knowledge gleaned from this chart aids one in strengthening one's moral fibre.

Hereditary diseases, if any, to which an individual is predisposed can be known from a study of the Shashtamsa, the 6th subsidiary chart. Health in general comes under this chart. The information obtained from this chart helps to banish fear of disease, as remedial measures could be suggested for meeting the crisis indicated in the chart.

The 7th divisional chart—Saptamsa is a most interesting chart. The evidence contained in this chart brings point and meaning in regard to birth, and prosperity of issues or children.

The Ashtamsa or the 8th divisional chart has a bearing mainly on longevity. One's duration of life can be anticipated with fair accuracy.

Navamsa or 1/9th division chart is of course the most important one. It can reveal the periods of stress and strain. Its main function is in regard to married life. It can give a clear idea of the character, temperament and mental and moral disposition of the wife, the number of marriages and whether one's married life will be happy or other wise.

Any person who has read books on Hindu astrology will have noticed that with the main chart Rasi is invariably given the Navamsa or 1/9th division chart. This chart is considered as important as the Rasi chart in assessing all the life events. It is said to balance the beneficial and malefic combinations present in the main horoscope. Its importance is so great that it is not only used for sex-determination, but in the system of Jaimini, it occupies a pre-eminent place as most important combinations are derived from the Navamsa.

One's profession or vocation can be ascertained with the aid of the 10th divisional chart or Dasamsa. This chart, properly interpreted, can be a guide to the trend of one's destiny and shows in what fields the possibility of good fortune resides. The Dasamsa chart indicates also the measure of success and the line along which one has to march to his goal. It designates the channels through which he should direct his efforts in order to develop his talents to the best advantage. It shows the contacts outside the family. A wealth of detail not apparent in the main chart can be gleaned from the Dasamsa.

While the Dasamsa chart has to do with one's career, the next one—Ekadasamsa or the 11th division chart denotes legacies, inheritance and sudden influx of money in chance-games, speculation and gambling.

The 12th division chart or Dwadasamsa, is a very interesting chart. Apart from revealing details about parents, their length of life etc., it deals with higher consciousness and links the past and future lives. An astrologer, skilled in philosophy can alone interpret this chart correctly because it deals with the knowledge of self or Atmagnana. It tells one about his past life and also about the future life.

The 13th, 14th, 15th and 16th divisional charts deal respectively with conveyances, education and general happiness and I do not propose to elaborate them.

Now comes the question of interpretation of these charts. While the main chart indicates the hidden factors which come into fruitition during this life, the subsidiary chart gives the details of the manifestation of the events. Generally planets in quadrants and trines confer favourable results. Planets in 3, 6, 8 and 12 denote unfavourable results. But malefic planets can confer beneficial results even when placed in the 6th in the subsidiary chart. Mercury is also an exception. He gives favourable results in the 8th house.

The intensity of good or bad results a planet can give, depends upon its inherent potency or Shadbala. Thus if the Sun for instance has 9 units, he is exceptionally strong. If he occupies the 10th in the main chart and the 12th in the 10th subsidiary chart, the native has a phenomenal rise in political field but has a sudden fall. Planets in combustion, even if placed favourably in subsidiary charts cannot produce good results. A planet in the 8th in a subsidiary chart destroys the event of that chart.

Thus the Varga or divisional charts are capable of telling us a variety of things, sometimes totally invisible in the Natal chart. I can only say that this discovery of the Shodasavargas in Hindu astrology opens a new and fertile field for investigation.

If astrological savants in Europe would try to understand the Hindu system properly and adapt it with suitable modifications, I am sure many a gap in astrological knowledge can be bridged over.